SWINDLERS & ROGUES IN FRENCH DRAMA

SWINDLERS & ROGUES IN FRENCH DRAMA

By

HILDA LAURA NORMAN, Ph.D.

KENNIKAT PRESS, INC./PORT WASHINGTON, N. Y.

SWINDLERS & ROGUES IN FRENCH DRAMA

First published 1928
Reissued 1968 by Kennikat Press

Library of Congress Catalog Card No: 68-26280
Manufactured in the United States of America

TO
L. H. S. AND W. D. S.

FOREWORD

THE swindles so frequently related in our daily papers offer little novelty after an examination of the tricks and deceits of those rascals who for centuries have given on the French stage an ample warning to the audience concerning the raw deals going on in its midst. The purpose of this book is to present the numerous devices of roguery in the many curious plays from the middle of the seventeenth century to the World War. An economic background has been sketched in to make clear the timeliness of these money-plays which fit so snugly into their periods.

For the student of drama a Bibliography has been added containing, besides works on drama and economics, a chronological list of the plays treated. The names of authors, plays, and certain of the principal rogue characters are indexed. After the names of the latter, the plays in which they figure are given, with the dates of the plays by which means they can be located in the chronological list.

The author wishes to thank Professor E. P. Dargan of the University of Chicago for his generous guidance and valuable criticism in the preparation of this volume, and M. Hauser of the Sorbonne for his suggestions regarding the economic side of the study. She acknowledges with gratitude the courtesy shown her by the Bibliothèque Nationale; by the libraries of the universities of Chicago, Harvard, and Princeton; and by the Art Institute of Chicago, which kindly consented to the reproducing of the Robert Macaire cartoons from its copy of Loys Delteil's

Le Peintre-Graveur Illustré: XIXe et XXe siècles, Tome XXI, *Honoré Daumier* (Paris, 1925), from which the adaptations used in the text have been made. All translations are by the author.

CONTENTS

. . . le monde est peuplé de gens qui veulent s'enrichir très vite ou qui, riches déjà, voudraient posséder davantage. La spéculation est au fond des âmes; le spéculateur est l'idole qu'on louange. De l'audace, une malice imperturbable, le sens commun . . . du vol, et les foules admirent.

—LÉON HENNIQUE, *L'Argent d'autrui*, Act III, scene 10

CHAPTER I

IN THE REIGN OF LOUIS XIV

Prétends-tu, maudit partisan,
    Le Ciel pour récompense
Du vol du pauvre paysan
    Et de toute la France?
Si Dieu te fait un jour pardon
    A ton impertinence,
Ce sera comme au bon larron,
    Au haut d'une potence.

—CHANSONNIER MAUREPAS (1681)

THE French money-play with its amusing get-rich-quick schemes and its many rogues and swindlers dates back to the days of the Grand Monarch and the theater of Molière. The fancy of more than one dramatist was caught by the intrigues of the crafty financiers and speculators of the day. The clever young Dancourt, a descendant of Guillaume Budé and a member of the petite noblesse, deserted the profession of law to become a dramatist and actor, depicting brilliantly the financial underworld of seventeenth-century France and acting the rôle of financier himself. The excellent actor Michel Boyron, better known as Baron, of the troupe of Molière, added a sketch to the century's portfolio of scheming business men. Edme Boursault satirized the character from the journalistic bureau of *Le Mercure Galant;* and Jean-François Regnard, writer of farces, caught with remarkable verve the gambling mania, a potent and ready means of acquiring a fortune at that time. And Alain-René Lesage created his Turcaret, who is not only the most perfect likeness of

the financier of the Old Régime but in many respects a
model for the business men of modern drama.

Besides boasting of these famous authors, the French
money-play may justly claim to mark a transition of great
importance in drama—the setting of the comedy of character and the rising of the comedy of manners. The extremely striking and difficult social conditions of Louis XIV's
reign were forcing writers to realize that a study of man
must, to be complete, include his environment. Why should
a period of such great culture be so overwhelmingly concerned about money? The Bourdaloues preached, the La
Bruyères exhorted, and the Molières poked fun; but the
absorbing interest in money continued. Everyone had become acutely conscious of its importance. An unwise government had bartered the revenues of the state for cash
and had thus delivered its people to the financiers.

There was a pressing need for money in the royal treasury. Banquets and fêtes must be paid for, armies equipped,
campaigns supported, pensions and kingly gifts bestowed.
The government revenues did not suffice, and Louis XIV
made use of a system of tax-farming already resorted to by
his predecessors in the sixteenth century. The only virtue
of the plan was the ready money it supplied: the vices were
innumerable. The system represented usury on a gigantic
scale, and France's condition is comparable to that of Molière's Cléante, the miser's son, whom the money-lender
has by the throat. The financiers who poured their gold
into his Majesty's coffers received in return the right to collect twice as much in revenues, thus pocketing half of the
state's wealth.

The financiers were already powerful under Particelli
d'Emery, the *surintendant de finances*. The struggle of the
Fronde, in reality a revolt against the men guilty of pillag-

ing the treasury, weakened them momentarily; but, under Fouquet, they swung back into greater power than before. The state became virtually dependent on them. Notwithstanding the war which Colbert later made upon the financiers, subjecting some to enormous taxes, arresting others as he had arrested Fouquet, and even resorting to capital punishment, they were still powerful because necessary to the government. The *partisans* or *traitants*, as they were subsequently called when the former title grew too odious, found numerous ways in which to increase their wealth.

Their principal source of income was, of course, the collecting of the regular public revenues: the *taille*, a poll tax on the lower classes; the *aides*, a tax on merchandise; the *gabelle*, a most hated tax on salt; various town and city customs duties; and import and export taxes. It would have been bad enough for France if the financiers had taken only what was legally allotted to them; but the opportunity for graft was too tempting. Accusations were trumped up against the people and fines added to their taxes. If a man could not pay promptly, his possessions were confiscated to a greater amount than the state allowed. The *gabelle* led to veritable atrocities on the part of the tax-collectors.

Besides this lucrative business, the *partisans* found other remunerative occupations. They engaged in the *huitième denier* (which meant collecting revenue on property that had changed hands) and in many *affaires extraordinaires*, such as inventing and executing new forms of taxation, creating new offices, and increasing wages. In these *affaires extraordinaires* the *partisan* was paid one-sixth of the sum he had contributed and was allowed to levy two sous a livre in collecting the new taxes. Moreover, he might engage in as many of these occupations as he chose.

A certain financier is said to have been interested in one hundred and twenty-two of them. Sometimes several members of one family were all draining the state at the same time. It is small wonder that these men were hated who, though taxes were already numerous and high, did not scruple to extend and increase them. The fertile brains that could suggest a new source of income, a new monopoly—as on the sale of coffee, for instance, or of snow and ice—received rewards known as the *droits d'avis* of which Molière gives an amusing example in *Les Fâcheux*. The bore, Ormin, wearies Eraste with his brilliant plan to secure the king four millions of livres by turning all the coasts of France into sea ports. Ormin then requests a modest loan which he will repay out of the reward to be received from the government for this lucrative idea.

War was, from 1670 until the end of his reign, an almost uninterrupted indulgence of the Grand Monarch; and the financiers found an abundant harvest awaiting them in graft on army supplies. They would buy more food than required and then sell the residue at a good profit; or levy a monetary tax on the people to pay for the support of the soldiers, retain that money and permit the people the pleasure of showing the army hospitality in addition to having paid for its food and lodging.

When Dancourt's angry Gascon of *La Loterie* wishes to find a comparison for the swindler Sbrigany, enriched by means of a very dishonest lottery, he cries out: "Hé donc, mon cher, vous voilà riche comme un Traitant en tems de guerre."

Though this form of graft does not seem to be referred to again in the seventeenth century, it occurs in later periods—as well it may, since the supplying of food and clothing for an army is tempting to a financier. The celebrated

Courrier de Lyon, represents a group of cutthroats of the year 1795 waiting for their leader who has promised them a new enterprise. They anticipate the pretty pickings that could be had from clothing the army of the Republic. To Chopart, one of the rogues, a horse-dealer by profession, it is suggested that he assist his country by supplying the army with horses, to which he replies that the French could capture few Prussian prisoners on the horses he would furnish. Another grafter of the stage, Gaudriot, of *Les Convenances d'Argent,* by D'Epagny, had been an army furnisher under the Empire and was surnamed "the Vampire" by the soldiers, who saw their rations decimated under his devouring eye. Scribe in his *Le Fou de Péronne* presents a certain Barnabé Guillaume Jacotin who had the contract for a whole army corps. At the time of the play he was being sought for 10,000 francs' worth of supplies for which he had received payment but which had never been delivered.

The many *fermiers, sous-fermiers,* and *commis* who were busily draining the resources of France in the seventeenth century formed not so much a class as a milieu, a *monde d'affaires,* the precursor of that of today. Most of these *partisans* were of low birth—sons of peasants, tradesmen, craftsmen—and almost invariably ashamed of their origin as soon as their questionable fortunes had been made. The striking exception to the rule is the *fermier-général* Raymond, who in 1693 began as a lackey and always treasured the sabots in which he had come to Paris. This low birth becomes as much a part of the financier of drama as his millions or his dishonest speculations. The ignorant valet Lucas of Dancourt's *Le Tuteur,* hoping that the letter he has found and cannot read will prove a *lettre de change,* observes that it would be no strange thing if fortune should smile on him: "Je ne serois pas le premier manant qu'elle aurait fait grand seigneur." This happens daily, and no one considers it a miracle. Who would take him, Lucas, for a peasant if he were seen in a fine carriage? ... "Je ne m'en souviendrois morgué pas moi-même."

The rungs of the ladder of success mounted by the seventeenth-century money-seeker are usually: service as a lackey, a job as clerk under a *sous-fermier*, the position of *sous-fermier* and then *fermier* and perhaps *fermier-général*. The nineteenth-century financier climbs a different ladder, but the method of the climbing and the nature of the climber have altered little. Although French industries, particularly the making of lace, silks, hosiery, arms, and linen, were notable under the Grand Monarch, great fortunes were not made in that way. The high cost of the monopolies which the king sold to the guilds and which had to be protected by frequent lawsuits, and the oppressive taxes demanded of all who would become master craftsmen, made manufactured articles very costly. Manufacturers were often driven into bankruptcy; and the plutocrat of that time, unlike the capitalist of a later day who is a creator of wealth, furthering the fortunes of many, is but a collector of already existing wealth whose profits benefit himself alone.

The lower class hated these *partisans* because of their obnoxious duties and the cruelty with which they performed them. The bourgeoisie blamed them for the creation of *billets* of one kind and another, which put the small *rentiers* at the mercy of the speculator. The nobles hated them for their ostentatious display of wealth. The financiers built sumptuous town and country houses or bought titles and old estates where they entertained lavishly, expending stupendous sums on their table, their carriages, their jewels, and their servants. They added to their prestige by becoming church trustees and marrying their daughters, *les petits lingots d'or*, to the impoverished aristocracy, thus weakening class barriers and incidentally establishing themselves, if possible, against future investigations and punishment, for the fortunes of a financier were precarious. Surrounded as he was by hatred, and having bitter rivals even in his own class, he rarely succeeded in keeping his fortune intact, even when he had kept clear of debt. Imprisonment was not unusual, and a financier's family was very likely to be deprived of its inheritance. Dancourt's Lucas, whom we cited a moment ago, hearing that his master's ward Angélique may be married to a financier, says sagely: "Elle seroit bien lotie. Aujourd'hui madame, et demain rien peut-être."

The seventeenth-century theater, when it chances to deal with the business man, makes of him either a greedy Shylock or some sort of tax-collector often practicing usury toward individuals as well as toward the state and sometimes engaged in other nefarious occupations.

The prototype of that unsavory homme d'affaires, the usurer, is Molière's miser, Harpagon, who is moved at the sight of his son's expensive ribbons to calculate the income they would bring if their value were loaned at double the legal rate of interest. Cléante, in his extremity, has recourse to the usurer, Maître Simon, who in turn seeks out Harpagon, ignorant of his relationship to Cléante. Harpagon, with a keen eye to his own interest, agrees out of sheer charitableness, to supply to Simon's client the 15,000 livres needed. He can, however, furnish only 12,000 in cash at a rate of 20 per cent. In place of the remaining 3,000 he will sell the borrower a number of interesting articles including furniture (in good condition), old muskets, games, and the famous stuffed lizard three and one-half feet long, which will look so well when suspended from the ceiling. Regnard in *Le Joueur* mentions among worthless objects sold by usurers: "des singes, des pavés, un chantier, du charbon." In the nineteenth century a certain coal barge served in many similar transactions. When Harpagon's terms and the identity of the usurer are discovered by Cléante, he cries shame on the insatiable greed which leads his father to make use of "the most infamous subtleties ever invented by usurers." But Harpagon gives no sign of a change of heart.

L'Usurier of 1685, a comedy by De Visé, discloses all the secrets of lending and borrowing and was intended by its author as a warning to the public. The work remained unpublished and was not popular on the stage because, to take the author's word for it, too many usurers saw themselves represented in the play.

Another comedy of the same year, *Les Façons du Temps* by M. de Saintyon, shows the money-lender, Griffard, who has been induced to assist young Dorante with a loan. Griffard, of course, has not the money himself, but, like Maître Simon, must borrow it from others. It can be had if the security is sufficient. Dorante must make out a personal note for the sum; he must also sign a document before a notary so that interest may be charged immediately, and this document must be countersigned by two lawyers and a guarantor. Dorante must also mortgage a piece of property though he owns none. This act constitutes a stellionate or fraudulent deal for which Griffard can have Dorante seized in case he default at the first summons to pay. As this would be of no value should Dorante die, Griffard insists upon diamonds or plate as further security for the loan. But Dorante has no valuables whatever, and the usurer takes his departure.

In 1823 we find in Scribe and Delavigne's *L'Avare en goguettes* an amusing copy of Harpagon, Gripparville by name, who has bought up a quantity of deteriorated canned goods which he intends to sell at a big profit in the village. Having political ambitions, he gives a banquet; but, like Harpagon, he wishes "bonne chère avec peu d'argent" and orders his cook to serve no refreshments. The canned goods happen to be delivered at this juncture, and the delighted chef opens and serves them to the guests. Gripparville is furious. He must pay for these supplies on which he can now make no profit.

The old-fashioned usurers and the modern ones are effectively contrasted in *Les Enfers de Paris* of 1853. Two young Bretons visiting Paris are conducted by Satan into that city's underworld where they meet money-lenders and speculators. They attend a meeting of the Usurers' Company at which the members express their willingness to lend to needy young men at a rate of 45 per cent. Satan steps into the group and scornfully compares these demoded Gobsecks, whose hands are dirty and who live on twenty-two sous a day, with up-to-date usurers who have a good tailor, eat three meals daily at the Café de Paris, and give generous tips. "You," says he, addressing the astonished group, "you are imitating Harpagon; you are short on linen and your hats are greasy. Come now, let's make a change. You may continue to steal, gentlemen, but, damn it! put on gloves!"

The great money-lenders of the state, the *fermiers*, are depicted with still greater vigor and disdain than the common usurer. Their vanity is scoffed at; their gross ignorance derided; and their dishonesty satirized.

Probably the first *partisan* to appear on the boards is Chappuzeau's Raymond of *Le Riche mécontent ou le Noble imaginaire*. This financier of 1662 is tricked by his vanity into paying 100,000 écus for a fake genealogy, prepared by his poor but astute rival, who, with the fortune thus obtained, wins the lady promised to Raymond. Unimportant as the comedy is, the display of vanity and credulity on the part of the financier is characteristic of the contemporary conception of such a person. The description that Raymond gives of his own affaris has something of the bustle which surrounds the modern boursier. All morning long he is besieged by long-winded men, suggesting enterprises, giving advice, seeking positions, paying fulsome compliments. No matter who it is, however, *receveur* or *rat de cave*, the financier must conserve their good opinion for the sake of business. A dog's life, surely!

The lightly sketched Harpin of Molière's *La Comtesse d'Escarbagnas,* is made the lover of an intriguing provincial countess, who is none too faithful to him. Harpin, suspecting her, angrily declares he will no longer provide money for her parties, and, thus drawing tight the strings of his purse, takes his departure from the countess, and unfortunately from the play. In him we see a vulgar libertine whom we know to be a rich, despised tax-collector but about whom little else is told.

Disdain for the *partisan* is vented on his widow, Mme Patin, in Dancourt's *Le Chevalier à la mode.* A marquise's shabby coach shamelessly crowds Mme Patin's great new gilded carriage, which, accompanied by six bedecked lackeys and a coachman with trussed up beard, fails to inspire respect in the marquise. Poor Mme Patin, alas! would give the two millions made by her husband in the king's service if only she might wear such a title! Her maid tries to console her with the wise observation that wealth is not always the concomitant of birth but that money will buy nobility. Mme Patin, in order to correct her fault in being a *partisan's* widow, decides to marry the Chevalier de Villefontaine excusing herself on the grounds that as her husband had made his dishonest fortune in Normandy, she, by marrying the chevalier, will make restitution to one of the noblest houses of that province. The chevalier, who is a shameless adventurer, demands all her property in recompense for the disgrace he will be subjected to in society for having married the widow of a financier. The investigations which the fortunes of deceased *partisans* often had to undergo are alluded to in the warning given Mme Patin not to make an enemy of the marquise as she might set on foot a ruinous inquiry into the source of M. Patin's fortune.

One of the first plays in which these men had the stage all to themselves was *La Rapinière ou l'Intéressé* by Jacques Robbe. Its eighteen performances indicate its favorable reception by the public. The marriage intrigue is hackneyed, but the scenes at the customs office in Genoa, where La Rapinière is *fermier-général,* are amusing. Wine is smuggled in as a gift to La Rapinière, who, in order to be under no obligation to his friends, confiscates it. The customs are cheated by various persons, among whom is a cook-shop keeper disguised as a marquis whose sedan is filled with poultry. Fun is poked at La Rapinière by a peasant carrying a basket of eggs which has under its false bottom an infant with a note showing that it belongs to the *fermier* himself. The author declares that if his portrait happens to be a likeness of someone, as people supposed it to be, the resemblance is wholly fortuitous, as he had in mind only the class of tax-collectors. Besides a *fermier-général,* the play exposes the doings of the *sous-fermier* Le

Blanc and the clerks Jasmin and La Roche whose graft is
sometimes three times as great as the recorded sums collected, who accept bribes and levy tribute, in kind, on the
peasants.

Boursault, who himself served as clerk to a *fermier* at
Montluçon, is thoroughly convinced of the tax-collectors'
heartlessness and dishonesty. There he had ample opportunity to study the character and methods of such men until his own humanity lost him his position. His tax-collector, Longuemain, of *Le Mercure Galant*, is a *receveur de
gabelles* and has stolen 200,000 francs from the revenues
and is afraid to show his face. He sneaks to the editor of
the paper *Le Mercure Galant* to propose a bargain. If the
editor, Oronte, will write a favorable article about him saying that he repents and will return 100,000 francs, he (that
is, Longuemain) will reward the editor. Longuemain begins by telling Oronte that one has to have gold these days:
virtue is no longer potent. For this reason he has permitted
himself little gains from time to time. When Oronte briefly
characterizes this act as theft, the *fermier* is much offend-
ed at so opprobrious a term: "... Frauder la gabelle est un
mot plus honnête." He excuses his act by an allusion to the
frequency of fraudulent bankruptcies of which scarcely
one out of ten is punished. These rogues make a display,
win the favor of the public, borrow money, and then de-
camp, a million écus to the good. Longuemain's arguments
do not move Oronte, and he drives him away with great
disgust.

A few years later, Boursault produced a similar character, one Griffet, of *Esope à la Cour*. It is Griffet's ambition
to be a tax-collector. He has served in various capacities
in farming offices, but now he wants the *non plus ultra*,
which is to be a collector himself. He is unmarried, aged

eighty-two, and worth 1,500,000 francs. Griffet presents himself to Esope, who is powerful at court, and requests the position. When asked by Esope what is the *vertu* of a tax-farmer, he replies that he has no idle *vertus*, but only those which are found in a strong-box, to which remark he zealously adds,

> Naked virtue hath too poor an air:
> Without gold there is no virtue anywhere.

Esope then asks whether, in all conscience, the position is worth the effort. Griffet replies that one cannot say yes, "in all conscience," for it is necessary to put aside one's conscience till one's pockets are filled. After that the reconciliation with conscience is easy and free of all care and one has only to live as an *honnête homme* on other people's money. Griffet offers Esope a bribe; but Esope answers with a description of hell, warning the aged Griffet that his end cannot be far off. The picture of hell is curious: it contains, among others, drygoods merchants who have given false measure, and court *modistes* who have flattered luxurious tastes by their style shows, and finally financiers and bankers who know no figures large enough to count the days they must spend in torment.

Baron adds little to the picture we have already gained from Molière and Boursault except the picturesque name "Basset." This financier, found in *La Coquette et la fausse Prude,* is of low birth as his name implies. This accident, however, does not disconcert him in the least, for he has money, and, as he shrewdly observes, "Avec de l'argent on fait tout." Basset is one of the coquette's suitors, and her maid advises her to take the financier, buy a government position, and use his money to make friends and even relatives, at the court. Above all his name must be changed from Basset to *Monsieur le Marquis*. But Cidalise refuses the financier.

In *La Critique du Légataire universel,* Regnard endows his financier with the diverting and serviceable trait of stuttering, calling him Bredouille. This trick, destined to confuse the client, is resorted to by Balzac's Grandet, his Baron Nucingen, and others. Regnard makes Bredouille a gourmet. Food occupies him incessantly. He must drink *bien frais* and have his meat cooked to a turn. He is even the inventor of *les poulardes aux huîtres* and other dishes. This culinary interest is quite common in the real financiers of the period. Bredouille is also grossly ignorant and refuses to *alambiquer* his mind about anything.

Dancourt gives droll glimpses of the hommes d'affaires. These sketches are but hints of what Dancourt might perhaps have done had he set himself the task of painting a complete portrait. Jules Lemaître has collected these *croquis* and constructed Dancourt's idea of the contemporary financier. There is about these unfinished farcical sketches more life and vigor, a better representation of the man in his surroundings, than would ever perhaps have been possible in a classical comedy. The many social and economic facets of this curious character are given in terse lines full of sly allusions and innuendoes. How did Rapineau of *Le Retour des Officiers* rise in the world, for instance? His shrewd brother lets the cat out of the bag. Rapineau once wore the livery of a lackey, which he would willingly have the world forget now that he has passed from wine-vault inspector, "le premier degré de la fortune," to the half-way post of *sous-fermier*. There is still a long stretch of road to go before he obtain his "million" and Rapineau hardens his heart and continues on his way, cruel, relentless, and selfish, leaving his sister to starve in the country, treating his brother insolently, and lavishing his wealth on Henrietta, who, doubtless with the approval of the audience, tricks and jilts him.

The position of lackey proves lucrative indeed to Simon of *Le second Chapitre du Diable Boiteux*. He serves in a financier's house and receives bribes from the lovers of his master's wife. Among these is an homme d'argent who, in order to annoy the husband, takes under his wing Simon whom the irate master had discharged. Simon is introduced into one affair after another until he eventually becomes the associate of his former master. Simon has acquired such a taste for making money that at the age of sixty-four he is still using his money "pour en gagner d'autre," intending some day to retire and amuse himself. The Diable Boiteux lectures him out of his miserliness by holding up as an example the financier Marsoin and the fine palace he has built in which he lives like a satrap, and even the young business man Oronte who has rebuilt on a magnificent scale the house of a *seigneur*. The lesson bears fruit; and when Simon returns to his wife, who, thinking him dead, had begun a life of great extravagance, he is ready to enjoy his fortune with her.

In spite of a financier's apparently spendthrift ways, he never forgets the exact amount that he is lavishing on himself and others and imparts the information loudly to all about him. M. César-Alexandre Patin, of *L'Eté des Coquettes*, who tears himself away from business for the pleasure of seeing the fair Angélique, couches his billets doux in the arid terms of finance. One could expect nothing else from M. Tarif. It is natural that he should boast of the price of his gifts. We find him in *Le vert Galant* at the house of his mistress, comfortably sprawled out in the most commodious chair, his hot wig replaced by my lady's hus-

band's best and cleanest night-cap, detailing to Mme Jérome the cost of the dishes which he has had sent in for her
delectation. The husband, a dyer by trade, finding Tarif in
so comfortable a pose, pretends no displeasure, but offers
the lover the still greater comfort of a bath in one of his big
dyeing vats. When Tarif comes out of the tub, he is a
bright green and the laughing stock of the town. It will be
some time before Tarif can again go courting another man's
wife.

Although Dancourt has not so perfect a financier as
Lesage's Turcaret, yet he has expressed, says Lemaître, the
dissolving force of the many dishonest and sudden fortunes
of the day. Having no culture behind his wealth, the financier used it simply to corrupt those about him. Dancourt is
interested in money as an unbridled force.

Turcaret was written at the beginning of the eighteenth
century when the financial condition of France was even
worse than before. In 1708, the year before the production
of the play, the government faced a debt of 700 millions of
livres with only 20 millions in the treasury. France would
then have gone bankrupt had it not been for the "miracle,"
the 30 millions brought by the merchants of St. Malo from
the South Seas, half of which sum was given to the king;
the 40 millions reluctantly furnished by the *traitants;* the
English victory of Malplaquet; and the interested pity of
Queen Anne. Louis XIV was now able to descend gracefully
what Michelet called *le Niagara de la banqueroute*. The
king was obliged to make a display of courtesy toward the
financiers, and they were then in the hey-day of their glory.
Samuel Bernard, one of their number, a man of great pride
and insolence, a frequenter of the best society, and at the
same time a fraudulent bankrupt and a speculator, had the

honor of being the guest of the king at Marly. But in spite
of the honors bestowed on him at this time, the *traitant*
was less beloved than ever.

The populace of Paris had every reason to feel itself
avenged on the tax-collectors in the character of Turcaret.
Lesage expresses the idea which was in every mind, and
Turcaret stands before us in a brutal light. He is a man of
disagreeable disposition and violent temper, *pas fort aima-
ble* on the whole: a libertine who has driven off his wife,
and a miser who refuses to aid his indigent sister so that
she is obliged to peddle secondhand goods. He is stamped
unmistakably with the low origin of a lackey, an origin
which he hotly denies, preferring the ambiguous title "homme d'affaires." To prove that he is of the élite, he opposes
the admission into a club of a *pied plat* and *homme de rien*
who has the impudence to aim so high. The quality which
results in Turcaret's undoing is a vanity so swollen that it
renders him an easy victim to all who would prey upon him.
Like the majority of parvenus, he is sure of the excellent
quality of his taste and boasts of it continually: the glassware and porcelain he bestows on the baroness must perforce be *d'un goût exquis*, for he has chosen them himself.
The house he intends to build for her will excel in size.
His generosity never prevents him from telling the cost of
everything; and when he tips Marine, he cannot help reminding her of his indifference to money: "Tiens, je donne
sans compter, moi!" The mania for figures even creeps
into his billets doux, and he writes to the baroness assuring
her that his heart will burn with an eternal flame as certainly as three and three make six.

In order to be thought a patron of the arts, he invites
the poet Gloutonneau to eat at his table; and although the

poet never has anything to say, Turcaret is satisfied for "il mange et pense beaucoup." He is also a subscriber to the opera, which he admires heartily: "Une belle voix, soutenue d'une trompette, cela jette dans une douce rêverie." His house is so luxurious that the slow-witted Flamand, his valet, becomes "soft": "Depuis que je sis chez M. Turcaret," says he, "je sis devenu délicat, oui!"

Turcaret may be vain and silly socially and the ready dupe of flattery, but he is hard and quick in his financial affairs. He is accused of being *l'usurier le plus juif*, selling his silver at the weight of gold. He resorts also to the common practice of making out notes for far more than the sum he lends. When reproached with such nefarious doings he protests that it is better to *prêter sur gages* than to *prêter sur rien*. We do not see him at work, and it is only in his conversations with his partner Raffle that we get an idea of his business dealings in the Rue Quincampoix. Turcaret places his dependents where they can best rob the public and serve him. The most notable trait of Lesage's play is its tone of relentless, pitiless satire. It is as hard and metallic as the gold that Turcaret steals from the public. There is not to be found in it, says Jules Janin, an honest smile, a look of sympathy; not a particle of good advice does it give nor a word of hope. It is a continual ricochet of *fourberies* from beginning to end. We shall meet many attacks on speculation and speculators, but not until the *Corbeaux* of Becque shall we again meet with a play as terse and terrible as this one. Du Bled describes it as "un grand vaudeville de mauvaises moeurs" comparable to a *comédie rosse* of the Théâtre-Libre.

The vivid portraiture of *Turcaret* naturally rendered the play obnoxious to the financiers, and tradition has it that they endeavored to suppress the play.[1] However that may be, it is certain that the actors were very unwilling to appear in the comedy as Lesage had written it and were probably to blame for its failure, which caused the rupture between the author and the Comédie-Française.

Alberic Second, commenting on the revival of *Turcaret* in 1857, shows how the type represented by Lesage had aged. Turcaret is tricked and fleeced and duped by the marquis, the chevalier, the baroness, by the valets, soubrettes, and everyone in general. That did very well in 1709; but the modern financier is served, followed, and adored: "Et de temps en temps, il lance à la Bourse une petite affaire dans laquelle il râfle spirituellement l'argent et les économies de tout son entourage."

There were other methods of making a quick fortune besides usury and tax-collecting. Among these was that peerless and eternal project, a fraudulent bankruptcy, which is as fresh today as ever it was then. There was also *agiotage,* that is, speculating on the difference in value between paper notes and specie, a lucrative side line for many usurers; and finally gambling.

Le Banqueroutier, a farce written by Noland de Fatouville for the Théâtre-Italien in the year 1687, has not been surpassed in its cynicism by any later play; and indeed, the depiction of milieu, except for a few antiquated terms, might pass for modern. The author has not scrupled to show the rough side of life under the Roi Soleil. He makes his Harlequin an arranger of bankruptcies with a wide knowledge of *les affaires délicates* such as antedating a

---

[1] A one-act vaudeville in prose by Barré, Radet, Deschamps, and Desprez, *René le Sage, ou C'est bien là Turcaret,* has for theme the writing of *Turcaret* and the effort of the financier D'Armanville, who saw himself in the person of the *traitant,* to forbid the performance of the play.

mortgage, lessening a debt, preparing a defeasance, and arranging bankruptcies according to first-class models. Nothing is so popular at present! Harlequin recommends to Persillet, who is eager to enrich himself by a bankruptcy, that he interest the public by talking of a rich marriage for his daughter, the purchase of a dukedom for himself, and the establishing of his son. These are three hooks which will catch all the dupes of Paris. To "faire son coup" one must be "dans cette odeur de fortune et d'opulence." Then Persillet must borrow a million francs, collect as much of the money as he can, and quietly leave town, having ordered his servants to say that they do not know where he is. When the storm blows over, the creditors will begin to listen to reason and will consent to a settlement of two-thirds of the debt rather than accept a total loss. When the terms are agreed on, Persillet will come up to the surface again with seven or eight hundred thousand francs in cash and all his best possessions safe: "Un homme qui a cette prudence une seule fois en sa vie n'est-il pas pour toujours audessus de ses affaires?"

When asked by her husband if she has the courage to sustain a bankruptcy honorably to the very end, for such high deeds cannot be repeated and it requires spirit to carry them through, Mme Persillet not only steels her soul against any pity toward her husband's creditors but hides away with care all the valuables which justice might claim. Harlequin, alias M. de la Ressource, then introduces to Persillet several rich men of Paris who are eager to loan him money. There follows the Scène du Prest, which Lintilhac calls "the prototype of the best dupe (gogo) scenes which will ever be written, without excepting Robert Macaire or Mercadet." Harlequin skilfully persuades the gentlemen that Persillet is "up to his eyes" in money already

and that if he borrows from them he will be doing them a
great favor. They fairly implore Persillet to take their
money. While they sip orangeade, which their host orders
for them, the latter impresses them mightily with his har-
assing business. He is simply *assassiné d'argent*. The
money is soon loaned to Persillet, who decamps, leaving
Harlequin to settle up. This he does by passing on to the
unhappy creditors contracts of sale in one of Persillet's
great undertakings, the conducting of the river Ourcq to
Paris with the intention of speculating on the price of the
water. These contracts will give the creditors first right of
sale—when the enterprise is realized. The creditors' black
costumes are truly prophetic, for they have forever buried
their money in the bankrupt's pockets. Isabella, the daughter of Persillet, enriched by her father's fraud, feels that
she has the soul of a princess, the only drawback being her
ungodly name "Parsley."

The farce of which *Le Banqueroutier* is so fine an example, is the ancestor of the nineteenth-century vaudeville,
which was, during the early decades of that century, almost the only dramatic *genre* to choose its subjects from
daily life and model its scenes on commonplace realities.
Lintilhac, a propos of Noland de Fatouville's farce, praises
the vivid scenes of the Théâtre-Italien with their timeliness
and intrepid realism which give the impression that between 1682 and 1697 "le rideau se levait sur la vie."

The *Banqueroutier* disclosed reprehensible surroundings and people: Dancourt's *Les Agioteurs* is a den of
thieves. The play swarms with rascals whose avowed purpose is to *duper les autres*. The old usurer Zacharie and his
godson the *agioteur* Trapolin "plus connu dans Paris, que
tout ce qu'il y a de plus illustre," do an excellent business
in speculation on paper money. Zacharie strolls about in

the cafés looking for dupes whom, when found, he sends to Trapolin to be fleeced. Trapolin does part of his business through his strawman Craquinet. In order that the public, which had taken umbrage at their association, may not know that they are still hand and glove, they have offices opening on different streets but so placed that there is a common wall in which the rogues have cut a door which they conceal by means of a wardrobe. Thus they can communicate and consult at will.

Trapolin knows the art of inspiring confidence by appearing rich: "Malpeste, c'est un des grands moiens de le devenir." He lays claim to but one praiseworthy trait, and that is honesty! His wizard-like skill in turning paper into gold and gold into paper is of great profit to himself. He gives Clitandre, for example, 9,000 livres in specie in exchange for 30,000 livres in paper; and he feels justly annoyed that Craquinet should lend 13,000 livres of paper to be repaid in cash at the expiration of six months and should make the note out for 15,000 livres only. When Zacharie hears of this abberation, he laments the capricious scruples that sometimes seize great men. Trapolin considers himself philanthropic because he lends to merchants about to go bankrupt, but he is careful to take as security all their silver and other valuables. He also lends his money under an assumed name so that he will have the legal right to keep the securities. Having explained all these little precautions to the shyster lawyer Durillon, he cynically asks whether he himself appears to be running any risk in these bankruptcies.

Trapolin and his godfather are untroubled by the market quotations on paper effects, for they are quite able to rig it by means of their many *bureaux d'intelligence*. As they are overburdened with paper notes, Zacharie recom-

mends that they force the value of paper down by 8 per
cent; and, when they shall have rid themselves of their
own, they will drive the price up to the usual figure, or
higher, if possible. The clerk Guillaume is called in and instructed to visit the various *bureaux* with the order that
paper shall drop. Besides these branch offices, the rogues
have the further assistance of a certain sheriff who posts
them on bankruptcies and of the lawyer Durillon who, an
adept in Paris business, secures loans for them.

An hour in Trapolin's office would give one a fair idea
of this world of thieves. Cangrène, an *agioteur;* Dargentac,
a rogue; Chicanenville, a swindler from Normandy; and
Daudinet, anxious to mortgage his rich parents—all come
in to do some shady business with the popular Trapolin.
Cangrène, declaring that he would not for the world do
aught to burden his conscience, comes to Trapolin for moral support in a certain deal. A friend to whom he had
loaned 600 livres in paper, without interest but on good security, payable in three months, could not meet the payment. Cangrène renewed the loan, this time for 1,000 livres
in paper payable in specie in another three months. Again
his friend cannot pay, and Cangrène takes possession of a
contract which the former had deposited with him as security. The contract is worth 2,000 livres, but Cangrène
has a shyster lawyer estimate its value at 800 livres. Thus
his friend must pay him an additional 200 livres to make
up the 1,000. The delicate point, however, which is trou-
bling Cangrène's conscience is whether he may consider
himself justified in retaining the six months' accrued interest on this contract which he had had since the loan was
first made. Trapolin cries fie on anyone for being so scru-
pulous and approves heartily of Cangrène's retaining the
interest.

Dargentac claims to be the scion of a noble but ruined house, now serving as steward in a family of which the grandfather had been a Dargentac steward. The high-born rogue boasts that he is gradually recovering his patrimony by ruining his master. Recognizing in Trapolin a cheat equal to himself, Dargentac dares to voice an apology for this world of *tripotages*. Everyone, says he, is excusable who has made a fortune; it matters little how. As he is progressing well in his rascality and Trapolin is advancing with giant strides in his, he, Dargentac, can speak freely before him. "Indeed you can," says the suave Durillon who is present, "you are among honest people." The proof of this honesty is speedily forthcoming. Dargentac, as steward, must pay a bill of 40,000 livres in specie. He has put the creditor off so long that the man has finally consented to accept half of the sum in gold and half in paper, evidently a clear profit for Dargentac, who wishes Trapolin to furnish him the 20,000 livres in paper. Trapolin, being the most obliging man in the world, is delighted to favor his client. He will let him have the 20,000 livres' worth of paper for 20,000 livres in cash. Dargentac makes a great outcry, insisting that paper is worth less than gold. Trapolin protests that *his* paper is exceptional, but finally decides to accept 15,000 livres. When Dargentac returns later with the money, Trapolin and his clerk begin counting it on the stage. Before they have counted long, Dargentac is informed by a coachman that his master is seeking him. His hasty departure is but a ruse to cover his retreat to Genoa with the 20,000 livres in paper. Trapolin finds that the sum left him by the fake Dargentac is much smaller than he had bargained for.

Chicanenville's visit is also disastrous. Trapolin's clerk, thinking to supply Chicanenville with the 1,000 livres he has come to borrow, gives him a sack which is supposed to contain exactly that sum but into which Trapolin had just slipped some 2,000 livres in gold received from Dargentac. Trapolin knows too well the reputation of the rogue Chicanenville to suppose that he will return the extra money, which is therefore a dead loss.

Daudinet is cleverly swindled between the homme d'affaires and his lawyer. When Trapolin refuses to lend Daudinet money without security, Durillon offers to allow Daudinet to give Trapolin a mortgage on a piece of his, Durillon's, property. Trapolin then consents to lend the client 20,000 livres for six months, making the note out for 22,000 livres to cover the interest. The dupe goes off rejoicing with his 20,000 livres, quite ignorant that these rogues can have him imprisoned for mortgaging another's property.

Women drift into this office too. The Baronne de Vapartout borrows paper money to gamble with, preferring the least valuable kind, as she is so apt to lose it! How she wishes all the paper she has lost at cards would turn into "oak leaves" in the winners' hands! Mme Malprofit must have money at once to pay for a trifle which she prefers not to inform her husband of. She already owes a large sum for a set of china which the pet monkey had broken to bits. The monkey is a costly animal. It has also eaten up two *promesses des gabelles* and spilled ink on a *billet de compagnie*.

The splendid realism of this clever play is lessened by the unlikely misfortunes which fall upon Trapolin, who is too clever to be so easily swindled, and on Zacharie whose *beau mariage* is thwarted. These conventional twists in the flimsy plot are all too evidently concessions to popular taste. But *Les Agioteurs* is to be esteemed notwithstanding. Not for a hundred years will there be such another company of rogues gathered together in a single play.

Running parallel to this shady speculation in the Paris underworld was the gambling among all classes, a rage which represented in its fervor and its disasters the speculation on the stock exchange at a later day. Many courtiers were ruined at the card tables, and many lucky or unscrupulous adventurers found themselves hobnobbing with royalty. By substituting the Bourse for tricktrack and by ultimately reforming the gambler by means of "honest industry," one would have in Regnard's *Le Joueur* of 1696 the framework and atmosphere for Ponsard's *La Bourse* of 1856.

Valère, the confirmed gambler of Regnard's play, engaged to Angélique, makes but a sorry suitor because of his devotion to cards. He breaks his many promises to reform and finally even pawns the jewel-set picture of herself which Angélique had given him. When Angélique discovers this, she bestows her hand upon Dorante. *Le Joueur* portrays a society where all classes meet about the green-covered gaming tables as they will later about what Mercadet calls "the well-spread table of the bourse." At tricktrack and lansquenet are gathered together marquis and bourgeois, banker's wife and duchess, lackey and duke. All injustices of birth are here avenged.

Géronte, Valère's father, in vain warns his son about this frenzy for gambling which has become veritable madness. Everything is staked: money, jewels, houses, contracts, even honor, which women lighlty risk. The same thing in very nearly the same words, but in poorer Alexandrines, will be said in the nineteenth century; and warnings such as the following will be as vainly given:

You were born to be the pillar of every gambling hall
Each filled for youth with deadly trap and fall.
A forest full of thieves is safer far
Than these bandit-ridden places ever are.
Choose of two evils, be thou dupe or duped.

—*La Bourse*, I, 7

The dupe and *fripon* are of necessity the leading characters in all get-rich-quick schemes; and later the bourse
becomes the thief-ridden wood where the rogue finds easy
victims, because the excitement of any form of speculation
blinds the novice who, like Valère, is sure that the next attempt is bound to be the successful one; and he eventually
curses the bourse as Valère the "maudit jeu de trictrac."
The speculator cannot be expected to keep even-tempered
in the face of fluctuating fortune, and the description which
Angélique's maid gives of Valère is repeated almost ver-
batim of more modern speculators:

Always sad or raging, furious with the pain
Of having lost so heavily or made so little gain.

In the pages of Regnard's play is to be found a handful of rascals whose faces are already familiar. There is
the usual low-born financier with a rich palace, a country house, a coat of arms, and a host of purchased ancestors whose portraits adorn his walls. The description of the
financier is made more piquant by being placed in the
mouth of the fake marquis, an imposter, an adventurer, a
chevalier d'industrie. This conventional type always wears
a borrowed name, speculates on the affections of some sus-
ceptible and elderly lady of means, and is betrayed by
someone acquainted with his past history. The betrayal is
performed by Mme La Ressource in this particular instance. She herself is a hard-hearted *usurière* though she

blushes at the word "usury," lending her money only on such honorable things as diamonds.

The last swindler of the group is Toutabas, a professional trickster, who goes about teaching his sleight of hand and using loaded dice. Toutabas's descendant, Robert Macaire, will later give lessons in the art of joint-stock-company swindling.

Popular favor passed from one card game to another. Some of the most disastrous were prohibited by law or were allowed only at court and not in Paris. What consternation in the salon of Mme Dorimène, the gambling hostess of Dancourt's *La Désolation des Joueuses,* when the habitués come dropping in with long faces, having learned that lansquenet is forbidden! Have the authorities really considered what a hardship they are causing? Sleeping, eating, and drinking could better be dispensed with. How is money to be secured now to pay off previous card debts and redeem jewels at the pawn shop? The little cashier is in despair and threatens with every breath to "kill someone." He has been lending the firm's funds to the gamblers, and now they will be unable to return the money and what will he do? Lansquenet has also been useful as a camouflage: A young son spends right and left the money he is borrowing from usurers and his contented father thinks he has won the money gambling; a wife receives a valuable jewel from her lover and the complacent husband congratulates her on her luck at cards.

Play these gamblers must, but fear of the fine of 1,000 écus keeps Mme Dorimène from inviting her guests to begin. Instead she suggests a migration to England, the Peru of gamblers, and then a journey to Holland, where gambling is unrestricted. Someone else proposes taking their

cards to the roof or to the cellar where they would be out
of reach in the one case and out of sight in the other.

A marquis arrives bearing the good news that a group
of gamblers have decided to play in the dilapidated abandoned houses of the *faubourgs* where they will be safe from
detection. Lisette advocates the better plan of retreating to
a boat and playing between the Pont Rouge and St. Cloud,
or even on to Rouen where Mme Dorimène will be half-
way to England. But play somewhere they must!

Angélique, Madame's daughter, is much disgusted with
the people who come to gamble at her mother's. Such ridiculous people; such bores! To make matters worse her
mother has chosen a husband for her from among them, a
chevalier who can make her a fortune at cards by means of
certain "infallible secrets" which he possesses. Her true
lover is frowned upon by her mother because he does not
gamble. In the nineteenth century husbands will be selected because they speculate on change and lovers rejected because they do not. Angélique's admirer, Dorante, sets his
rascally valet, Merlin, to catch the chevalier, whom he sus-
pects of being a cheat. The two swindlers soon recognize
each other, having met before at a fair under the disguise
of a wine merchant and an ox merchant. Indeed, as the
valet points out, an adventurer is liable to represent himself as a marquis, chevalier, merchant, abbot, or financier.
The chevalier is driven off. The assembly then decides to
celebrate the betrothal of Dorante and Angélique by a
game or two for which the knave Merlin promptly offers to
furnish the decks.

In the passion for gambling every law of etiquette is
forgotten. When Mme Orgon, the *joueuse* of Dufresny's
comedy by that name, refuses to pay her maid's wages because of the poor style in which the maid has been serving

suppers at her card parties, Lisette angrily describes the
mob of gamblers in her mistress's house who prefer the
green cover of the card tables to a white table cloth, and
pass the chicken around from hand to hand, snatching a
wing or a leg in the midst of their game. They drink, eat,
swear, and groan, playing all the while. How can Lisette
serve an orderly meal in such confusion?

Besides trusting to cards for a ready fortune, clever
swindlers used to set up lotteries which attracted suckers
from far and near. Among the shrewdest of these scamps
is Dancourt's Sbrigany of *La Loterie,* the Neapolitan who
establishes a lottery in Paris. He is a very honest man, is
Sbrigany; and he is running the lottery just to please the
people. Every ticket will draw a prize; most of which, as it
turns out, are handkerchiefs into which the dupes may
weep for the loss of their money. The few big prizes will
not be delivered until later, which means that they will not
be delivered at all. Sbrigany has increased the scope of his
lottery to include the giving of clandestine presents which
could in that way be received with *bienséance,* as, for instance, the Chinese chest which a *partisan* intends to fill
with rich stuffs and present to the wife of a *raporteur,* "qui
a fait prendre un bon tour à une mauvaise affaire."

The Neapolitan uses his daughter, as he does everyone
else, for his own profit. He had encouraged her attach-
ment to Eraste, a young customs officer, in order to be able
to smuggle his wares into France. Now she must decoy a
sheriff who will be useful in protecting her father in the
lottery swindle. Sbrigany takes the additional precaution
of putting an iron grill at the door of the lottery, where he
stations two formidable looking Swiss guards. Lisette, his
daughter's *suivante,* hints that a fortification might not

come amiss in case of a riot. Sbrigany has little fear, however, as he has given specially marked tickets drawing good
prizes to the few men who might prove dangerous. As for
the rest, Sbrigany knows the Parisian public. The duped
will make no complaint because of their pride; those who
have lost but little will jeer at the greater suckers; and
those who have escaped altogether will rejoice that Sbrigany should have outwitted their fellow-citizens. Lisette
warns him that such a trick as he is playing will prove a
valuable lesson to the whole city; but Sbrigany does not
care, as he has no intention of repeating the same fraud.
Lisette feels sure that after this experience there will be no
need of police ordinances to forbid lotteries.

Before the day is over, Sbrigany is assailed by many
malcontents. The peasant Bastien is furious because he
has drawn bedroom slippers, toothpicks, cold cream, and
toilet water. The Gascon demands his money back, refusing to accept the "miniature" prizes and declining to let
Sbrigany lead him about by the nose with his handkerchiefs! Mme la Procureuse arrives with three porters to
carry off her prize which she supposes from the wording of
her ticket to be a "buffet furnished with silver" but which
proves to be merely a bodice ornamented with silver thread.
The irate people threaten to drown the swindler and burn
the lottery. Eraste's uncle, the *partisan* of the Chinese
chest, promises that if Sbrigany will dower his daughter
with the 20,000 écus won on the lottery, and marry her to
Eraste, he will buy up the worst of the malcontents and
rescue Sbrigany himself. Here the financier is indeed *bien
dans son rôle*.

By the end of Louis XIV's reign French audiences had
grown accustomed to laugh at a stingy Harpagon, at Tur-

caret *traitant* and parvenu, at bankrupts, *agioteurs*, and gamblers. These types are strictly relegated to the vaude-ville stage, however; and the attitude toward them is one of scorn and hostility. Late in the eighteenth century, for the first time, members of the bourgeois class are presented to French audiences as serious and respectable people, and financiers are occasionally conceived of as honest.

CHAPTER II

FROM THE REGENCY TO THE RESTORATION

On s'habitue de plus en plus à entendre parler sur la scène de bénéfices et de pertes, d'inventaires, de billets à ordre, d'échéances et de banqueroutes.—F. GAIFFE, *Le Drame en France au XVIIIe siècle*, p. 370.

THE Regent found finances in an incredibly bad condition. One remedy after another proved futile. A court of justice was formed to try the tax-collectors and, by means of fines, replenish the treasury. This was unjust and as vain as the other schemes. It was then that John Law, who had long been the friend of Philippe d'Orléans, succeeded in persuading the government to adopt his great credit scheme. Law was looked upon as the most brilliant financier in Europe, and his plan to save France from ruin by means of a bank issuing notes secured by actual property was financially sound. The Bank of Law was incorporated in 1716. Its success was phenomenal: industry revived throughout France. About a year later Law decided to take over the monopoly of trade in Louisiana which the merchant Antoine Croizat was eager to rid himself of. The West India Company was then established, which, though nominally separate from the Bank, was in reality a part of the same system. This company was soon united to the East India Company forming the Compagnie des Indes.

Speculation on Mississippi shares became the great excitement of the day. The Rue Quincampoix, a short street where bankers were accustomed to meet, grew so crowded and noisy that police were required to clear out the *agioteurs* of an evening in order that the neighborhood might sleep. Strange tales are told of the sudden fortunes made in that street. Shares mounted by leaps. A man, so the story goes, wishing to sell his two hundred and fifty shares and being too ill to go in person, sent them by his servant with orders to dispose of each at 8,000 francs. The servant found upon reaching the Rue Quincampoix that shares had jumped to 10,000 francs. He retained the difference of 500,000 francs and multiplied it four times. Had it not been for the Regent who debased the currency in order to have more money for his mistresses, and had certain Frenchmen been less jealous of the fame of Law, France might have come safely through her difficulties with the gifted Scotchman at her helm. But his plans were wrecked by the Regent, and thousands of French people were ruined, so that the name of Law became execrated. Unfortunate as the outcome of the system was, it taught the French ultimately the value of maritime commerce, of credit, and of the spirit of co-operation, although its immediate effect was to make the French wary of any credit scheme. French industry had a relapse because of the terrible fiasco but began to recover ground toward the middle of the century.

This period seems to have produced no money-plays relating to the Système de Law. Possibly the subject was too bitter a one for the stage; or perhaps there was really no occasion for comedy to satirize Law and the speculators of the Rue Quincampoix, as the harm had been accomplished in the short space of four years and Law had left the country.

It may be in reference to the lively interest betrayed in Law's bank that Marivaux composed in 1828 his *Le Tri-*

omphe de Plutus, which pricks the worshipers of money
and the financiers. Conceived by the graceful Marivaux,
Plutus is much less terrible than Turcaret. He is a frank,
bluff fellow, rather likable on the whole; not so handsome,
it is true, as the versifying Apollo, but so rich and so generous withal that he wins the favor of everyone, even Apollo's betrothed whom Plutus courts to prove that no one can
withstand the god of treasure. He is a shade vulgar, to be
sure, and speaks of the fair Aminthe as a *morceau à cro-
quer;* and after tritely comparing her to Venus, expresses
the hope, in the young lady's very presence, that if he marries her he may be no such cuckold as the husband of Dame
Venus. Though Aminte finds Plutus *ridicule* at first, the
richness of his gifts soon causes a quick change in her sentiments, and she transfers her affections brusquely from
Apollo to his rival. Apollo comforts himself for his defeat
by the thought that it is only natural for men to prefer the
god of vices to the god of virtues and that such preference
brings no disgrace on the loser. Plutus has the one thing
desired above all others—money—which never grows old
and wrinkled. In the vaudeville at the close of the comedy
the power of money is declared. Without it one has no esteem; but, once possessed of the *métal salutaire,*

> Our every word,
> Although absurd,
> Charms and pleases:
> Praise increases.
> Would you honor, credit, rank?
> A day will quite suffice.

No favor will be granted at a mere request, but if one adds
money to the prayer,

> The most captious
> And refractious

> Now steps lively
> Most obliging.
> All goes smoothly, swiftly, surely—
> A day will quite suffice.

The shepherdess of pastoral days married for love alone, but modern ladies choose otherwise:

> Were he clown
> Or idiot grown,
> A master-fool
> Or vandal cool,
> If he but have a rich gold mine,
> A day will quite suffice.

And suitors too have ceased to look for gentleness and charm:

> Good revenues,
> Contracts, écus
> Far outweigh
> Old-time virtues.
> All such knots are quickly cut—
> A day will quite suffice.

So all the world burns incense at the altar of Plutus.

A small fragment of the Mississippi Bubble floats down into the nineteenth century. Memories of the Rue Quincampoix are in the scheming mind of Dickson when in *Le Diable d'Argent* of 1857 he tempts Peterbott into a speculation on Mississippi shares. Peterbott calls the Mississippi a "cours d'eau inventé par Law" (Dickson corrects the other's pronunciation to "Lass"). The plan proposed by Dickson is that of cornering shares so that they will rise in value. Thereupon he and his partner will throw all their shares on the market, selling "retail" what they had bought "wholesale" and realizing a profit of 300 per cent.

Tribute is paid to Law as a financier by the speculator

Lafontas, whom we shall meet again. Lafontas calls Law the "Napoleon of finance," a man of such intelligence that the best financiers since his day have modeled all their schemes on the pattern of his. Lafontas is but one of the hundreds of stage promoters who have misused the sound scheme of Law.

The eighteenth century does not seem to encourage the appearance of financiers in drama, and it is not till Saurin's *Les Moeurs du Temps* of 1760 that we find a financier at all comparable to those of Dancourt and Lesage. The public hatred toward the business men had softened somewhat because of a change in the type itself. Money and education had done much to improve their tastes and manners, and they had shown themselves generous patrons of art. Many having entered business with a fortune, are cultivated. No longer are they social outcasts suspected and suspicious; and the continued raillery at their expense, springs less from hatred than from habit.

The Géronte of Saurin's play remains the conventional figure of earlier days. This rich parvenu, a descendant of Monsieur Jourdain "avec des visions de noblesse et de galanterie" proposes to marry his daughter, in spite of her opposition, to a marquis. The latter is delighted with this *mariage d'argent* as he will have in his father-in-law a new sort of steward. "Whereas most stewards ruin us," says he, "I intend to ruin this one." Nearly a century later the the Marquis of Presles will be ruining M. Poirier and calling him an honest steward hard to replace. Géronte can see no objection to the match, as such marriages are in style.

Like Turcaret, Géronte, is immensely proud of his own untutored taste and boasts of the way in which he has furnished his house. He, too, would pass for an intellectual and hires an attendant to supply him with ideas. Not having esprit, he flatters himself that he has common sense, and, looking complacently upon his millions, thinks of himself as "le premier homme du monde." Like M. Jourdain his "lumières sont petites" but "il a du discernement dans sa bourse." Indeed, he is fully aware of the value of lucre: "Money, by Heaven! That's what I call merit. I want merit that brings in something. Tell me what a man has and I'll tell you what he's worth. Money is the only real thing there is. Intelligence, birth! What yearly income do they afford?" These are eternal characteristics of the parvenu the world over and accompany the type wherever it crops up.

Saurin has created a good, if conventional, financier but without representing him in his business milieu. It remains for Beaumarchais, writing according to the theories of Diderot, to present business characters in their natural setting. The great genre, tragedy, was waning; the classic comedy had grown stale. It was time for the rise of a genre which should represent seriously the new class slowly forcing its way upward. To meet this need, Diderot wrote a bourgeois drama, his *Père de famille,* which was played the year after Saurin's *Les Moeurs du Temps.*

It seems strange that the clever Beaumarchais should have written so calm and virtuous a business play as *Les deux Amis ou le Négociant de Lyon,* played in 1770. His hommes d'affaires are all jewels of honesty. Aurelly, the financier of Lyons, is unwittingly exposed to immediate bankruptcy on account of the sudden death of a fellow negociant in Paris. Aurelly's friend, Mélac, knowing the condition of affairs, tries to soften Aurelly's rigid attitude toward bankruptcy; but the latter insists that no distinction should be made between an honest and a dishonest bank-

ruptcy, as the safety of commerce does not admit of such
subtle discriminations: failures that are not intentionally
fraudulent are usually blameworthy as due to lack of caution.

Mérac, sure that the unavoidable disaster will kill his
friend, secretly tides over the difficulty by the use of the
public funds of which he is a collector. Aurelly would have
been none the wiser had not the inspector, Saint-Alban,
made a tour at that critical juncture and exposed Mérac.
Eventually Mérac is exculpated and Aurelly saved. A servant, being unable to remember the name of a stockbroker
among the financiers of the play, describes him as using
certain obscure phrases: "Paris 2½, Canada 30"; and he
is easily recognized by these market quotations.

The sincerity of Beaumarchais' attitude toward his
financiers is hard to determine. Be that as it may, *Les deux
Amis* marks the appearance of honest business on the stage.
In time of peace, says Aurelly, the financier has the good
fortune to be his country's hero. At last industry and patriotism join hands.

The financial idealism of this play was met with the
following jibe:

> J'ai vu de Beaumarchais le drame ridicule.
> Et je vais en un mot vous dire ce que c'est:
>   C'est un change où l'argent circule
>   Sans produire aucun intérêt.

It is difficult to forgive the witty Beaumarchais, a speculator trained by the financier Paris du Verney in all manner of business affairs, for not writing a comedy on this
milieu he knew so well, unless one accept Lanson's interpretation of Figaro as not so much the defender of liberty
as the representative of the low life of speculation which

Beaumarchais had had so many opportunities to observe: "In fact, what Figaro represents, is the world of *faiseurs* of all sorts, politicians, writers or financiers, ambitious, intelligent, unscrupulous, who run after positions and money."

Beaumarchais, himself, was a curious combination of courtier, author, and financier. In 1764 he went to Spain, a country at that time attractive to speculators, hoping to get an exclusive trade concession in Louisiana for a French company like the Compagnie des Indes. He was eager also for a contract to supply the Spanish colonies with negroes, to colonize the Sierra-Morena, to develop the industry and commerce of Spain, and to furnish supplies for the army of that country. With such enthusiasm for business he should have been born a century later. His fortunes were extremely uneven, and his career checkered with wealth and severe poverty. At the age of sixty-five he still had the courage to attempt the reconstruction of his shattered fortune in the midst of creditors, debtors, and lawsuits.

The theme of honest business and the representation of a financier in his proper milieu are both present in Sedaine's masterpiece, *Le Philosophe sans le savoir* (1765), in which the ideas of finance are so modern that Faguet sees the whole nineteenth century seething in it. Indeed the play might have been written to illustrate the industrial ideas of Saint-Simon.

The son of this financier-philosopher, Vanderk, overhearing his father's profession insulted, challenges the offender to a duel. Vanderk, though overcome with grief at his son's resolution, allows him to fight. The young man's opponent is the son of a man whom Vanderk had but lately befriended in a financial way. The young people shake hands on the duelling ground, and no blood is shed. The play in its simple and touching realism introduces a new manner to the French stage, and Jules Janin calls Sedaine "le Révolutionnaire sans le savoir." Sedaine is revolutionary, not only in his dramatic style, but in his ideas on commerce. When his son speaks of the prejudices with which business is regarded and how all bankers are supposed to be usurers, Vanderk contrasts the signature of a business man which is respected the world over with the money of a king which would be valueless did not the worth of the metal guarantee the impress. Vanderk ranks only the magistrate and the soldier above the financier. The negociant, however, is a cosmopolitan figure serving all nations; he is *l'homme de l'univers* in whose hands is the fate of all countries. The financiers are silken threads which bind the world together and keep it at peace.

A realistic stage-setting represents Vanderk's office where his desk is seen littered with papers. Large supplies of coin are carried in, and Vanderk cashes a letter of credit before the audience. It is significant that this financier is a nobleman. Obliged to leave Holland because of a duel, Vanderk had sought refuge in France, where, forced to earn a livelihood, he had taken up business, feeling himself in no way dishonored in so doing. After the French Revolution, many aristocrats of drama will follow his example unblushingly.

Equally honest, though of less noble family, is "Vilson," the English manufacturer-hero of Falbaire de Quingey's extremely sentimental melodrama, *Le Fabricant de Londres,* played with very poor success at the Comédie-Française early in the year 1771. This would-be touching picture of domestic life was much more favorably received by the German public, who doubtless admired the stiffly starched little Wilsons and the self-sacrificing "Fanni." Wilson has recently lost his dear "Clariss," who bade him on her death bed make Fanny, who with her mother had found refuge in the hospitable Wilson home, the step-mother of the two children she herself must leave. Fanny is courted by a nobleman but refuses his attentions that she may give her heart and hand to Wilson. The marriage is consummated during the second act, and the happy pair returns to the shop only to be greeted with the tidings of two bankruptcies which reduce Wilson to poverty. The heroic Wilson determines on suicide in order to leave Fanny free to marry her rich suitor; but, when about to throw himself into the Thames, he is accosted by Lord Falkland who, to make a more advantageous marriage, had deserted Fanny's mother when Fanny was born. His wife is now dead; and having in vain sought his mistress and his daughter, he is also on the point of consigning his body to the black waters of the Thames. Having heard Wilson's tale of woe, he eagerly offers him money, and no sooner is the generous offer accepted and Wilson restored to his bride than Falkland discovers in Fanny his long-lost daughter and in her mother the woman he had seduced and whom he now intends to marry. The French audience can scarcely be reproached for having been unmoved by this domestic melodrama.

The realism of *Le Fabricant de Londres*, which is considerable, met with no sympathy in France. The first four acts take place in the room back of Wilson's shop, from which glimpses can be had of the shop itself and the rooms where the weavers are at work filling orders. David, the clerk, writes a business letter on the stage to protest against the quality of wool received from a certain firm; and he then makes up the pay-roll of the men, performing his calculations aloud. *Lettres de change* are presented for payment and are met by Fanny's dowry and her diamond earrings. But even this generosity is insufficient, and the bailiff comes at once to carry off the furniture. While he is busy dismantling the house, the dejected workmen file out through the shop, declining with deep emotion the gift of a gold chain which the unhappy employer has taken from his little daughter to pay their wages.

The atmosphere of the play is one of such rarefied virtue that creatures of flesh and blood could scarcely live in it. Honesty is, temporarily at least, in vogue on the stage, as other plays of the same decade show. In Mercier's *L'Indigent*, which is, by the way, an ancestor of such socialistic plays as Pyat's *Les deux Serruriers* and Serret's *Un mauvais Riche*, the wealthy De Lys refuses to seek for his lost sister in order to keep all the inheritance for himself. How can he live on the pittance his father had found sufficient? Indeed, says his dishonest attorney, M. du Noir, a financier cannot shine without great expenditure of money, for he has neither birth nor illustrious actions to distinguish him. De Lys attempts to seduce a pretty factory girl who virtuously repulses him and bids her father return to the debtors' prison rather than accept any kindness from such a villain. Who can fail to divine that this pretty Charlotte is De Lys' lost sister? The lawyer who makes the discovery supports her in her claim as joint heir, and De Lys discovers at last that even he has a heart and is able to repent of his misconduct.

The honest lawyer, busily occupied at his desk, sadly regrets the condition of society. Never were people so eager after money! So many loans; so many swindles. A usurer goes bankrupt, and everything is fixed up for his benefit. It is veritable robbery. Heirs can hardly wait for death in order to seize their share of the property, and their brother's too, if possible. A financier locks his daughter up in a convent that he may use her dowry on extravagant living, and a father would deprive his little children of their property for the sake of a second wife. How honest a lawyer must be to protect men against their own wickedness!

Such criticisms of society are to be expected in this philosophic eighteenth century, and playwrights killed comedy by exchanging her common sense for tiresome moralizing. One of the worst of these offenses is perpetrated by Chamfort in his *La jeune Indienne*, in which the Indian "Betti" who has been seduced by a shipwrecked American, accompanies him to Charlestown where she is confronted with civilized society. Instead of being impressed with the excellence of a mode of living based on the possession of gold, the young savage is eager to return to her cave and the chase. How terrible that one's happiness should depend on *ce métal stérile*, and how stupid of her lover to be afraid of poverty! Belton explains how powerful money is, and Betty is shocked at the harm that might be occasioned by wicked rich men:

> If gold has so much power, how fearful you must be.
> They can of you and of your lives dispose so easily.

Belton is indeed so afraid of poverty that he is arranging to marry the rich Arabella whom he had once loved; but Betty convinces him of his perfidy to her, and Belton marries her all the more willingly as his father's old friend and beneficiary Mowbrai dowers her richly.

La Brouette du Vinaigrier, by Mercier, has again the theme of the honest business man who is unavoidably ruined by the bankruptcy of a firm on which he is dependent. Delomer, seeing his fortune collapsing thus, wishes to take advantage of those as yet ignorant of the state of his affairs and orders his clerk Dominique to borrow as much money as he can. But Dominique reminds him that to borrow now will bring ruin on others and cannot mend his own business. Surely Delomer is too honest to have recourse to such an act:

> Ah, Sir! do not yield to that unworthy weakness which the first attack of misfortune brings. Do not break this circulation, the soul of commerce; respect it even in the midst of your reverses; equity and honor will overcome all difficulties. Think of the wrong that you will do; twenty families will be plunged into poverty and they will accuse you. They will be destitute and you still have resources.

Dominique at length persuades Delomer to sell all he possesses, which will cover the amount of his indebtedness. By so doing his credit will remain intact and he will be able to face the world, an honest though a poor man. Delomer is, however, not reduced to this extremity. A fortune is trundled on to the stage in the wheelbarrow of the vinegar merchant, Dominique's father, who offers all his savings on condition that his son and Delomer's daughter, who are in love, may be allowed to marry. The old man apostrophizes his sacks of coin:

> Pernicious metal! You have done enough harm in the world to do good at least once. I have been hoarding you for a great moment. Now is the time so greatly desired! Go and establish the peace and security of a house which love and virtue will inhabit. I will sometimes go and enjoy the use they make of you: the father, the daughter, my son . . . . they are all good people.

With the close of the Old Régime the *parvenu traitant* is still affording a spectacle for French audiences, but beside him stand the honorable Aurelly and the proud Vanderk expressing a new and enlightened view of finance, a consciousness of its world-wide significance. Even a financier of the stage may be something more than a swindler robbing his fellow-men. Unfortunately the dramatic descendants of Aurelly and Vanderk are few indeed.

The New Régime opened with a period of uncertainty, terror, and licentiousness. Society swarmed with the curious types of speculators who had come to the surface in this great upheaval, but the theater took little interest in them. This new heterogeneous society preferred tearful tragedies. There are, nevertheless, a few plays which in some degree represent the business men of the time.

Crusophile of Charlemagne's *L'Agioteur* (1795) is a rich speculator to whom a certain attorney determines to marry his daughter in order to further his business interests. Crusophile is caught in a fraudulent affair, and the unhappy girl is set free. Crusophile is the kind of rogue which is to multiply so rapidly: an unalloyed scamp, whose sole passion is speculation, whose morality is nil. He is brazenly *coquin* in order not to be a dupe. The picture of society as the resort of rascals whose one idea is "money" was, strange to say, enthusiastically received by the public. Unfortunately Charlemagne was not a sharp observer; and he missed, says a journalist of the time, one of the most striking characters of the period, the elegantly dressed aristocrat who was to be seen flitting about from shop to shop laden with merchandise and drawing samples of cheese from his amber-scented pockets.

The *nouveaux riches* are represented in Pujoulx's comedy, *Les Modernes enrichis*, by a certain Victor Truchant, who, after a fraudulent bankruptcy in 1789, had amassed a fortune as a contractor and had settled in Paris under the name of Saint-Victor (the adoption of "Saint" is a favorite trick with the speculator). In Paris Truchant discovers that he is living in the same house with a man whom he had ruined by his bankruptcy. Truchant tries in vain to have the man forced out of the house. Meanwhile, by a very unlikely event, Truchant is ruined. A swindler persuades both him and his associate that the government intends to investigate the fortunes of the newly rich. The frightened Truchant turns his money over to the rogue and retires to the country.

Fraudulent bankruptcies were extremely prevalent, as one might expect, at a time of so much political and economic disturbance. Fourier calls them the most ingenious and the most impudent form of rascality that has ever existed; and Alphonse Toussenel sarcastically dubs these bankrupts the "Bayards of the moneyed feudality, the noble wounded of the great battles of industry." Louis Picard, a favorite dramatist during the first two decades of the century, undertakes in his *Duhautcours* (1801) to correct this reprehensible form of speculation which is a subject "better befitting tragedy than comedy." In his Preface, Picard admits his indebtedness to *Le Banqueroutier* of 1687, from which he has drawn the general plan of the play and the leading characters—a dupe who wishes to enrich himself *à toute vitesse,* and a *fripon* who makes it his business to arrange bankruptcies. The biting, delightful farce which treats its theme so lightly and deftly far surpasses the heavily moralized treatment of Picard's comedy.

The tempter Duhautcours finds the weak-willed Durville easy prey and soon persuades him that it is legitimate to cheat one's creditors. Duhautcours, in preparing Durville's bankruptcy, recommends that the latter sign his property over to his wife and give a magnificent ball to keep the public from suspecting his dishonest intentions. Durville is finally declared bankrupt, and a meeting of creditors called to sign the terms. The meeting is held; and the creditors are about to sign when Durville's friend, Franval, an *instrument de grâce,* divines the fraud, unmasks Durville's true financial standing, and forces the would-be bankrupt to pay all his debts. Durville, colorless and weak, repents and reforms. Franval, the *raisonneur*, with megaphone to mouth, proclaims down the century the moral of the play: "Respect au malheur; indulgence au repentir; guerre éternelle aux fripons."

Charles Etienne wrote a play very closely resembling *Duhautcours*, which he called *Le pauvre Riche, ou la Séparation de biens*. This was received in 1803 by Picard, then director of the Théâtre-Louvois, but was apparently suppressed by him, perhaps, as M. Allard suggests, because Picard was a little jealous concerning his own play. This play, taken in connection with *Les deux Gendres*, shows Etienne's interest in money, that subject of paramount importance in life. Etienne's name is almost forgotten, but it should be recalled in regard to the comedy of manners and the development of realism in drama.

It was wholly beyond the power of Picard to stem the current of fraudulent bankruptcies. They become a more and more lucrative speculation. A swindler either makes terms with his creditors—terms which are ruinous to the latter—or he decamps with all their money as the *agioteur* of the following lines:

> Just look at this scurvy rogue,
> Gambler and robber discreet!
> Last year this swindling scamp
> Shook the dust of the town from his feet.
> He is pitied by all, as I know,
> And so in his schemes will persist.
> Let him *fail* again two or three times
> And we'll see him a capitalist.

> —FRANCIS, *et al., Le Capitaliste malgré lui*, II, 11

The subject is a very popular one in drama throughout the century. The melodrama paints the bankrupt black; the vaudeville makes him a jest; and the *drames* of our own day allude to him gravely or cynically.

Bitter melodramatic imprecations are frequently hurled at the financier. The villain of Desnoyer's *Le Facteur ou la Justice des hommes* is rich "thanks to a most shameful bankruptcy; after three years all is forgotten. He is now a banker, an elector, a baron, and member of a bureau of charity. Such is human justice." This insolent financier promises his creditors 25 per cent of his capital, retaining two million francs for himself. "They will bless me for that," says he. "If I gave them a cent more they would think me a fool." The bankrupt has nothing to fear if the creditors declare themselves satisfied. He need not even leave town. The creditors hold the key of this door to wealth, says some character in another melodrama, and offer it to anyone who will but pay them something. These terms make a "comfortable bed to rest in and there are millions under the pillow."

Dire woes result from a fraudulent bankruptcy committed by a young scapegrace, Edouard, and his business partner, Frédéric, in *Le Banqueroutier* of 1826. The affair caused a great stir at the time; but, such speculations being à la mode, people called it an *affaire malheureuse* and promptly forgot it. Not so the honest business man, Montfort, however, to whose daughter Edouard has become engaged. This bankruptcy, which he in no way associates with his future son-in-law, had caused his own ruin and the ruin of several firms depending on him; the suicide of his father-in-law, who had made the unfortunate investment for him; the death of his wife; and the dangerous somnambulism of his daughter. Edouard, to whom Montfort relates this series of catastrophes, recognizes with shame that his own dishonest act had been the cause of these terrible events. After further horrors, Edouard is shot and his friend imprisoned.

A very romantic treatment of the theme is given by Jacques Bornet in *La Banqueroute* with its *cri du sang* and the incident of hair turning suddenly white. The banker Dussolin is an immoral rogue who has abandoned an illegitimate son and intends to marry his daughter to a man of sixty for the sake of his money. In order to conceal a premeditated bankruptcy, he uses his daughter as his secretary. She, however, shrewdly detects the fraud and, with the assistance of the lawyer Daniel, who proves to be her father's deserted son, forestalls Dussolin's plans. She discovers the secret cupboard where he keeps the money of his creditors and his correct balance sheet. Possessing herself of these things, she returns the money to the creditors, thus saving her father's honor in spite of himself. For this he is most ungrateful and wishes for his lost son who might have been rascal enough to help him in his crooked deals.

The farcical vaudeville, *Une Assemblée de Créanciers*, by Théaulon and Lubize, is much more in the spirit of Noland de Fatouville's *Le Banqueroutier* than either *Duhautcours* or the melodramas just related. Badinaud, the bankrupt, is a weak and cowardly soul who would like to make his escape across the border. Not so Mme Badinaud, his wife. She wants the bankruptcy carried out in real style. All the funds are safely in her name, and she is prepared to swear that Badinaud possesses nothing but "son imtelligence et sa bonne volonté." The whole affair is intrusted to Lombard, true son of this century of speculation, who devotes himself particularly to furthering bankruptcies. While in Paris, do as the Parisians do, urges Lombard. You must be able to say: "J'ai été aux eaux, j'ai vu la mer, j'ai joué la comédie ... j'ai fait faillite." Lombard has, in fact, a bankruptcy company, "entreprise utile, morale et philanthropique." A millionaire who wishes to pull off a big bankruptcy calls on the company to furnish eight or ten fake creditors. These persuade the real creditors to sign the document which ruins them but enriches the speculator. Lombard, experienced in handling these "wild beasts" of creditors, knows what to expect. Among them will be some fools, a few honest men, some who are indifferent as to what they get, a sprinkling of recalcitrants, and a certain number of rogues. Persuasion will succeed with all but the rogues. These are always the first to cry *au voleur!* and must be given special privileges—"il faut bien que tout le monde vive!"

The play progresses. Some of the creditors sign at once. Others are not moved till Lombard shows off the pitiable Badinaud, dressed in hired rags and instructed to whine and hang his head. Unfortunately Badinaud is fat: "ca n'excite pas la pitié ... si vous aviez pu maigrir un peu ... mais nous sommes si pressés." All the creditors finally sign except Dumont. Lombard at last finds his vulnerable spot. He is about to become a father. Lombard has a messenger summon him to his wife's bedside and persuades him that a young son is already calling him. Dumont signs and hurries out followed by the other creditors. At the foot of the stairs they meet Mme Dumont and realize that they are victims of a trick. Rushing back they discover the gleeful rogues sitting down to lobster and champagne. The irate creditors are appeased when they learn that the stolid German at the table, whom they take to be an Englishman because he is eating beafsteak, is to marry Mlle Badinaud and pay all her father's debts. And so the play ends with one more trick on the part of the rogues.

The frontier most convenient for the escaping bank-

rupt is Belgium. So in the skit of 1829 by Dumersan and
Gabriel called *Les Rouliers ou la Route de Bruxelles* it is
no surprise to find the road to Brussels being used by the

The bankrupt Macaire and his partner Bertrand leave France for safe
haven of Belgium.

swindler Valbrun, who by the slow means of a *diligence,* is
escaping with the money of his creditors tucked away in
his purse. Accidents will happen, even to crooks: the stage
coach overturns, and Valbrun loses his purse. The precious
object is tossed by the hand of Providence into the posses-

sion of the penniless Didier who is sighing in vain for the
innkeeper's daughter whose rich father spurns his suit.
Didier tries to find Valbrun to return the purse, but that
gentleman's fears had spurred him on toward Belgium.
Shortly after, there arrives news from Paris of a disaster to
the innkeeper: a fraudulent banker has run off with his
funds along with those of other creditors. But there is no
cause for alarm. Didier, the hero, holds those very funds in
his hand. They are restored to their owners, and Didier
marries the innkeeper's daughter.

This vaudeville affords a diverting song on the escape
to Belgium.

> Brussels offers an asylum
>   To many a clever scamp
> And especially in the autumn
>   They are known to decamp.
> They flit by like swallows
>   Carrying our cash.
> They'll not return when Springtime follows . . . .
>   They wouldn't be so rash!
>
> —Scene 11

The speculator Saint-Joseph, a contemporary of the
above-named Valbrun, recommends to a friend a bankrupt's well-tried horse:

> A banker sold me this goodly steed,
> A banker of wealth who, within one year,
> In spite of the clamoring public here,
> Rode three times at topmost speed
> To a sure retreat in Belgium dear.
>
> —MAZÈRES, *La Fin du Mois,* scene 8

Vauléon, a brother-speculator in the next decade, explains his departure and that of so many others for this
land of refuge:

I tell you I'm leaving for Brussels today.
For angels rebelling 'tis Botany-Bay:
For the debtor cleaned out, the fraud and the cheat,
There never was known a better retreat:
Above all for those whom France cannot bear
Because of their shrewdness and industry rare:
That is the reason I'm settling there.

—M. G. MALVOISINE, *Le Ver rongeur*, V, 8

A vaudeville with the significant title *Paris et Bruxelles, ou le Chemin à la mode* sends the speculator off to safety with a gay crack of the whip:

Air d'un marche
Click, clack, Postillon, clack! Give her a whack!
　　Let's hit the track!
　　To Brussels town we'll make the tour.
　　Speed up, man, your tip is sure.
　　The long whip shrieks,
　　The paving creaks,
　　There's the frontier
　　And we are near!
How many fêted are at home
Who suddenly begin to roam—
　　Inconstant they
　　To run away.
There's Mr. Rich, a broker of fame
Who likes to live in gay Paree
　　And yet, all the same,
At the end of the month away he'll flee!
Click, clack, Postillon, clack! Give her a whack!
　　Let's hit the track! etc.

—Scene 4

With the rise of the joint-stock company, bankruptcy augments as a speculation and becomes increasingly common. This system is the same but the gains of the speculators are much greater and the losses affect more creditors. Details of these colossal swindles will be given later. The cynical realism with which they are handled is already felt in Ernest Feydeau's *Un Coup de Bourse* (1861). Moïse Silberstein drives his son the banker into bankruptcy: "In our business," says the old Jew, "which does not depend on work and is but a form of speculation, of gambling, the only way to get rich quickly and safely is by failing. That's what I did and that's why I'm not so hard up today as people think." When the bankruptcy has been compassed, Moïse offers to pay his son's creditors 50 per cent of the debt. So generous a reimbursement is rare. Indeed, Fourier calls it "honest" because so unusual. With the five millions still in his pocket Moïse intends to set his son up in business again.

The bankrupts alluded to in the foregoing pages—Dussolin, Lombard, Silberstein, and the rest—are but a few of the many such swindlers who follow in the footsteps of Duhautcours and Durville, whose fraudulent bankruptcy opens the swindles of the nineteenth century.

The Old Régime produced a money-play in certain respects fundamentally different from that which accompanies the rise of industry in the nineteenth century. The early financier, whether tax-collector, usurer, or bankrupt, had been looked upon as belonging to a class apart and was interesting particularly as a figure to be laughed at or hissed (save in a few exceptional plays). The public cared little about his actual business. The turmoil of the French Revolution, for which the system of tax-farming was largely responsible, and the swiftly changing politics of the succeeding years, aided in opening the doors of society to the financier. He ceases to belong to a class apart; he is a neighbor one meets on any street or in any house, and above all at the bourse. He is no longer considered a stain on the society of the salon, sufficiently different from the rest of the gathering to be noticeable, but is gradually accepted as an integral part of it. The nineteenth-century public, keenly interested in the steadily increasing possibilities of money-making, now sees in the financier a sort of hero and demands of the money-play an accurate report of his speculations, which, on account of personal experience, the public is capable of understanding and appreciating. Although many of the conventionalities of the Old Régime persist in the nineteenth-century money-play, the latter is pervaded by a new and very different spirit.

The Hunchback who made a fortune renting his back in the Rue-Quincampoix

CHAPTER III

THE NEW SPIRIT

Voyez-vous, mon garçon, dans le siècle où nous vivons il faut être plus positif : je veux faire de vous un industriel .... —J. ANCELOT, L'Escroc du grand monde, Act II, scene 3.

THERE is materialism in every age, even in the most aristocratic and idealistic, but never did it become such a tremendous romantic force as in the nineteenth century. Never before did it find its way so universally into poetry, novels, and drama. Never had the stage been so free to reflect realistically the lives of the middle classes; and perhaps the middle classes had never been quite so interesting as when they set about the building of colossal fortunes, inventing one huge speculative scheme after another. The old aristocracy, finding that glory and distinction must be sought elsewhere than at court or in the battlefield, turned toward industry and joined the bourgeois in the pursuit of wealth. Class barriers had already begun to weaken under the Old Régime because of the intermarriages between the nobles and the financiers. The Revolution had swept away, in theory at least, many of the traditional barriers still left standing; but it was, above all, steam, with its enormous effect on industry, which brought the final leveling influences of material comfort and wealth to all classes.

The person most responsible for the steadily increasing growth of French industry was that imaginative and daring genius, Claude Henri de Saint-Simon, who spent his life and energy trying to show France her way to salvation through industrial prosperity. Ultimate human perfection and the abolishment of war were to be attained, and a brotherly Christianity seeking particularly to better the conditions of the poor. This socialist, preaching eagerly on the text "Tout par l'industrie, tout pour elle" drew numerous converts who, in after years, realized many of his great plans, not only in France but in foreign lands as well. His was an imagination capable of conceiving a Panama Canal, and his devotion to the cause of industry became so passionate a faith that upon it he built a religion and founded a church.

Saint-Simon, a reformed speculator, who had seen a vision and become a prophet of industry, was a choice subject for ridicule. A vaudeville of 1832, by Vander-Burch and Langlé, *Louis-Bronze et le Saint-Simonien*, which represents the Poissy prison of which Louis-Bronze is jailor and to which industrials are sent to learn honesty, is a parody of Casimir Delavigne's *Louis IX;* and François de Paule is replaced by Père Bouffantin, a caricature of Père Enfantin, described by Taxile Delord as a "socialist pope in sleeve-protectors with a swivel chair for a throne and a railroad office for a Vatican, who preached the religion of Saint-Simon which was no religion but a science, the science of business: stock exchanges, railroads, banks, factories and companies."

While Père Bouffantin of the parody is preaching, he tries to steal a few of Louis' clothes. After explaining the meaning of communism and citing *Le Globe*, which had received that year the subtitle of *Journal de la doctrine de Saint-Simon*, he promises rivers flowing with tea and chocolate, sheep ready roasted gamboling in the fields, trees producing apple preserves, harvests of clothes, snow of wine, and rain of pullets and other French delicacies. But of

one thing Père Bouffantin warns his hearers—none of the
money which they sink in shares in industrial enterprises
will ever be refunded. A character of the play announces
that virtue is now divided into bonds, God into shares, and
morality has become a coupon book. The saint of this new
religion is described as a tramp in the most threadbare of
clothes, in battered hat and ragged shoes—this new saint
who delivers people not of their sins but of their money.

After citing the famous words "A chacun selon ses
oeuvres et sa capacité," another socialist of the stage sings
a droll interpretation of communism:

> To put an end to our wretchedness
>   Our latest rules decree
> Children shall all be parentless
>   And parents childless be.
> No more advantages of birth,
>   No heritages sure . . . .
> How very much we shall be worth
>   When everyone is poor!
> —SAINT-HILAIRE *et al.*, *Encore un Préjugé*, scene 6

It is with such parodies that the French vaudevillists
derided the socialistic ideas of Saint-Simon and his industrial schemes. It was, in fact, his doctrine of industrialism,
rather than his socialism, that bore fruit; and the push he
gave the ball of industry in the first quarter of the century
sent it speeding along with continually increasing momen-
tum.

For some years after the beginning of the nineteenth
century there was no great flare of industry, but rather a
wavering unsteady flame which needed all the fanning
that Napoleon I and his intelligent minister, Jean-Antoine
Chaptal, were able to give. Expositions were inaugurated to
bring manufacturers together and to introduce new meth-

ods. The program of development was carried on by Louis XVIII who arranged for expositions at intervals of four years after that of 1819. Gold and silver medals were distributed; decorations of the Legion of Honor and the Order of St. Michael and the title of "baron" were bestowed upon the most active manufacturers. A comedy-vaudeville, *Le Fabricant ou la Filature,* of 1823, by Francis and Brazier, shows the home of a rich manufacturer with his factory in the distance. Dermont, as he is called, has established a model concern and in recompense has received a gold medal from the government. He urges his men to work harder than ever now that the king has rewarded them so generously. He enumerates in one song the time-honored French industries—perfumes, silk, velvet, and other stuffs; in another he celebrates the progress of industry.

> Chaillot makes the rugs from Turkey,
>   Lyons gives *florence* and *pékin,*
> Paris the perfumes of Araby,
>   And from Rouen there comes *nankin.*
>
> France beloved, in thee all grows:
>   And nature bows at thy decree.
> Thou need'st no help from friends or foes
>   But every land hath need of thee.
>
> —Scene 7
>
> We all admire the progress
>   Of native industry
> And see that every workman
>   Is working steadily.
> Our monarch need not fear
>   For the future days of France—
> The more the hands to make her rich,
>   The more for her defense.
>
> —Scene 13

Here is a new patriotism and a novel paladin!

Louis Picard and Eugène Scribe, with their many collaborators, people the French stage with this bourgeois class so valiantly ready to defend its country. Picard is often rather vague in his allusions to commercial activities, but Scribe adds the few determining lines which transform a *commerçant* into a *marchand de bois, de fourrures, de mercier, de bonneterie,* or perhaps into *a confiseur,* and turns the stage into a shop or factory. Failure to understand the subtleties of deep emotion, an exaggerated use of the little event to turn the tide of his plays, lack of literary style, and an ideal *à hauteur de comptoir* kept him from being a great dramatist; but Scribe was unconsciously preparing the way for the social comedy in these vaudevilles which flattered the long-neglected bourgeoisie and represented observations of actual life which had no place in classic tragedy or romantic drama. As Hippolyte Parigot says, "Il ne dit plus: *condition* avec Diderot; il ne dit point *couleur locale* avec Victor Hugo. Il se prend aux moeurs." Scribe is, indeed, with his actuality and his clever intrigue, the dramatist of his time and of his craft.

In 1817, when the French drygoods store was still a gloomy boutique with its small stock of silks piled away on dark shelves, Scribe conceived, in *Le Combat des Montagnes,* his dapper little clerk Calicot (the cotton cloth of that name had just been invented), with mustache, black cravat and spurs, whose battlefield was a counter and whose lance a yard stick. Scribe and his collaborator H. Dupin were jesting a little at the expense of those warlike clerks of the Restoration who longed to be considered conquerors of Europe condemned to a forced rest. But they had to make amends at once. The shopkeepers of Paris were furious at the caricature and made war on the Théâtre des Variétés where the vaudeville was having a run.

The authors yielded to public opinion and immediately wrote another vaudeville, *Le Café des Variétés,* in which shop-keeping folk are most respectfully handled. Does a clerk wear spurs? Does he wear mustaches? Indeed not! Why should he blush at being a clerk rather than a soldier when his business is the most useful of all occupations? The merchant Bernard Lerond states this emphatically:

> 'Tis he who spreads abundance
>   By his industriousness;
> 'Tis he whose useful influence
>   Binds all lands to us.
> Although to noble victory
>   All states should honor pay,
> And though the arts should lauded be . . . .
>   'Tis commerce brings the happiest day.
>
> —Scene 5

A contented merchant of La Scribie is Vert-Bois of the Rue St.-Jacques, who rejoices at hot weather when he can sell "le silésien, le bouracan et le camelot"; and who rubs his hands with glee at the cold when out of his shop go "la ratine, le louviers et le velours."

The little boutique, dark and grimy, where Scribe found his Calicot and his Vert-Bois, is destined to grow under the magic touch of the nineteenth century. Its metamorphosis is already sensible in *Les trois Quartiers,* of 1827, by Picard and Mazères, the theme of which is the rejuvenation of France by the blending of wealth and aristocracy. The three quarters are the Rue St.-Denis with its shopkeepers, the Chausée d'Antin and its bankers, and the aristocratic Boulevard St.-Germain. A certain Després arranges a match for his friend Desrosiers with a girl from each class successively. When the shopkeeper's daughter is found too poor, and the financier's daughter discarded as not noble enough, the Comtesse de Montfort is settled upon. But she, learning how Desrosiers has treated her friends, rejects him for a banker. Jenny, the daughter of finance, weds a poor viscount; and Georgette Bertrand of of the Rue St.-Denis marries a clerk. Her father's shop is a lively place: sales are discussed, money counted, and customers served. The attitude throughout the play is one of great respect for this honest shopkeeper, the "doyen des marchands de nouveautés de la rue St.-Denis."

A still more pretentious store is described in *Le Lansquenet et les Chemins de fer* by Bayard and Dumanoir (1845). Old M. Quincampoix has come to Paris and finds it necessary to do a little shopping:

> I never laid eyes on so big a store:
> Monstrous stairs and enormous door,
> Mighty counters and giant clerks.
> And in this store with the great big works
> Of bigness everything had a share . . . .
> Except the kerchief I purchased there!
>
> —Scene 2

Did the old fellow, perhaps, do his shopping in the Belle Fermière or Le Pauvre Diable?

None of the French department stores that we know today were establishments of any consequence until twenty years later when Sardou produced his *La Maison neuve,* which might represent the rising Bon Marché or the Belle Jardinière, which was winning fame for its ready-made garments. The play contrasts the dingy shop of old Paris with the *magasin de nouveautés,* such as Zola describes in his novel, *Au Bonheur des Dames.* Genevoix, an old-fashioned *commerçant,* is very proud of his excellent silk shop in the Rue Thévenot. René, the husband of Genevoix's niece Claire, is in partnership with him. Both of the young people rebel at the dinginess. Claire complains bitterly of having to keep accounts in her glass cage, listening to the eternal stacking of bolts of goods and the going and coming of clerks. She and her husband resolve on an establishment of their own and open Le Bouton d'Or in the Boulevard Malesherbes with all the pomp which a professional *lanceur* can give. Old Genevoix watches the expensive venture anxiously from his shop, La Vieille Cocarde, which, ever since his grandfather had cornered red, white, and blue ribbon in 1789, had stood the shocks of business, even the "terrible échéance de février." The young people are glad to accept Genevoix's aid when they have all but ruined themselves financially and morally in their new enterprise.

It was not until after the middle of the century that French textile industries were fully reformed. Steam was, however, gradually being introduced here and there. By 1832 twenty-four steam engines were at work in Lille. In a play of the following year, *L'Escroc du grand monde,* Jacques Ancelot presents a progressive individual by the name of Dubourg who announces that his new steam-run machine for making waterproof hats will be in use "Thursday next." He needs but fifteen workmen to run his five machines; whereas, under the old system, he had used three hundred men.

A factory episode furnishes material for a thrilling recital in Etienne Arago's *Les Aristocraties,* of 1847. Mlle Laurence is visiting the factory with her aunt. The sight of the great machines, the gigantic arms steam-driven, the excitement, the noise, confuse the visitors; their clothes are suddenly caught in a moving chain and they are being dragged to death when the hero, Valentin, the director of the factory, leaps to their rescue. He, in his turn, is caught

by a wheel and would have been crushed had he not had
the presence of mind to detach the cable. This modern Ri-
naldo is rescuing his fair lady from the giants of a new age.

Scribe, writing from his usual bourgeois point of view,
notes with evident satisfaction the cases of nobles who
have thrown in their lot with the manufacturers. He presents in *L'Ennui* the Count Derfort, who, finding himself
penniless, seeks work in a factory, quells a strike, and succeeds admirably in his new occupation. Another of his aristocrats, D'Havrecourt, celebrates the place that industry
has taken in the life of the old nobility:

> They thought me proud of my birth,
> My forebears and family name:
> But a penniless marquis will forsooth
> Turn industrial all the same.
> A many-windowed factory tall
> Replaces our ancestral hall,
> And on our ancient grass-grown wall
> (May my dead fathers pardon it!)
> I have, by work, our arms rebuilt.
>
> *Uno Femmo qui so jotto par la Fonôtro,* scene 3

A drama by Guerville, *La Sonnette du Diable,* permits
the noble De Cerny to explain that he has gone into manufacturing because the old aristocracy is dead and because a
man no longer offers his sword to his king but his life to his
country. Instead of shedding blood on the battlefield, he
himself keeps three hundred families occupied. Now that
a fortune is the only patent of nobility, he intends to double
and triple his capital in order not to be crushed by the luxury of some valet enriched at the bourse.

In this great development of industry the character
which seems to incorporate most truly the ideals of Saint-

Simon is the civil engineer. He is the hero of an age of constructions: canals, roads, bridges, railroads, and the rebuilding of cities. By 1855 (the date of Ernest Legouvé's *Par Droit de Conquête*), he has become the French matinée idol of whom Francisque Sarcey says, when discussing the revival of this play in 1878, that he represents active science; and, as the only progress then admitted as possible was the subjugation of nature, he was elevated to the post of missionary and apostle of progress. The protagonist of the above-mentioned play resembles a mythological hero in his conquest of natural forces. Under the materialism of the nineteenth century there is always a lurking romanticism. It crops out in this self-made *enfant du peuple*, occupied in the construction of canals, roads, drainage works, exploitation of mines, and so on, who considers himself the equal of the ancient preux of France. Engineers have exchanged the sword for a compass and are repelling floods, fires, mortal pestilences—foes more terrible than the robber of old. Sure of the nobility of his calling, Georges Bernard aspires to and wins the hand of the noble Alice de Rochegune. He finds a supporter in Marquis de Rouillé, a devotee of science, who points with pride to the steamboat invented by the Marquis de Jouffroy, and nurses the fond idea that the old aristocracy might regain its prestige through the study of science.

Under Napoleon I the French civil engineer extended roads through France and beyond the Mont Cenis pass and the Simplon, down the Dalmatian Coast, and along the Rhine Valley—13,000 leagues of them. Under the Restoration the roads were kept intact but the attention of the engineer was turned, particularly toward the lengthening and multiplication of canals. Before 1830, 900 kilometers of navigable canals had been added to the 1,200 previously existing. By 1848 could be counted 2,000 additional kilometers.

Speculation very soon took an interest in canals, roads, and bridges. As early as 1821 appears a vaudeville skit, *Les Joueurs*, in which the financing of such enterprises by means of shares is alluded to:

> Into shares all is divided:
> Canals and bridges, balls and shows
> Are by industry exploited
> And everyone for coupons goes.
>
> —MOREAU *et al.*, scene 10

Mme Dalincourt of Bonjour's *L'Argent*, of the same decade, reviews her stock anxiously: regrets her *métalliques* which are not selling well, and wishes that she had bought canal stock instead as it is much better. But of all allusions to canals, that in a contemporary vaudeville, *Les Entrepreneurs*, by Brazier, Dumersan, and Gabriel, is the best. An old bourgeois, M. Jobin, living in retirement at Ivry, is so much a prey to the speculation frenzy that he will allow his daughter to marry only a successful speculator who will take him into business partnership. His daughter is in love with the neighbor Jaquinard's son, but her father remains obdurate. Jaquinard, in order to cure Jobin of this craze, disguises himself as a M. Filtré, promoter of a most original scheme. The sea is to be brought to Ivry by means of a canal. The town will become a seaport with baths and an oyster market. Filtré is adequate to the great scheme, having already undertaken to purify the Seine by sending it through casks. "Are we not," he urges, "in a century of canals?" And then he enumerates those of Languedoc, Ivette, Orleans, Briarre, and Ourcq, predicting finally that Jobin will ride to fortune on this new canal through

Ivry. What could Jobin do but accept Jaquinard's proposition? His one concern is that, with the sea brought so near, he and his wife may be disturbed at night by storms. When Jaquinard sends workmen to demolish Jobin's house, the latter comes to his senses, renounces speculation, and marries his daughter to Jaquinard's son.

A jesting allusion is found in *Le Diable à Paris*, by Brazier and Gabriel, to the construction of bridges and to stock in the same. In a dialogue, Filoselle and Jean discuss the former's investments.

Says Filoselle:

> Sur un pont nouveau
> J'viens d'en prendre un'douzaine,

Jean (aside):

> Ça n'fait-y d'la peine,
> V'là son argent dans l'eau.

Jean concludes to let the stock alone for:

> Les spéculations
> S'enfoncent avec les actions.

And his decision is probably a wise one.

France was as slow in applying steam to methods of transportation as she had been in using it for manufacturing. The idea of a steamboat was not a new one: the Marquis de Jouffroy d'Abbans had invented his *piroscaphes* of 1776 and 1782, and before him Denis Papin had had a similar idea. It was not, however, until Fulton's invention that France awoke to this important use of steam. By the middle of the century she had in all less than four hundred steam boats, mostly river-going boats or coasters. Although there was the Mediterranean service of the Compagnie des Messageries Nationales about 1835, transatlantic traffic did not develop to any great extent until after

1847, and was not really successful until taken in hand by the Péreire brothers in 1861.

The principal episode of *Le Bateau à vapeur* celebrates the voyage on the steamboat "Elise" sailing from London to Rouen in 1816. The traveler Moufflet describes the very hot journey:

> Such a boat you never saw:
>   Its heat is dreadful toasting
> And not a bit of me is raw
>   For all the way 'twas roasting.
> A chimney serves her for a mast,
>   A furnace is her steering-gear,
> She has for sail a flaming blast,
>   And oars yield place to bellows here.
> Never again, without a doubt,
>   Will I travel on a boat so dire . . . .
> Before long, if you don't look out,
>   There'll be a shout:
>   "The stream's on fire!!!"
>
> —H. SIMON *et al.*, scene 9

By far the most important application of steam is that to the railway. Here again France neglected an early invention of her own. The excessive force of the huge steam engine invented by Cugnot in 1770, which escaped control and ran through a wall of the Arsenal at Paris, proved discouraging; and the idea was abandoned for half a century. The first passenger road to be built—the dean of all the French railways—that from Paris to St. Germain, was ready to carry passengers and goods in 1835. Concerning this road Thiers made his famous short-sighted remark: "Il faut donner ça à Paris, comme un joujou; mais ça ne transportera jamais un voyageur ni un colis." Interest in the enterprise grew intense, notwithstanding. It was fanned

by the far-seeing Saint-Simonians who urged the establishment of railroads above all else. By 1842 a railroad system
was planned with lines radiating out from Paris in all direc-
tions. The government proving unequal to the great building program, it was handed over to some thirty or more
small companies, which fused later leaving France with six
great lines. The 1842 railroad project was completed by
1860, and by 1870 the French railway system was much as
it is today. The telegraph appeared as an adjunct to the
railroad, and in 1858 Europe and America were united by
cable. The railway-age proper cannot be said to have fairly begun until 1845, but the excitement occasioned by the
great plans and the tremendous speculation which accompanied the designing and building of the railways is one of
the interesting phenomena of the nineteenth century.

In a later chapter the extreme importance of the railroad in drama will be shown. For the present, mention
need be made only of a slight vaudeville of 1832, *Les Chemins en fer,* by Etienne Arago, which burlesques this great
excitement. M. Chauchaud feels that France is in a rut and
is wholly lacking in that enterprise which has marked England's career. He himself is crazy on the subject of railroads and longs to get this great idea into the minds of the
French. He would establish trains leaving Paris every five
minutes for all parts of the world, carrying civilization to
the pyramids of Egypt. (Chauchaud begins to doze.) His
route should go via Peking and Constantinople. Here Chauchaud dreams and excitedly orders his workmen about:)

Hey there, men, just lay these rails right along the way. Spread
them along! Dry up that arm of the sea! Fill up that abyss! Cut
down that mountain! That mountain is in my way. All aboard! We
lunch at Naples; dine at Cairo; have our coffee right at Mocha, an
ice in Siberia, and we shall get back to Paris in time for the show.

An excellent parody, this, of Michel Chevalier's Système de la Méditerranée. This famous economist and follower of Saint-Simon conceived a railroad from every Mediterranean port; a line from Barcelona to Madrid and Lisbon; another along the north coast of Africa; railroads to awaken Asia; the canals of Suez and Panama. Then indeed would the globe be a *ravissant tableau*. With railroads, canals, steamboats, and the banks necessary to facilitate their construction, not a nation will be found to make war on another; nor will there be any hungry classes to stir up civil strife. At least so thought Michel Chevalier.

Balzac, so fond of grandiose dreams, apparently has this same Mediterranean system in mind when, in *Quinola*, he assigns to his Alvaros, the richest banker of Catalonia, a monopoly on the Mediterranean.

The Second Empire accomplished many of the dreams of the Saint-Simonians. Napoleon III was thoroughly in accord with them, a devotee of the religion of "progress," eager to relieve the poor, to better agriculture, rebuild Paris, improve communications between nations, and establish peace. He is christened *le saint-simonisme couronné*. Under his régime, construction of all kinds redoubled. The city of Paris was rebuilt. The inspiration for this widening of Paris streets, and the replacing of old buildings by new, dates back to the cholera epidemic of 1832 when the Saint-Simonist paper, the *Globe*, urged Louis Philippe to undertake public works for the sanitation of the city.

Throughout the early years of the century there had, of course, been more or less speculation on real estate. With the Revolution of 1789 and the confiscation of royalist property by the government, syndicates known as *bandes noires* were organized. The members of these companies, many of whom were boiler-makers and scrap-iron

merchants, carried on a profitable business, demolishing
the old châteaux and selling the building-materials for new
constructions. It is to the tender mercies of such a band
that M. Poirier would confide the historic Château de
Presles rather than purchase it for his spendthrift son-in-
law. Every year brought an increase in demands for edi-
fices of one kind or another. People desired comfortable
living-quarters to correspond with their new luxury in
dress. Toward the end of Louis Philippe's reign, the architect Lesoufaché began erecting convenient houses with
larger doors and wider windows and no gables, thus per-
mitting the light to penetrate into the streets below. There
was also, about this time, much interest in the building of
arcaded streets or *passages* in Paris.

Among the episodes of the vaudeville, *Les Entrepreneurs,* which merrily mocks the excited speculation on new
constructions, is one in which Jaquinard, whom we have
met before, disguises himself as a promoter, Accéléré, and
proposes to buy Jobin's house in order to turn it into a sort
of *diligence* station, an immense and lucrative affair. Jobin
has no sooner given his eager consent than Jaquinard reappears as one, Duplatras, with the magnificent proposition
of building a city within the village of Ivry on the very site
of Jobin's house. It is to have a *faubourg,* four public
squares, and six large buildings. Needless to say, this city
on a postage stamp is never realized.

In *L'Anonyme,* of 1826, the busy contractor Courville
is building a "joli petit village suisse" on the banks of the
Seine, La Folie Courville. He is trying to persuade the capitalist Dubreuil to take a chalet for 40,000 francs, or to
allow a street to be named after him: "Rue Dubreuil en
lettres blanches ou bronzées, car c'est la mode aujourd'hui
de lancer son nom à l'immortalité ... sur une pierre de

taille." Courville is an untiring entrepreneur: he opens new quarters, deals in villages, and speculates in provinces.

The new arcaded *passages* and the old-fashioned uncovered streets of Paris are engaged in a law suit in a vaudeville, *Les Passages et les Rues*, of 1827. Dulingot, the speculator of the play, invests all his money in arcades. In a lengthy song he mentions the *passages* Delorme, Feydeau, Vivienne, du Caire, du Pont-Neuf, Choiseul, and one to be constructed in the quarter of Montorgueil. The theme of the song is Dulingot's great eagerness to buy more shares in these arcades, no matter how many there may be:

> Qu'il en vienne, qu'il en vienne
> Je prendrai des actions!

It was during the sixties that Baron Georges Eugène Haussmann, prefect of the Seine, remodeled the French capital. Among the new buildings erected were five or six theaters and the Grand Hôtel, containing seven hundred and fifty rooms, then the largest hotel in Europe. Factories had to be housed and room found for many new enterprises. Industrial companies vied with each other in the luxury of their respective buildings. Never had there been so much speculation on land and houses. D'Avenel tells interesting tales of the masons and contractors who made fortunes during this period of intensive building: of Duphot who covered the *rues* Castiglione, Mont-Thabor, Rivoli, and Miromesnil with structures; and of Joseph Thome, a partner of Haussmann's, who accumulated sixty million francs. Construction companies would submit plans for a new quarter. Even before the plans had been adopted, the companies would quietly buy up the land involved at a low price. If their plans were accepted and the quarter boomed, the profits might reach 500 per cent.

A certain Verdelier of *Le droit Chemin,* drags Baron d'Amblard into a speculation of this nature, a new section of Paris to be known as the "Cité d'Amblard." Verdelier's friends will pretend to buy lots so as to boost prices, and work will be started on a few buildings to serve as bait. The plan is promising but Mme d'Amblard, who is not a speculator, refuses her husband the money for the scheme. Verdelier himself lands in prison.

Among the persons who hope to inherit the property of César Girodot is one, Tancrède Lehuchoir, a swindler, who, when asked what he would do with the fortune were it willed to him, replies that he would buy the Palace of Industry for a *cité ouvrière* which he would divide up into small quarters and rent to the poor at the highest price possible. Resenting the sneer with which his wife greets his proposal, the contractor snaps out: "I'm not ashamed of the business which has made me rich and keeps you in luxury, my dear. Don't forget that!"

The inexperienced speculators of E. Plouvier's *Les Fous* are led by the banker Kant into a real estate deal. He proposes that they buy up some lots at a low price and then resell to contractors who are to erect houses. These contractors will count on paying for the land by the sale of the houses, for the construction of which Kant will advance funds. When the houses are almost completed, the banker will find himself obliged to withdraw his credit. The contractors, unable to pay their workmen, will be forced to give up both houses and lots. Kant is himself tricked, however, by a false plan of the new streets in Paris and buys up the wrong block of land.

Besides excitement over the rebuilding of Paris, the Second Empire was noted for the development of mining and metallurgy and for a craze over mining-stock speculation very similar to that in railroads under Louis Philippe. Although several great foundries existed in the thirties, none developed modern methods until the middle of the century. Even then much of the pig iron made in France came from little charcoal furnaces. This was, of course, a great handicap in the building of railroads: rails had to be imported from England over a heavy tariff; and in some cases blast furnaces were erected along the route to provide iron for the new road.

Mining stock seems scarcely to be mentioned in drama before the forties. From then on it occurs frequently and many of the most pretentious money-plays of the Third Republic turn on the exploitation of mines. At first the native products of coal and iron are most attractive to the characters of drama. It is a visit to a "newly discovered" coal mine at Lyons which serves Mercadet as an excuse for not being at home to his pressing creditors; and it is on iron in the Basse-Indre Basin that he makes his coup. Boursicoff tries to trap M. Gogo's supposed inheritance in a bogus coal-mining company. Theodosia, a woman speculator whom we shall meet again in other enterprises, promotes, in 1866, a marvelous coal mine lying between Argenteuil and Bois-Colombes and extending nobody knows how far, the existence of which no one had ever suspected before.

France's attention, along with that of the rest of the world, was turned to foreign mines during the gold rush to California in the fifties. The excitement brought much fake mining stock to the market. The gold rush is celebrated in a melodrama called *Les Chercheurs d'Or du Sacramento* by Fournier and Duplessis. Passion for gold wrecks the life and character of Georges de Montalègre. He takes his wife to California with him where he neglects her in his mad and selfish search for wealth. He violates an Indian tomb, thinking to find treasure there, and incurs thus the wrath of the dead Indian's son. He is finally betrayed and left to the tender mercy of the toughs Kentucky and Tabasco. Learning of a secret passage in the mountains, he tries to escape with all the gold belonging to the party, after seeing his wife captured by an Indian enemy. The reader need not be alarmed on the lady's account. A gentleman who has been watching over her comes to her rescue at the opportune moment.

The plays that follow this one are full of allusions to stock in gold, silver, and copper mines in the Americas, Africa, or the Near East. Montjoye, learning that his South American gold mine is rich in copper, keeps secret this valuable information, allows the mine to fail, buys up the stock for a song, and reopens it to exploit the copper. This trick ruins his partner but puts Montjoye on easy street for the rest of his life. The financier Calandel makes a trip to Arkansas to investigate copper mines reported to be there but which, he finds, are not in existence. Algerian mines are alluded to in Ponsard's *La Bourse* and in Feydeau's *Un coup de Bourse*. Silberstein, in his struggle to avoid a bankruptcy, tries to get the concession to work a gold mine in Hungary. Twelve thousand shares in the zinc mines of the Sierra-Morena, in the province of Estramadura, Spain, are among the possessions of Bourtibourg; and Boursicoff alludes to fake platinum mines which are not definitely located. The question of mining companies under the Third Republic will be taken up in a later chapter.

Chemistry did its share toward creating a new era in the nineteenth century. Many existing industries were improved, many new ones created, decreasing materially

French dependence on foreign nations. Among the most important contributions of chemistry were the production of India rubber; the use of gelatine for foods and glue; the invention of the daguerreotype, electroplating, and matches; and the revolutionizing of the soap and candle trades. Mention of soap recalls the unbounded enthusiasm of Prudent, the cautious speculator of Sardou's *La Famille Benoîton,* before the soap factories of Liverpool: "Twenty-five million kilograms of soap a year! That is sublime, Madame. It was there that I felt all the pride of human power—at the sight of all that soap!"

Improvement was made in the distilling of liquors; the making of cotton prints; the manufacture of perfumes, glassware, and paper. Use was made of sulphuric acid to extract soda from marine salts. In the process of improving charcoal, hydrogen gas was discovered and applied to the lighting of Paris streets in 1815. A propos of this discovery, the ready Scribe comes forth with *Le Combat des Montagnes,* in which figures Antimèche, the *artiste lampiste,* a god of light, who proposes to illuminate Paris with an immense lamp having an infinite number of branches—branches not wicks, for gas is the declared enemy of wicks. The principal invention celebrated in this fantasy, however, is the rollercoaster already the subject of a previous vaudeville, *Les Montagnes russes.* Speculators invested large sums in the construction of these "mountains," the idea for which had come from Russia and which were a popular form of diversion. Scribe includes among his *montagnes* Niagara, the mountain of water. Gas and incubation are the chief novelties offered by our old friend Jaquinard when he appears for the fourth time to Jobin as Faitout who contracts for absolutely everything.

Once upon a time
  Argand lamps they burned.
My gas is not so dear
  And a vast deal more clear.
On the coldest winter days
  I save the wood supply,
And to heat the fireplace up
  On paper do rely.

Oft there are no pullets
  For finicky gourmets;
But I have a passion
  For incubation!
I make a thousand chicks at once
  With neither hen nor cock;
And some day I'll make them
    (This is new)
Without an egg in stock!

—*Les Entrepreneurs,* scene 12

New inventions, of course, flocked to the expositions, and the vaudevilles make the most of this chance for mirth. *Industriels et Industrieux,* by Desvergers, Dubourg and Laurencin, derides old Bonnard, a capitalist, lured thither by his daughter's fiancé, who is determined to make him invest his money. The rogue pins a placard to Bonnard's back, bearing the information that he has 60,000 francs to invest. Inventors in search of capital to manufacture their inventions besiege him. The possibilities for investment are numerous and attractive: indestructible hats, incombustible paper, cabbage-leaf cigars, locks which call out a burglar alarm, collars to prevent a wry neck, and umbrella bayonets. The last named is a gibe at the gun with a tricolor umbrella invented to protect the comfort-loving soldiers of the bourgeois monarch who complained of the discomforts of sentinel duty.

In another vaudeville of the same year, *La France et l'Industrie,* the authors, Tournemine and Guénée, represent Enterprise complaining that such inventions as six-wheeled non-reversible carriages (which, if the truth be told, all turned over) and streets paved in bitumen (which had proved cloacae) had been refused. She now appears armed with seven thousand other inventions equally good.

Quentin of Sardou's *Les Femmes fortes* evinces great admiration for American inventions: a whisk broom descending from the ceiling to brush one's clothes; a bed that can be turned into a bath tub; a button which when pressed sends one's soiled shirt up the chimney and returns it through the door washed and ironed.

The authors of *Les Entrepreneurs* produced a similar skit called *Les Actualités,* in which the credulous Gobetout, a victim of all new ideas, takes it into his head to establish in Algeria a colony with all modern improvements. His daughter is in love with the artist Ducrayon, but her father insists on having a "progressive" son-in-law, one who has either invented a railroad, a new religion, a subway bridge, or a balloon. With such industrial ideals Gobetout may properly boast of being a man "qui marche avec son siècle."

Among these progressive individuals of drama none is more amusing than the hero of Bayard's *Monsieur Gogo à la Bourse,* in whose multifarious activities may be seen a comprehensive review of the many industrial and speculative projects of the century. He is ruining his wife and daughter, having left the Rue des Lombards, where he was a respectable *épicier-droguiste,* for the Rue des Filles St.-Thomas near the bourse. Returning from a tour of inspection of all the enterprises in which he has shares, Gogo appears on the stage, loaded with samples of all kinds: a kettle in one hand, canned milk in the other, a bottle in his pocket, books, loaf sugar, packages under his arms, and newspapers peeping from under his coat. He triumphantly produces bouillon for dinner; also beer, soup, and the papers which he never reads. His appearance and his enthusiasm bear out Mme Gogo's despairing recital of her husband's investments: canals, boats, banks, mines, forges, manufacturies, swamps, plains, bridges and *voitures* of every sort:

> ... batignolaises, béarnaises, citadines, dames blanches, dames françaises, favorites, hirondelles, orléanaises, omnibus, parisiennes, tricycles, lutéciennes, sylphides, zéphyrines, cabriolets, mylords, cabriolets compteurs ... urbaines, dandys, gondoles pour Versailles, et pour Saint-Germain, messageries pour toute la France!

The poor lady is sure that the family will soon be so destitute that there will not be ten centimes left for omnibus fare in spite of all Gogo's shares in these boats and vehicles. The interest in these conveyances was quite timely. The first omnibus line, in 1828, instead of proving a nuisance as was feared, was so popular that dozens of other lines followed bearing the names indicated by the distressed Mme Gogo. The service on the Seine, which had begun in 1807 with the slow "Cagaillotte" and "Zéphir," was much improved by 1829; and by the year of our vaudeville, a decade later, there existed a Compagnie générale des bateaux à vapeur de Paris à Saint-Cloud among whose boats were the "Dames Blanches," "Hirondelles," and so on. The *messageries* refers to the Compagnie des Messageries nationales, which, having abandoned the sea for the land, was at this time sending coaches throughout France. The company was driven back to sea again in 1850 because of railroad competition.

Industry in many and varied forms enters into the life of the nineteenth century and into its plays. Unfortunately

the increased and improved methods of manufacture, the
new inventions, and great enterprises opened the way to
unlimited speculation, most of it nefarious. On this phase
drama dwells at length, satirizing, mocking, condemning
her financier protagonists. We step into a world of money
interest, of financial scandal; into a society of parvenus
and cheats. The acquisition of wealth has apparently become the sole ambition of every class from the nobility to
servants. To be as rich as one's neighbor has become a
right. Vallès calls this war of interests, this clinking of millions, this noise of locomotives, this growth of towns, "a
stirring poetry, the sacred poetry of the nineteenth century."

The Roller-Coaster of a Century Ago

CHAPTER IV

LE DIEU MILLION

Il n'est qu'une seule idole
Que l'on adore à deux genoux;
Il n'est plus qu'un mot qui console ...

. . . .

Il n'est qu'un but, qu'un dieu, c'est l'or!
—E. SERRET, *Le mauvais Riche,* Act IV, scene 1

THE New Régime goes down on its knees before the golden calf. Or, at least, so says drama. Duhaut-cours seemed to speak prophetically when, standing on the threshold of the century, he proclaimed the nineteenth century a period in which "tout le monde se vend." A Jewish age this, remarks a speculator in Scribe's *Le Veau d'Or:* gold is the only idol worshiped. Dalincourt, an adorer of the god Mammon, devotes two pages of Alexandrines to his praise: money alone brings happiness; it governs the world and reigns in all hearts; it is equal to God. The least intelligent of human creatures may be skeptical of God, but he will put his faith in money. Another worshiper, Danvilliers, waxes eloquent in his hymn to money. Once upon a time, says he, feudal lords ruled their separate little kingdoms all over the land, but now all people are subject to our empire; the god of the world is Money and his kings are millionaires. A certain marquise drolly confuses religion and finance by promising God a church if he will direct her speculations profitably. There is not a civilized soul, says the blatant Jean Giraud, who upon rising in the morning does not recognize the sovereignty of money—

money, the great motive power of the age, the goal of work-man and millionaire, the sole aim of industry, the force that divides families, the only title to respect.

Though the public may sling mud at millionaires, it adores them just the same, says one of Feuillet's compla-cent and self-confident bankers. A speculator's daughter names money as the most powerful of forces, one which kings cannot resist. The wife of a *brasseur d'affaires* is re-proached by her husband for calling money a grotesque di-vinity: "You insult money, Annette," says he. "It is some-times magnificent." The very shadow of the golden calf is adored. Let a man be supposed rich and the world is at his feet. Mathieu of *Les Fous,* becoming disgusted with soci-ety which fawns upon him believing him able to bequeath a fortune at his death, wills to his speculating banker all that he has: a cane, a Rabelais, and sixty francs' worth of furniture, stating that everyone has been kneeling before him who had been nothing but the shadow of the golden calf.

A new aristocracy is rising, the aristocracy of money. To the financier are now open the gates of the *faubourg* St.-Germain, and the *faubourg* itself haunts the office of the financier. Palaces are built nowadays for business men, observes one character of drama; and another says that many a financier is almost a nobleman, to which his wife replies that many a nobleman is almost a financier, from which the son concludes that all ranks of life are uniting as the hope of enjoying the gifts of fortune is lessening the dis-tance between them. A speculator says to a millionaire: "My dear sir, we are the true aristocracy! We have the money! Therefore we are the great lords! Money needs no ancestry; it is always quality. With money you can do any-thing!"

The old motto of *noblesse oblige* has become *richesse oblige,* which Scribe's Piffard explains as an obligation to augment one's wealth. The same thought is put in the mouth of a wealthy and wicked banker who is made to say to a poor man that riches impose certain duties, of which the first and most binding is to become richer. Another writer contrasts the modern idea of virtue with the conception of it in earlier days. It was once *plus faire que dire;* it is now as a broker says, talk much, do little, and look out for yourself.

Ideas of honor have altered also. A financier does not seek satisfaction from his wife's lover in a duel. He ruins him on the stock exchange. Mercadet displays a five-franc piece, exclaiming, "This is modern honor!" As for honesty, honesty is money! "With money one can have everything: honor, love, happiness! I want money!" This is the cry of the bandit-speculator of Felix Pyat's *Les deux Serruriers.* Augier's financier Roussel salutes money as the only nobleman in France, the only powerful man, the only honest man! When one speculator says ironically to another that he "esteems" him, the latter replies with a significant pun:

Oh well! That is of small account;
Do folks "esteem" today? . . . . They but discount!

It would be a long task to gather all the many allusions in contemporary drama to the dishonesty of the new aristocracy. There are many such remarks: An honest man is a hindrance in a business deal; no man can make millions honestly. When a man has "arrived" nobody asks how he did it. A certain banker considers whether he shall continue to vegetate in the path of honesty or follow the wide highway to riches: "Voilà le grand mot de la vie." He will be neither the first nor the last to try that tempting course,

and public opinion will not be hard on him: "Qui donc dis-
cute l'or? on le ramasse ... on ne l'essuie même pas!" Another homme d'affaires, Brassac, admits that he has a bad
reputation but that it is easily explained: if a financier has
any reputation at all it is certain to be a bad one.

The children of the aristocracy of wealth have been
trained to consider a fortune indispensable to happiness.
They quote the teachings of their elders that money is an
ever present necessity. Marriage must be a step toward
balls, fêtes, carriages and a sumptuous *hôtel*. The financier
is approved of as a husband, for, as a sage character remarks, no sentiments are so solid as those based on arith-
metic. Love, says a quondam seamstress, is like a Swiss
muslin dress, very pretty and pleasant for summer wear;
but money is like brocaded satin: it lasts forever and can
be dyed after that. Mercadet explains to his daughter that
marriage must be considered *en affaire* and that a poor em-
ployee cannot possibly be in love. He has no time for that:
he has to work. The father of the terrible Benoîton family
has inculcated in his daughters the valuable idea that a
good marriage is inseparable from lace, velvet, and a *calè-
che*. Marriage is an "opération tout à la fois conjugale et
financière." Emma of Léon Laya's *Le Duc Job,* although
in love with Jean who is of noble birth, cannot make up her
mind to marry him because of his comparative poverty.
Finding him asleep one day, she sits beside him and busily
figures on a scrap of paper her dowry, his income, and her
needs: gloves, hats, carriage, and so forth.

Emma has certain traits in common with Thomas Love
Peacock's Lady Clarinda of *Crotchet Castle,* who plays fast
and loose with poor Captain Fitzchrome because her father
is dangling before her eyes a speculator who can give her
"a town and country house, and plenty of servants, and a

carriage and an opera-box"; and because, with such a husband, she could make her friends who have "married for

The speculator discovers too late that the lady's immense fortune is an immense *blague.*

love, or for rank, or for anything else but money" die with envy at her jewels.

Such an education as this creates the class of women which Augier calls *lionnes pauvres,* married women, such as Séraphine, whose desire for luxury leads them to supplement their husband's inadequate salary by taking a lover. It seems that the critics, dissatisfied because the heroine is not made to suffer for her crime, recommended that she be punished with smallpox between the fourth and fifth acts in order that poetic justice might be respected. Séraphine is not an extreme example of how the stage treats the luxury-loving daughter of the moneyed age. Their frivolity and *légerté* are proverbial. They are spoiled darlings of fortune who "love to leave the house with lots of money and come back without a penny" or protest that nothing gives them so much pleasure as "to be on the go continually, to shop, to spend money and to waste it."

Young men not only seek rich wives but sacrifice their careers for money. An artist of Scribe's *Le Mariage d'Argent* cannot be satisfied with his art, and wonders why speculators and fools of all sorts think that they have the exclusive right to make money? The artist of *La Chasse aux Millions* gives up his painting to make a fortune on the bourse. There is Achille of *Le Duc Job* who sacrifices music to speculation. "Music?" queries Achille. "I haven't touched my piano for a year—I have the music of the pit," and he begins to shout out market quotations—30, 60, 80! A young musician of drama writes a symphony which he calls *Le Veau d'Or*, justifying himself with the argument that the arts should be inspired by the times. An adventurer composes a book on the *Art de faire Fortune*, which, he feels sure, must attract the money-loving public. The very theme of the society novel has changed, observes one of Augier's characters: in the novel of the Old Régime when a man of low degree was in love with a daughter of the nobility, he won her by making a name for himself; today a poor young man in love with a rich girl tries to make a fortune to gain her approval.

The desire for luxury is as keenly felt in the servants'
quarters as in Madame's salon. The valet dreams of a bed
with rich hangings, servants behind his carriage, a crowd
around him at the bourse greeting his entry with prolonged
whisperings, a signature commanding respect, friends,
wines, and the joy of eating the dishes he is now condemned
to serve. The dream is not altogether a vain one, for a fortunate speculation has put many servants into the drawing-
rooms of their masters. Jean Giraud to whom René's father has been obliged to sell his estate, insolently reminds
René that he, Jean Giraud, son of the former gardener, is
now the proprietor of the estate. "Times change, eh?",
says he. "Where we were once the servants we are now the
masters."

Servants frequently imitate their masters' speculations
so that financial enterprises in the kitchen form a sub-plot
to those of the drawing-room. Durosay of *L'Agiotage* leads
both master and valet to the bourse. A groom in Scribe's
O Amitié stops a guest in the antechamber, begging that he
secure certain bonds for him; the guest is obliged to acqui-
esce in order to escape the speculator in livery. A cook is so
anxious about fluctuations in stock that she lets her chocolate burn. A valet and maid, confident of the fortune they
are about to make in speculation, refuse to work; the re-
fusal proves premature, as the bubble bursts, and Fran-
çoise and Robin swear to confine their gambling to parlor
games in the future. A domestic eavesdrops to get information about the market, misunderstands, speculates in the
wrong way and loses; when he returns home late from the
bourse, his master storms that the world is going to perdi-
tion and wonders what his ancestors would have said had
they seen a valet at the bourse. We hear servants learnedly
discussing investments and recommending real estate as

against bonds. A rather tiresome sub-plot occurs in *La Bourse*. The master falls a victim to a stock-jobber; and his servant is swindled by the broker's servant, who is also a speculator. Both Pierre and his master neglect their sweethearts, lose their money, and are very nearly jilted by the incensed girls.

Such universal hunger for wealth could never be appeased by the patient accumulation of sous in a *bas de laine*. Even successful manufacturing is too slow, and France with the cry "Millions!" on her lips rushes madly toward speculation. Vaudoré, a promoter of 1839, likens this epidemic to a springtime which quickens the pulse and awakens ambitions: everybody wants shares; industry and commerce, which had been creeping like snails, are now running at breakneck speed. Any enterprise is feasible if only it promise immediate gain, says the intrepid Mercadet. Speculation is for all of us, exclaims one of Augier's financiers. And so it seems from the words and behavior of one dramatic character after another. It is a great game to be penniless one day and win millions the next. Lafontas speaks of this eagerness to get rich quick or to increase already big fortunes: "Speculation lies at the bottom of the human soul and the speculator is the idol of the day: audacity, imperturbable trickery, common sense,—even theft, and the crowds look on in wonder."

Paris is caught in a terrible fever, and women too are suffering from the contagion. One hears the fair sex talking of shares, liquidations, quotations, shorts—a bourse jargon. Such is the lament of a character in *Le Roman* of 1825 who compares this frenzy to that shown by the men in the Rue Quincampoix under the Regency. But the women were not so untouched by that craze as the speaker thinks, for the Système de Law had many fair victims;

and Rambaud describes quite elegant women who from
1789 to 1814 cornered soap, candles, tobacco, spices, tis-
sues, and in their salons discussed the *baisse des suifs* and
the *hausse des cuirs*. The women of the third decade are
described thus in *Le Capitaliste malgré lui:*

> Many a woman of Paris
> In this speculating age
> Is cleverer than her husband
> And doubles his meager wage.
> While Madame bravely speculates,
> Monsieur, the selfish bear!
> Remains at home and takes a nap
> And wakes a millionaire.
>
> —FRANCIS *et al.*, scene 14

One of the most typical promoters of shady companies
is the busy Theodosia, who breezes through Sardou's *La
Maison neuve*, trying to sell stock to everyone she meets.
At one moment she is enthusiastic over the cork trees of
Bou-Sada in Algeria; at another over coal mines; or again
she is helping to form a company which shall have exclusive
rights in handling velocipedes at the Exposition grounds
(probably an allusion to the World's Fair of 1867). She
grows eloquent over the possibilities of cork: the trees
have not been exploited since the time of the Romans. A
company will be formed; and she will have 500 shares,
which she will sell as soon as stock goes up a little. In a
short time she will soon have her million! The public will
take to cork: it is so useful. Excellent floors can be made
of it, and think how elastic streets paved with cork would
be! When we meet Theodosia in the second act the cork
trees are *au fond de l'eau* and she is selling stock in the
wonderful coal mines already mentioned. She bobs up in

the third act with a tip from her financier that there is to be a rise in stock and fortunately she is *à la hausse*.

It can well be imagined what questionable characters choke up the salons of an age where money is the sole arbiter. Society tends to become a band of thieves, says Pyat's Oscar, in a country where money is everything and honor and merit count for nothing; where a man must become rich to win citizenship; where in fine, one is driven to make a fortune no matter what the means. Mosca of *Un Parvenu* complains that the parvenus have become a pest. There have rained down brokers of all sorts, bankrupts, and impudent ignorant speculators whose fortunes have been won by a coup de bourse. We meet usurers, no longer speaking a German brogue, but *décrassés* and elegant, who use their money to corrupt women; fraudulent bankrupts just back from Belgium; jailbirds who have submitted to a few years in prison in order to enjoy a greater fortune at the expiration of their term, sure of the tolerance of society. Such is the case with Fayolle in Capus' *Qui Perd Gagne:* they keep you a few months in prison, he explains, tell you that what you have done is a licit financial operation which, however, you must not repeat. There is a person mentioned in *La Bourse ou la Vie* by the same author who, preferring an income of 100,000 francs to 60,000, committed certain acts which sent him to prison, but who upon his exit, will enjoy the 100,000 francs.

This society is full of "la chevalerie industrielle et la noblesse alimentaire" growls André of Donnay's *La Douloureuse,* and he proceeds to name Ardan of starch, Ratinel of rubber, Godefroy of bouillons, and others who are *barons de la galette,* veritable medieval barons who, instead of ravaging the country from their feudal towers, are ambushed in their business offices and from there send by

telephone or telegraph the orders of purchase and sale
which will ruin thousands of people and even set nations at
each other's throats. In this heterogeneous society we shall
make the acquaintance of the *grands bourgeois* whom
Fabre describes so powerfully, capitalists grouped in companies and in banks with minions all about them, the laws
in their favor, the press at their service, and such ministers
as Duvilard of Guinon's *La Décadence* always ready to go
"fifty-fifty" in a nefarious business deal.

As we shall be for some time in the company of this
host of capitalists, sharpers, and rogues, let us join them in
the toast proposed by Feuillet's banker of *Le Roman parisien*—a toast to "Le Dieu Million"—and then turn our
attention to the transactions that are carried out in the
name of that powerful deity.

CHAPTER V

THE BOURSE

Adieu: jasez, courez; moi, je vais à la Bourse.
—COLLIN D'HARLEVILLE, *Les Moeurs du Jour,* Act I, scene 7

IT IS at the bourse, the "Hôtel de ville of the new republic," as Vallès calls it, that the financial activity of the nineteenth century is concentrated; and the bourse looms up in drama as the throbbing center of life, its name on every tongue, its victims and its favorites legion. It has a mysterious occult power which gives wealth, or takes it away, in the proverbial twinkling of an eye. Its charm lures even the best of men and destroys in them all sense of right. It is, in other words, a modern sphinx, a modern fate. At the bourse is what all men desire, namely adventure; and drama is full of the great adventure of the stock exchange.

The first Paris bourse was established by Philippe-le-Bel near the Pont-au-Change in 1304. It was later moved to the main court of the Palais de Justice and then to the Rue Quincampoix, the same which won great fame by reason of the excited speculation at the time of Law. Michelet describes vividly the terrible fury of the provincials from all over France—the monks, lawyers, lords, the women—who speculated madly in this renowned street. The bourse changed habitation six times after that before settling where it is today on the site of the convent of the Filles St.-Thomas. This was in 1818. On November 3, 1826, the present handsome building was inaugurated.

In order to understand the allusions in the plays which are to follow, we must call to mind the gray colonnades of the bourse and the excited throng of speculators which gathers every day on its steps. Their shouts can be heard down all the adjoining streets, and as one passes that way it is not difficult to imagine one's self in the Paris of 1826. One must replace the lumbering autobus that passes before the perron by an old-fashioned cab, and the automobiles by cabriolets; make a few changes in the cut of coats and trousers; replace the Rue du Quatre Septembre by buildings; and deprive the bourse of its wings. The most important place inside the building is the railed-off *parquet,* within which is the *corbeille,* inclosed by a circular railing, corresponding to our pit. Here the seventy *agents de change* transact business. These official brokers are, as a rule, men of high standing and integrity, and we shall not find many of them among our fraudulent speculators. The unofficial brokers, known as *coulissiers,* buy and sell unlisted securities in the *coulisse* or lobby. It is here, according to Proudhon, that the bourse rumors are started: "Le canard financier y éclat sous les bigarrures les plus merveilleuses." Our speculators will have much to do with these false reports and with the unlicensed brokers, known as *remisiers* and *courtiers marrons,* the latter dealing not only in *rente* (government bonds) but also in industrial stock. The pit is open from noon till 3:00 P.M.; the lobby from 11:45 P.M. till 4:00 P.M. Without the building is the *cours du ruisseau,* on which curb market a great deal of *tripotage* ("jobbing") is carried on. This spot, known as the corner of *les pieds humides* or *les chapeaux gras,* is the gathering-place of swindlers, confidence-trick men, and fools who deal in valueless stock. All around the square are unreliable establishments which advertise dubious investments. Women are sometimes to be seen in the crowds around the bourse, although they are not allowed within the building.

The importance of the bourse is strongly manifested in drama by the third decade of the nineteenth century, when the example set by Morand, the speculator of *Les Moeurs du Jour* (1800), who, enticed by the *agioteur* Basset, leaves the society of his friends for the stock exchange, is followed by many dramatic characters. All feel the lure of this game of chance; some are filled with respect, enthusiasm, even awe. Others express vehemently their fear and hate. The popularity of the bourse as a subject for drama increases from then on; and plays of every decade testify to the interest taken in its activities and to the crowds willing to trust their fortunes, or the fortunes of others, to its uncertain moods.

Saint-Joseph, a broker in a play of 1826, encourages General D'Ambreville to hie him to the Rue Vivienne, exclaiming that everyone is taking the street to the bourse in search of a fortune. And to be sure, certain characters in the play are very much involved at the said bourse. Another broker of the same year, Durosay, in Picard's *L'Agiotage*, is more explicit as to the crowds which haunt the stock exchange. He begins by exalting the bourse above all things and then tells of the men who show themselves in that place openly, of those who speculate incognito, and of others who do not appear but who are speculating none the less—in fact, everyone is doing so. The bourse is the rendezvous of all industries and talents; of all classes which meet there in perfect equality—for no aristocracy is to be found there. Indeed, it serves as a melting-pot for the social prejudices of the Old Régime. Even in the eighteenth century, Voltaire was struck by the cosmopolitanism of the stock exchange, not so much that it brought social classes together as that it represented a spot free of religious fanaticism: Jew, Mohammedan, and Christian be-

have there as if they were all of one faith, and the name of
infidel is given only to bankrupts.

Still another broker, of the same vintage as Durosay,
resents the scornful tone employed by one of his acquaintances in alluding to the bourse: one must not speak thus of
a place where so much money can be made—besides perfectly respectable people go there. Vaudoré, whom we met
some pages back raving about the beauties of speculation,
describes the innumerable opportunities of the bourse,
where, trembling, the speculator makes or loses a fortune,
where he takes the plunge with honor—and comes up to
the surface, with his honor still intact, be it noted. Everything happens at the bourse! *La Chasse aux Millions,* contains a song extolling the bourse as the temple of Fortune,
where copper becomes gold and through which flow the
precious floods of Pactolus.

Some ten years later, drama is reiterating the importance of the bourse. This time it is a young fellow newly
come to Paris who is an easy prey to speculation, Chabanais of *Les Enfers de Paris.* He is delighted over his happy
idea of speculating at the bourse; such a fine affair he has
gone into; bound to be a big success! Chabanais' friend
objects to this *tripotage;* and the former protests eagerly
that it is blasphemy to speak of dishonesty at the bourse,
that it is a most trustworthy place unjustly maligned. Unfortunately for Chabanais his confidence is ill-placed, and
he never sees his funds again. More sober, more justifiable,
praise is spoken by a broker of Ponsard's *La Bourse:*

> Of the modern universe it is the heart, the hub;
> It is a knot, which drawing all minds in,
> Binds London to Vienna and Paris to Berlin;
> The bourse is now the ruler of the world
> Whence peace doth come or bolts of war are hurled.
>
> —III, 2

A similar hymn of praise is chanted by the speculator
Féréol of *Les Fous*, in which he calls the bourse the masterpiece of modern civilization, the axis of the modern world.
The pit which seems so empty is in reality brimming over
with gold; it is "le berceau des plus belles opérations,"
from which results either peace or war.

Quite a different note is sounded, however, when the
onlookers behold the whirlpool of destruction toward which
the victim is being swept by the current of the bourse, or
when he himself realizes his peril. The tone becomes skeptical, or stern with warning, or bitter with the vituperation
of the loser. *La Bourse au Village* contains some wary
peasants who look askance at this spot where one grows so
suddenly rich:

> I know that on Change one grows rich *tout de suite;*
> But this money about which you talk,
> If it arrives just a little too *vite,*
> It is likely to go for a walk!
> (Such money does nothing but travel!)
> When to the Change your footsteps range
> It is your change they'll take from you.
> For today we have but one great Change
> Which changes all your change for you!
>
> —Scene 2

Lecardonel, the speculator of *Les faux Bonshommes,*
speaks loudly against this devastating bourse to which he
gently lures his prey, referring to its *écueils perfides*, warning against the terrible storms of the ocean called the
"Bourse" where the rudder of honesty is soon broken. Delatour speaks in much the same terms when in *La Bourse*
he tries to save his friend Léon from the *rivage avare* of the
stock exchange: it is a *tripot*, a *caverne*, a *casse-cou;* it is
a sphinx which finds for every Oedipus a thousand victims:

> Alas! How many enter with victorious air
> But leave, pale, mute, hearts full of care!
> How many tears upon this spot with failures strewn!
> Beneath this vaulted roof what imprecations and what ruin!
> —I, 4

Madeleine, maid to Camille, Léon's betrothed, is deserted by Pierre, who, now that he, like his master, is gambling at the bourse, has no further use for her. She calls down the wrath of heaven upon the bourse, praying God to destroy with a thunderbolt the accursed spot. The good Lord doubtless takes pity on her, for Pierre is ruined and restored to her; but the bourse stands unharmed waiting for other prey. One of these numerous victims speaks out his lamentations in Rasetti's *Les Parasites*. His name is Barreau; and he is an incorrigible schemer, who, unable to break away from the entanglements of speculation, flings insults at the bourse, calling it Saturn devouring his children, a Minotaur demanding new victims daily.

Thus the tongues of the dramatis personae declare how powerful a factor the bourse has become in life and on the stage: how it awakens respect, wild enthusiasm, fear, despair, hate. It is a power dividing Paris into two parts: *Paris qui rit* and *Paris qui pleure*.

The atmosphere of the bourse, an air of rush and excitement, pervades many plays, even those which contain little definite speculation. One is always meeting some broker who in the midst of other matters will pull out his watch and exclaim, "L'heure de la Bourse!" and tear off the stage. Or perhaps he will say impatiently, when summoned to dinner: "Est-ce qu'on déjeune quand on est dans les affaires?" His carriage is always waiting to roll him off to the bourse, the tourney-ground of these modern warriors. Jean Giraud expresses excellently this mad haste: "We are go-getters, we are. We finish one piece of business and then try something else. We can't wait on the duffers who travel by stage coach."

The business man finds it difficult to get time for affairs of the heart: he has to see to such trifles after bourse hours. A banker says to the lady of his choice that, as the bourse happens to be closed, they can take a walk together. Ordinarily the bourse leaves him only Sunday afternoon free, and he must, therefore, do his courting as quickly as possible. A certain speculator so far confuses his love and his business as to ask for a young lady's hand at the bottom of a bill, informing her father that he wishes to marry her no later than the *fin courant*. The financier Balardier, likewise addressing the father of Caliste, whom he wishes to marry and on whom he has tried to make a favorable impression by a slight duel, says: "Vous pensez que mes actions sont *en hausse?*" A husband is often so overwhelmed with his affairs at the bourse, his hands so full of telegrams and papers, his mind so occupied with business deals, that he leaves his wife exposed to the attentions of other men. Such is Didier Benoîton, once witty, artistic, amiable, and now conscious of nothing but business. His life is "like a train suppressing time and distance."

The absorbed speculator is wont to reply with market quotations to inquiries regarding his health. This idea is developed with sundry puns in *Les Joueurs*. The speculator Jacques Morin falls ill and replies to the doctor's questions that his health is "falling" (*baisse*). The doctor reassures him with "Elle se consolidera," and is about to say that he will seek the nature of the malady when Morin eagerly interrupts with "De la rente?" The final diagnosis of the case is "la spéculomanie, espèce d'épidémie que je range," says the physician, "dans la catégorie du somnambulisme."

Bourse jargon is occasionally defined on the stage for the benefit of some novice. Bassot of Picard's *Un Jeu de Bourse* gives a lesson in terminology to the retired merchant Gautier: "Shorts, premiums, futures, strong, steady, liquidation, being *à cheval*, that is to take no risks: the *cours du ruisseau* which means the quotations made after closing hours."

One of the scenes most redolent of the stock exchange is to be found in *Les faux Bonshommes* by Barrière and Capendu. Péponet has a fair daughter promised to a broker but beloved by the artist Octave. The latter has been disinherited by his rich uncle, Vertillac, because of his profession. Realizing that his one chance to obtain the daughter of Péponet is to take up speculation, he joins his uncle and proves himself a wholly competent broker. He appears at Péponet's house in a great haste (for time is capital much too precious to be wasted!) and talks business so hard and fast that the poor ex-silk-merchant is wholly bewildered and deeply impressed. Without the slightest intention of doing so, he finds himself buying stock in two railroads and thinking how happy his daughter would be with such a fine business man. Octave in the midst of this mass of business asks for Péponet's daughter's hand; but hardly is the question out when Vertillac enters, and Octave apparently forgets all about the trivial matter. He quizzes his uncle on a certain railroad concession, on the purchases of various customers, and so on; while poor Péponet, in mortal dread lest the marriage shall not be concluded, tries to get him back on the subject again. But Octave, just as he is about to leave, tells his uncle to conclude the arrangement while he runs over his mail. Vertillac makes the formal request for Emmeline's hand, and Octave informs the delighted Péponet that he will have the con-

tract drawn up and they can sign "entre deux Bourses."
Péponet hardly has breath left to exclaim over this marvelous son-in-law, who talks so fast that Péponet cannot
get in a word and is so busy that he almost forgets to
ask for the daughter's hand. "Nous signerons entre deux
Bourses!" How happy the girl will be with such a husband! Octave returns like a whirlwind a little later with
the marriage contract; he has only an hour, so Péponet
must sign at once, for Octave is due at a stockholders'
meeting and he has already lost ten minutes. Octave carries things with such speed that Péponet is led to give twice
as much dowry as he had intended. When the marriage is
finally solemnized, Octave deserts the bourse for his neglected painting. As Jules Janin observes, Octave has the
truc of an *agent de change* and the *fiou* of a banker.

Besides representing the hurry and excitement of the
bourse, certain dramatists have even ventured to produce
scenes on change either in serious or in comic vein.

In order to give the full significance of the scene at the
bourse as depicted in Pyat's *Le Brigand et le Philosophe*,
it will be necessary to review the plot briefly. In the wilds
of a German forest (attacks on speculation were for prudence' sake sometimes laid in foreign countries) a band of
brigands under the command of the outlaw, Oscar, take
prisoner a countess from a neighboring city. Oscar be-
friends the lady, and she offers him her support should he
decide to give up his wild life and come to the city. Oscar
does go to the city, but he does not give up his trade of robber: he merely changes his methods, robbing now at the
bourse under the protection of the law. The harm, he explains, is not in thieving but in the way it is done. Steal
with the Code in your hand. Then when you are at last decorated, the officers of the law themselves will salute you.

Oscar does not hesitate to use dishonest means; but though he is suspected, he is not caught. The second act shows us Oscar operating at the exchange. Within the building there is an excited crowd in which the speculator moves, spreading a false rumor of war between France and Germany. While the value of stock is low, thanks to this canard, Oscar buys heavily, so that when the rumor is denied and prices spring up again he has made a fortune. Oscar is finally brought to justice because of his other crimes, which are many. In true melodramatic fashion he is proved to be the illegitimate son of the countess.

The *Ver rongeur* by Malvoisine, belonging also to the thirties, contains the speculator Balainville, who had once been a smuggler but is now a broker at the stock exchange. With the capital gained by smuggling and by adulterating army supplies, Balainville plunges into the sea of the bourse expecting to come out with his million. It is in the interior of the bourse that we find him in the second act. He is accompanied by his wife to whom he points out the sights of the building, informing her with a show of masculine importance that as she is a woman she must go to the gallery since the fair sex is not allowed on the floor:

> The approach to the parquet is closed to the fair sex
> Through fear of the chatter. . . .

Madame retorts promptly,

> Nay, you forbid us the hall
> For fear that our skill would ruin you all!

Her husband informs her that here, at least, her whims are of no consequence. He then describes in Alexandrines the Paris bourse, with its handsome staircase, its grisailles by Abel de Pujol, and painted arch and cornice which appear to be sculptured. Balainville is quite supercilious about the

structure of the building and regrets that the clever architect did not make a plaster colonnade for the façade, as that
would have harmonized better with the imitation vault-
ing of the interior. Having sent Madame to the gallery,
Balainville is soon hard at work, red in the face and mop-
ping off the perspiration. He is surrounded by clerks whom
he sends on various financial enterprises. One is to buy up
wine in Bordeaux and ship it to London to sell; another is
to corner wheat crops in Saumur to be sold at a high price
in the midst of winter when the people are starving. Another agent is ordered to the Hôtel Bullion to buy up the
masterpieces of Poussin, David, and Gérard which are being sold at auction, and export them to Brazil. While busily
engaged in cornering and exploiting, Balainville is assailed
by the usual mob, offering to buy or sell stock; and finally
he goes down in the quicksand of the bourse.

An antisocialistic vaudeville, *La Propriété c'est le Vol,*
of 1848, stages the bourse in ruins as the symbol of a once
prosperous society now wrecked by the application of
Proudhon's motto, "Property is theft."

A play of later date, to which the author Léon Hennique gave the significant title *L'Argent d'Autrui,* shows
people entering and leaving the bourse, groups standing
here and there, calm or excited. Almost everyone has a list
of stock quotations and a pencil. A lively hour of speculation follows, during which one individual declares that
there is nothing left him but suicide and another cries out
that all men at the bourse are rogues. Whereupon, the
speculator Lafontas remarks: "Si on apprenait un jour ce
qui se trame d'infâmies, de crimes, dans cette boîte, au
long de cette boîte, par et à cause de cette boîte!"

A burlesqued scene at the stock exchange occurs in *La
grande Bourse et les petites Bourses,* a vaudeville by Clair-

ville and Faulquemont, in which the whole family is bourse-mad, including the five-year-old son. The husband, M. Gobergeot, pawns his wife's cashmere for funds with which to speculate; she does likewise with his dress-suit; and neither knows what the other has done. Their daughter is to marry a country boy, Dutillet, who arrives on the scene with an inheritance. Nothing will content the family but sending him to the bourse to speculate, though he is innocent of all knowledge on the subject. Colombe, the daughter of Gobergeot, has also been promised to Carottin the broker. This Carottin startles the family with the latest news from the bourse, to wit, that four railroads are about to coalesce and only people holding stock in all four railroads may profit. There is at once a wild scramble in the family to buy. A little family bourse is held then and there, and one kind of stock is traded off for another until each member has some of the four different kinds. Now the Chinese banker Fich'ton-kan is in charge of all their funds, and Fich'ton-kan is no more honest than one would expect a man with such a name to be; he absconds, and the bubble bursts. The unhappy family is in tears when Dutillet, to the surprise of everyone, himself included, finds that he has made a lucky investment on the real bourse and becomes a millionaire. Gobergeot decides to return to his regular job, which he had almost lost on account of his three months' absence spent in speculating.

There is a very amusing bourse scene staged in a vaudeville called *La Bourse au Village,* by Clairville, Lubize, and Siraudin. A peasant named Bourèche has been so impressed by the bourse during a visit to Paris that on his return to his native village he determines to inaugurate a similar institution there. His fever is contagious, and the little town goes mad over speculation. Bourèche has in-

stalled a little curb market, which meets by the gutter in
the main street, and a big bourse, which is held at one
o'clock in his own house. Bourèche fires everyone's ambition by telling about a boy from the home town who went
to Paris in wooden shoes and now has servants "dorés sur
toutes les coutures." His name is Fillerin! It is a quarter
to one, almost time for the big bourse to open; and Bourèche runs his wife and daughter, Marianne and Denise, out
into the *coulisse*, as women are not allowed on the parquet.
In come the peasants by two's and three's, whispering to
one another or keeping silent, their notebooks in their
hands. One o'clock strikes, and they begin shouting at
once like demons, around a wooden tub. All one can hear
is cabbages, turnips, carrots, etc. Floquet, the fiancé of
Denise, cannot get time to marry her, much less to shave,
so he tries to get shaved by Malcuit, the barber, while the
bourse is in session; but Malcuit does a very hasty job in
his hurry to be among the speculators.

The punning is as fast and furious as the speculating.
Malcuit, who does not trust the financial transactions of
Floquet, threatens to "execute" him, that is, force him to
sell. Floquet, unacquainted with the term, is terrified at
what he deems to be speedy death, until Bourèche explains
that all he needs is a "cover" or guaranty. Floquet, quick
to adopt the suggestion, appears at the liquidation wrapped
in a cotton blanket. At the liquidation, names of stocks are
punned on: "docks" being pronounced "dogues," two dogs,
César and Pataud, are offered for sale; *petites voitures* are
represented by wheelbarrows, and *mobiliers* by furniture.

The bell rings and all become silent. A peasant announces the close of the market: "Asparagus high—mel-
ons strong—turnips erratic—cucumbers bearish—radishes
returning to former price—carrots inactive—beans calm."

The meeting closes with the announcement that the liquidation will take place at three o'clock in the afternoon. Poor Marianne sighs over this new and terrible state of affairs: the place is going to rack and ruin, the fields are deserted, the town ungoverned, and the policeman has let lovers have the run of the wheat fields because he is speculating in potatoes. At the liquidation the peasants appear laden with their vegetables. In the meantime, the rogue, Truchelu, who professed himself too virtuous to speculate, has run off with Denise. News reaches Bourèche in a letter that Fillerin, the pride of the town, has failed on the Paris bourse. This cures Bourèche of the bourse fever; and he even has qualms at letting his daughter marry Floquet, who has shown a penchant for speculation. Just then, in walks Truchelu, virtue incarnate, a man who would never speculate and ruin himself as Jean Fillerin had done. At this news, however, Truchelu cries out that he too is ruined, being an associate of Fillerin. Bourèche then gives his daughter to Floquet, *fin courant*, and Truchelu closes the play with:

> A la Bourse, on va *courant*,
> *Parcourant* et *discourant*,
> Et de son compte *courant*
> Le jobard est au *courant*
>   Fin *courant*.

Besides these scenes, there are interesting descriptions of bourse activities contained in other plays. In the vaudeville *Les Joueurs* a lengthy song describes the ordinary daily events that occur at the bourse, in part, as follows:

> Entering we see
> A man in agony—
> A market slightly "bear"
> Has crazed him with despair.

Yon happy fellow there
With such a joyful air
Near whom the crowd collects
Offering its respects
Bought shares at six and then
Sold them all for ten.

.   .   .   .

A sudden silence falls
And loud the stentor calls
    Announcing noisily
        The day's decree—
The prices all would know:
Then behold the show
Of joy or crushing woe!

—Scene 7

The song continues, recounting the ringing of the bell, the
closing of the parquet, and the continued business in the
cours du ruisseau. An exciting moment at the bourse is
witnessed from the street by one of the characters of *L'Agiotage,* reminding one strongly of the present-day scenes
in the same spot. Laurent says he had just crossed the
Rue Vivienne when he saw signs of great confusion about
the bourse: brokers, stock-jobbers, speculators, running
around and asking each other questions; carriages collid-
ing; one man swearing at his coachman; another beating
his horse; some pale, frightened, tearing their hair; others
lamenting the fate of their comrades or threatening to pur-
sue them. What a spectacle a bourse revolution is to an
observer who knows how to be content with small daily
gains! exclaims Laurent.

Throughout the plays which we have been reviewing
society seems to move in an excited throng under the grey
colonnade in the Rue Vivienne, some joyously contemplat-
ing newly made fortunes, some grimly seeking to outwit

the sphinx in their turn, others turning desperately away. There is the restless hurry of this bourse throng, and scene after scene reproduces the typical operations of the stock exchange. Not only are scenes represented, but frequently the plot of a play turns with the tricky weathervane of speculation, blown so often by a false rumor of war or peace or twisted about by the efforts of a powerful banker.

Robert Macaire

CHAPTER VI

PLAYS OF THE STOCK EXCHANGE

> Ce temple grec est un tripot
> Plus fréquenté que les Eglises.
> On y parle un étrange argot,
> Ce temple grec est un tripot.
>
> Un peu plus tard, un peu plus tôt
> Tout le monde y fait des sottises.
> Ce temple grec est un tripot
> Plus fréquenté que les Eglises.
>
> —ANTONIO SPINELLI

THE plots of many of our plays depend directly on some coup de bourse. Two parties are speculating: one as a bear, the other as a bull; one is ruined, the other makes a fortune. This reversal or *système de bascule* might be represented by the tipping of a pair of scales first on one side and then on the other. The coup may be brought about in various ways. A clever speculator gets inside information about the market and anticipates the rise or fall in stock. Promoters boom shares by dangling promises of enormous dividends before the public. Occasionally a financier is successful in cornering stock, the price of which is then entirely at his command. The price of stock may also be affected by the concerted effort of a ring of bankers or companies who buy up or unload heavily and simultaneously, thus raising or depressing prices at will. A very common method is to spread a false rumor at the bourse. This report may concern the reputation of a financier, a stock company, or a political event, such as peace or war. Industrial stock or the *rente* will then soar or tumble.

> With us the bourse is a dreadful coward,
>   And money in France a poor poltroon:
> For no cause at all the national bonds
>   Faint right off in a deadly swoon.
> Let Persia or China give birth to a prince,
>   The three per cents will feel the shock, O!
> And all we need to lower the *rente*
>   Is a cold in the head of the king of Morocco!
>
> —Dumanoir *et al.*, La Balançoire, scene 5

There is usually in addition to the coup de bourse a decided element of contagion, the fever of speculation spreading from one person to another and even attacking a whole family. Not infrequently a slight marriage intrigue depends on the coup. The *système de bascule*, some device for rigging the market, excitement over speculation, and in addition a slight love theme are present in most of the stock-exchange plays before 1870.

In a vaudeville with the apposite title, *Un Jeu de Bourse ou la Bascule*, by Picard, Wafflard, and Fulgence, the fathers of two sweethearts are speculating. Bélanger, a rich lawyer, refuses to let his son marry Sophie, the daughter of a poor man, M. Gautier. But M. Gautier is speculating on a bull market, and Bélanger on a bear market; stock goes up; Sophie's father makes a fortune, and Gustave's father loses his. Then it is Gautier's turn to hunt a better match for his daughter. There follows, however, another *coup de bascule*, and the old order of things is re-established. This time Bélanger, having profited by his lesson, no longer sneers at Gautier's poverty but gives his son in marriage to Sophie. There is an unlicensed broker in this little comedy who is true to type. He enters upon the stage, rubbing his hands with satisfaction: four bankers ruined, six capitalists have failed, twenty unlicensed brokers must leave the bourse . . . . so much the better . . . . more business for those who remain. When asked after his health, he replies with the *cours de la rente*, "78, 30." He assures the audience that there is nothing half-way about his transactions: he either loses the funds intrusted to him or doubles them; in case his client wins, he himself is content with half the profits. According to his system he is always safe: "J'achète à terme, et à l'échéance je dois la différence; il n'y a donc que mon honneur de mis en avant." Bassot, for such is his name, knows all the tricks of the bourse: the courtesies one can show, the alarming reports one can spread, and the servants one can dress as messenger boys and send thither. The fact is he has thought up a trick that will make him roll in wealth: it is to bribe some telegraph operators so as to get news right from the source; but they are so "damned honest." Though Bassot could not bribe the telegraph operators, he now cooks up another scheme with his associates. They spread the rumor that the great wall of China has fallen down on account of an earthquake and that, as a result, Europe is threatened by an invasion of Kalmoucks—all civilization is about to be submerged. The falsity of the rumor is discovered, up goes the *rente,* and Bassot decides that another country would suit him better. He and his friends embark for England, where they plan to start up an insurance company.

La Fin du Mois, by Mazères, points to that dread moment of liquidation when there is always some unfortunate speculator ruined. This time it is Colonel De Baldy, who is a bear when he should be a bull. His prudent wife, having suspected his position, is speculating *à la hausse* through his own broker, the unctuous Saint-Joseph, who complacently serves both husband and wife, collecting his pay from both. When the fatal day comes, Georgina is able to save her husband from ruin and her daughter from the broker, to whom De Baldy would have married her.

A much more serious comedy of the same year, 1826, Bonjour's *L'Argent*, has a similar plot, though this time the money lost at the bourse is balanced by that gained on the indemnities which were paid to the nobility under the Restoration. M. Dalincourt, the banker, is speculating under the unfortunate guidance of a swindler, Chalet, who is planning to marry Dalincourt's daughter and retrieve his fortunes. Dalincourt refuses to allow Jenny to marry Jules de Belleville because his father is poor, destining her for Chalet, whom he believes well off. Dalincourt's speculations prove anything but fruitful. In the meantime M. de Belleville has become rich, thanks to the law of indemnities; and he in his turn objects to the match because Jenny is now poor. Chalet, pursued by the police for forgery and sundry other crimes, leaves the country. Dalincourt, with a foreign loan to negotiate, is not altogether destitute; and he persuades M. de Belleville to consent to the match between the young people.

The reaction of the public to this play is enlightening as regards the attitude toward realism in the twenties. The play stirred up a good deal of anger among the spectators because of its sinister tone. The *Figaro,* however, praised it as showing more than a mere profile of vices. The critic Delaforest takes exception to the play on the grounds that money-getting is a necessity of life and not an evil, and that the people engaged in it are by no means all wicked. He says of Bonjour's work: "His picture is horrifying without being instructive. The society which he has depicted is a veritable gang of cutthroats. This is, to tell the truth, nothing but a libel in five acts against gold and silver mines."

One of the most significant and best-known plays dealing with speculation on the stock exchange is Picard's serious bourgeois comedy, *L'Agiotage,* written in collaboration with Empis. It preaches earnestly against speculation on the government bonds, illustrating its precepts by the effect that such behavior could have on a whole family. The plot is fashioned in about the same manner as those of the preceding comedies. The dignified hypocritical old Dormeuil and his married son, Saint-Clair, a lawyer, are buying and selling stock on the bourse secretly, each afraid of being discovered by the other. The clever broker Durosay has led Saint-Clair into temptation, and along with him, Germon, a young farmer. Even the valets do not escape. Marcel, a manufacturer from Lyons, uncle to Saint-Clair's unhappy wife Amélie, comes to the rescue of the family at Amélie's request. Marcel soon realizes what the father and son are doing. He warns Saint-Clair but to no purpose, the latter being convinced like many another gambler that his luck is infallible. In fact, he does not trust to luck alone: he has made a scientific study of the bourse and has prepared himself to understand it by reading politics, social history, and newspapers. Saint-Clair, however, makes the fatal mistake of getting on the wrong side of the market, and away goes his money. What Saint-Clair has lost, his father would have won had not the broker, who had been speculating with his funds, pocketed the gains and escaped. Saint-Clair sees nothing left him but suicide. Marcel intervenes, saves the young man, and gets Durosay arrested, having recognized in him a notorious character of Lyons. Thus all things are made right in the end.

This comedy follows a rather conventional pattern, but it is not without a certain naturalness which Picard succeeded in instilling in his plays. The *système de bascule* enters with the father's gains at the bourse which might well have replaced the son's losses had the father not been swindled. We have also a good case of the contagiousness of speculation sweeping as it does through parlor and kitchen alike. Moreover, Saint-Clair is a lawyer accustomed to see others suffer from this malady and yet unable to protect himself. There is an observation in the *Globe* of July 27, 1826, a propos of this disease: "This malady must be universal, and contagion inevitable; gambling and stock-jobbing appear to be characteristic of the times."

This same year, so fruitful in bourse comedies, contains one called *Le Spéculateur* by Riboutté. Alexis, son of the respectable M. Duvernet, has become a passionate speculator, even inducing his father to follow his example. The family is living in such great luxury that M. Ménard, worthy manufacturer of Avignon, when he visits Duvernet, is both shocked and alarmed. He had intrusted money to Alexis, and the latter has become so blinded by speculation that he would have used the money himself had his father permitted. Indeed he needs it sorely, for he has been risking his money on the strength of a rumor of war, which proves false and leaves him big differences to pay:

> I am in speculation the man of the age.
> War is declared by a mighty power:
> A courier from England within the hour
> Has informed me at length of this great event
> And to use this advantage my thoughts are bent.
>
> —I, 4

As no further news comes, his valet Dupré offers to play the rôle of courier and with great mystery spread the news of war at the bourse; but before he can do so, the expected courier arrives, but with news of peace, and Alexis loses 3,000,000 francs. Ménard shows clemency toward the unfortunate speculator without more preaching than one would expect, and indeed allows his son to marry the sister of Alexis.

Des Granges classifies this play as a *drame larmoyant* rather than a *comédie de moeurs*. Very little effort is made by Riboutté to reproduce the milieu of speculation: he contents himself with having chosen that for a subject. The *Globe* reproaches the author with not having observed "ce qui se passe sous les hangars de la Bourse." The only real *fripon,* continues the article, is the valet, *courrier de Bourse;* but the schemers of today do not wear livery; they dress in black suits and are the best friends of this banker or that. The valet of *Le Spéculateur* actually dates the play back fifty years.

Eugène Scribe, who in his materialistic interests is, par excellence, the dramatic spokesman of the reign of Louis Philippe, and the successor to Picard in popular favor, describes speculation on the bourse in *Le Voyage dans l'Appartement* and in *La Passion secrète*. The former treats of a certain secretary-general who speculates with secret state funds; the latter of a woman who, attracted to the bourse by the conversation of her banker husband, speculates there without his knowledge. By a successful coup he makes a fortune which ruins his less fortunate wife.

The central figure of *Tout pour de l'Or,* a curious melodrama of the forties by Dinaux and Lesguillon, is one Verdier, a dastardly rogue who lies, murders, and betrays both master and country. He finds himself on the brink of financial ruin, and financial ruin is the only shame he knows: money is his one desire, for it represents pride, pleasure, and power. His opportunity to make a coup de bourse comes in a thrilling way. France is at war, and the enemy is at her gates. A messenger, Fernand, enemy of Verdier, is wounded while carrying a dispatch from Napoleon to the city officials; and he rushes into the château where Verdier happens to be, seeking someone to carry his message on. Verdier stabs him and steals the message. In it Napoleon urges the city not to capitulate, as he will soon come to her aid. Verdier, instead of delivering the dispatch, suppresses it in order to make the *rente* fall, he being just then *à la baisse*. Paris will capitulate. With his certain knowledge, he will be able to crush those who have ruined him. To-morrow France will belong to the enemy and he, Verdier, will be rich *jusqu'à l'insolence*. He will triumph, and his gold will protect him from the hatred of the public. Verdier triumphs with an enormous coup, but justice finds him out at last and he is killed.

There was published in 1846 a play called *L'Argent,* by Julien Coeur, which was never played, probably because the Alexandrines are many and tedious and the moral too bald. It is constructed in the usual way. The speculator Marcel is short of funds and intends to marry his daughter to Théodore, a devotee of the bourse. She is, of course, in love with someone quite poor and well out of the financial circle, the poet Maurice. The virtuous Paulin tries to cure his brother, Marcel, of the bourse malady; but all in vain. Marcel invests heavily in a bull market and loses his fortune. Chance, kindly to some at least, has guided the poor poet, who, staking his all *à la baisse,* wins what Marcel has lost. There can after that be no further hesitation about the wedding. It may here be remarked that Alexandrines held their place tenaciously in drama in spite of the tendency of the subject matter to become realistic. Although the moral can be uttered in them with great effect, they are a poor medium for the description of financial schemes.

From the theatrical pulpit François Ponsard, who in his turn, succeeded Scribe in popular favor, thunders forth as late as 1856 the eloquent Alexandrines of *La Bourse*. Indeed the protagonist of the play is no other than the stock exchange itself, beside which all the characters are mere pigmies. Under the shadow of this great power the following plot unfolds: Léon Desroches is in love with Camille Bertrand, but her father is looking for a richer suitor. Léon goes to Paris, hunts up a broker friend of his, Delatour, and proceeds to speculate on the stock exchange. Camille meanwhile prevails on her father to allow her to marry Léon and come to Paris in search of him. Camille finds him very much changed and becomes anxious when she discovers that he is speculating, for nothing ruins a good disposition so fast as "the bad air of the bourse." Her neatly turned protests are of little avail. What can poor little Camille do against such a rival as the bourse? She extracts a promise from Léon that he will speculate no more, stipulating that if he breaks his word he must no longer expect to marry her. But Léon has become deeply involved, having invested not only his own money but that of M. Bertrand, his prospective father-in-law. Léon, hoping against hope that the falling *rente* will rise, conceals the danger from M. Bertrand as long as he can, but is finally obliged to admit that their money is lost. Camille, hearing that Léon has failed to keep his word, refuses her hand and promises to marry the exemplary Reynold. Now Reynold has taken Léon under his protection, saved him from suicide, and placed him in certain mines of which he, Reynold, is the director. Here Léon proves himself a hero; and Reynold, seeing that Camille still loves the reformed speculator, brings the two together again. The bourse has exercised its baleful influence not only over Léon and M. Bertrand, but over nearly all the characters in the play. There is a young society man, Alfred d'Auberives, in the grip of the monster who cries out: "Cette Bourse, morbleu! n'a donc rien dans le coeur!" Mme Julie d'Argental, a friend of Camille, strongly advises her against marrying a man who has once caught the fever of speculation, for she herself is married to a financier. The coarse Simonnet, an old hand at the bourse, and well trained in its ways, represents its spirit of heartlessness. A poet asks him if he has no scruples at exploiting honest, credulous people. Scruples? Not he! So much the worse for the fools; victory belongs to the crafty. The contagion is felt even by Léon's valet, who repeats all the experiences of his master with exemplary faithfulness, until the parallelism becomes wearisome.

This play contains more polemic against the bourse than actual observation, but Ponsard was giving the public what it wanted; and as late as 1867 he was the *roi du théâtre,* in spite of the fact that Dumas *fils* and Augier had already written some of their best work. Although Ponsard realized that the trend of the theater was toward realism, he is but superficially realistic. He stands, says Latreille, midway between the exaggerations of romanticism and the conventions of classicism, urging liberty in art. He disdains the intrigue of Scribe and opens up the way for such realists as Becque. He is interesting also as virtual head of the Ecole du bon Sens, in which he was joined by Augier and Latour, who were seeking to steer literature between the rocks of fantasy and routine. This school serves as a transition from the romantic drama to the social comedy of the Second Empire.

Events of the famous *Question d'Argent* by Dumas *fils*, are closely related to the Paris bourse and its operations. The plot itself develops out of the fact that M. Durieu has lost 30,000 francs in speculation on the stock exchange. It is because of this loss that he decides to intrust the remainder of his money to the very successful financier Jean Giraud. The latter's success is due to his wholly unscrupulous methods—"les affaires, c'est bien simple, c'est l'argent des autres"—but this causes Durieu little concern, much less in fact than it causes his honest wife. Jean has promised to convert 40,000 francs into 60,000 by the end of the month. He refuses to disclose his plan, and Durieu has no reason to suppose it the more honest for that. Jean is a parvenu seeking to establish himself in good society. He needs Durieu's name and reputation for honesty to protect him, and he therefore wishes to go into partnership with him. The speculation with Durieu's money is Jean's way of keeping his partner faithful. The parvenu's second need is social position, and this he seeks by means of a marriage with the noble and virtuous Elisa de Roncourt, whose father is financially embarrassed. Jean wishes to assure himself full value for his money and, noting Elisa's sentimental air, asks René if the young lady's virtue is still *at par*. When courting Elisa, Jean makes the fatal mistake of telling his fiancée that he is putting all of his money in her name so that he cannot be forced to pay his creditors in case of a failure: "Je suis dans les affaires; je les fais sur une grande échelle; l'échelle peut casser. Il est bon que, dans ce cas, je retrouve par terre une bonne somme qui m'aide à me relever."

The lady resents this dishonesty and breaks off the match. Meanwhile the end of the month is approaching and Jean carries out his coup de bourse. He has bought stock as though he were expecting it to go up. Instead, it falls and he loses three million francs. He then carries over, or postpones, payment (*se fait reporter*) and spreads the rumor that he has gone to Havre on his way to America. This, he informs Durieu, is a *malice de Bourse*. Jean, without leaving Paris, has by this coup made a fortune both for himself and his associates.

Durieu has a rather sudden change of heart and refuses, though reluctantly, this money won by means of a lie. Jean Giraud realizes that his adventure in high society is over, and he departs, conscious that his financial ethics are unwelcome in certain circles but not knowing why. Indeed the reader is sorely puzzled at Durieu's sudden access of virtue. Being a man of affairs, he must have known that 20,000 francs are not won honestly in a few days; and as a frequenter of the bourse he must have known Jean's reputation, which was none of the best. When the coveted money is in his hands, he, like a weak soul, is afraid to take it and reluctantly returns it to the speculator, consigning himself henceforth to the safe mediocrity of 3 per cent bonds. Mme Durieu does all the work that Durieu's conscience should have done. She is his mentor as well as his financial secretary.

The *Question d'Argent* is amusingly parodied by Siraudin and Bourdois in a skit called *Avez-vous besoin d'Argent?* Jean Giraud appears as Jean Gigot; Durieu as Pluvieux, wine merchant; René as Raisinet; Elisa becomes the laundress Lisa; and her father, D'Argent-Court; finally the Countess Savelli figures as Mme Çavaty, the baker's wife. Jean is ostensibly an umbrella-vender, but the umbrella is a mere accessory: the principal thing is business, he explains to Raisinet, and upon the latter's query regarding the nature of the business, he laboriously explains:

"Well, now, business—well, business is other peoples' profits; and money is the other fellow's pocket. And the important question is to get as much money as possible out of that pocket without getting your hand caught in it: that's where you've got to look sharp!"

Now Jean has *pignon sur rue* and *terres au soleil,* but he must have *la considération!* Therefore he plans to marry Lisa. He makes his fortune over to the said Lisa, who at once plans to spend it on frivolities, but Jean forbids her to touch it, disclosing his deep-laid scheme to "beat it" one of these days leaving *la clef sous la porte.* His dearest wish is to go bankrupt and—to assure himself a nest egg for a rainy day—he generously leaves to his creditors all that he has not made over to Lisa, which is nothing. Lisa is disgusted with him for openly discussing his rascality: "c'est bête comme chou, mon bon"; and she refuses to marry him. Now Jean is speculating with money belonging to Pluvieux and Mme Çavaty. He appears as in the drama with the capital and interest as he had promised. Both Mme Çavaty and Pluvieux virtuously declare they will not accept the interest as it comes from too impure a source. Nevertheless they both pocket it, to Jean's great disappointment. Raisinet then berates Jean as a *filou* for having offered to enrich him, as *canaille* for having sought to make rich a penniless girl, and as a *malhonnête homme* for having attempted to increase Pluvieux's fortune: to all of which Jean Gigot insists that he himself is a coward and will not fight. Raisinet ends by declaring Jean lacking in moral sense. And Jean leaves the ungrateful group to return to the bourse. Pluvieux informs the public that one has to pay now to get into the bourse, and it is lucky one doesn't have to pay to get out, for one never has any money left. And Raisinet to the same tune sings:

> Everything on Change has value:
> Even nightcaps quoted are;
> Secondhand clothes are at a premium
> And cornet shares are soaring far.
> And nobody wishes anything more than
> Tin, tin, tin, tin, tin. You bet your life!
> No, nobody wants anything more than
> To filch her money from the baker's wife!
>
> —Scene 8

Emile Augier sends a number of his characters to the bourse. We find the hard-headed Roussel of *La Ceinture dorée* losing his fortune there and the brazen Vernouillet of *Les Effrontés* carrying out a coup by means of his paper, *La Conscience publique*. Vernouillet is speculating for a fall in the *rente,* when he reads in a rival paper, *Le Courrier,* that the tsar of Russia has visited the queen of England. This will send stock up in value, so he orders Giboyer to write a dispatch dated Petersbourg, for *La Conscience publique,* to the effect that the tsar has departed. The lie, Vernouillet explains, can be corrected after the liquidation which is due at the bourse the following day. We are not informed as to the outcome of the coup.

Vernouillet represents the early stages in a speculator's life when he makes his first important dishonest deal in order to get funds to establish himself quickly. The later stages are represented by Charrier, a highly respected banker whose early fraud is crusted over with the years, and who is suspected by no one. Weiss says in his comment on *Les Effrontés* that it is a true picture of society under the Second Empire in the *pêle-mêle* confusion of honest and scandalous fortunes, in the fellowship between respectable business men and intriguing adventurers. The true dramatic situation lies in this companionship between the honest man and the rascal. This Augier sensed; but in spite of his usual courage and in spite of the frankness becoming popular on the stage, he did not dare make Charrier a truly honest man.

Another popular dramatist, Sardou, has likewise made use of the bourse in his *Famille Benoîton* through which speculation runs rampant. Benoîton, a manufacturer of mattresses, and his son-in-law, Didier, are devoted to business and the stock exchange; the older son of Benoîton dabbles in stock, and the young boy of six plays at bourse with his companions all day long. This would seem to promise a sharp attack on speculation, but there is so little reality in the characters and so little solidity or consistency in the plot that the general effect is feeble. Parigot condemns Sardou for continuing to write vaudevilles after the manner of Scribe when the comedy of manners and the social comedy are already well developed. Sardou has merely retarded the progress of drama; whereas, Scribe, coming when he did, sent it forward. Nevertheless we owe Sardou thanks for his amusing parody on American business life in the play called *L'Oncle Sam*. The conversation between Sam Tapplebot and his crafty precocious son, Ulysses, is worth quoting. Sam is asking Ulysses about Nicaragua stock, to which Ulysses replies that he hopes his father has none. Sam has none; but, unfortunately, he is under contract to sell six hundred shares to Ulysses at the end of the month. Ulysses informs him that he has cornered the stock and that his father will have to buy it from him at $40 a share in order to sell it to him at $30.

SAM: Is there a corner [*coin*]?

ULYSSES: There is.

SAM: And I didn't catch on! Oh! Ulysses, I'm ashamed of your father!

ULYSSES: You say, sir, three thousand?

SAM: Three thousand.

ULYSSES: That's a dead loss of six thousand dollars . . . .
SAM: Not a penny less . . . .
ULYSSES: Well, give me two thousand and I'll fix things up . . . .
SAM: Oh! Thanks! Ulysses, you're a good son . . . .
ULYSSES: Glad to be of service, sir. (*Aside*) He's breaking, the old soul! He's breaking.

Although many of the plays treated, thus far, signal out the bourse as the great factor of the age, not one of them dares put before the audience the true grimness and sordidness, the daring and suffering of the actual events that occur there. Picard composed a pleasant warning with regard to speculation; Ponsard shook his finger at his young speculator Léon Desroches and then rewarded him with a sugar plum. Jean Giraud's speculation is, after all, hardly more than a salon *divertissement* for a group of well-to-do people who do not even get their fingers burned as they richly deserve. We see Jean particularly as a social ignoramus in an aristocratic circle, but scarcely as a business man robbing and ruining his fellow financiers. We have only a hint of his transactions: the prudish ears of René, Durieu, and the rest refuse to be contaminated by listening to Jean's own explanation of his coup de bourse.

The first writer to leave this saccharine treatment of financial dishonesty was Ernest Feydeau in his *Un Coup de Bourse,* which proved too realistic for production and was not even published until 1868, some seven years after its composition. In his Preface Feydeau tells how he had been urged by his friends to write a drama which should depict the true character of the great financiers of the bourse and he determined to put on the stage the Cyclops and Titans of the money world and the battles he had seen them wage ambushed in their offices. He refused to reproduce Ponsard's glib bankers, or the *faiseurs* created out of

Augier's brain, or the petty *carotteurs* wittily sketched by
Dumas *fils,* for in all of these characters there is nothing,
says Feydeau, "of that fever, that grimness, that frightful
self-control, nothing of those coalitions, of those crafty
tricks, of those terrible hatreds which drive and hurl into
a furious mêlée all these men who are seeking to control
their fellows." The fate of the play was precisely what
might have been expected. The actors of the Comédie-
Française were enthusiastic at the reading, but when it
came to accepting the play for production, they demanded
that it should be remade after the pattern of Ponsard's
L'Honneur et l'Argent and Léon Laya's *Le Duc Job*. The
softening element of love must come in, and the harsh
treatment of the financier must be smoothed down. Feydeau protested hotly: he was not trying to write a pleasant
play but a true one. The play became known to the financiers of the time, and the author was asked to read it to a
group of them. They listened solemnly through the five
hours of reading and then filed out in silence. Some years
later one of them congratulated Feydeau on having written the play. "It seemed harsh at the time, and unjust," he
said, "but after what I have seen taking place at the bourse
I am glad you wrote it."

We have here our first portrayal of the Israelite as a
big financier actively engaged in business and surrounded
by the usual army of parasites. Adolphe Silberstein is running a bank supported by shareholders, with whose money
he is speculating. His father, Moïse, slumps about his son's
office, complaining that since his bankruptcy he has no
funds, and yet at the same time secretly intrusting huge
sums to a broker for speculation. In the employ of Adolphe
is Henri de Buffières, whose place has been obtained for him

by his uncle, Saldagnac, the Silbersteins' doctor. Henri has seen enough of the Silberstein dealings to realize that the bank is a hoax and that the money he himself has invested in it is as good as lost. He informs his astonished uncle of his observations, who determines to study carefully the Silberstein operations on the bourse in hopes of winning back his nephew's lost money. The play is full of business excitement: it is laid in 1855, the period of the Crimean War, and every new dispatch from the front has its effect on bourse quotations, so that the bank is constantly being shaken to its foundations. A telegram announcing a ministerial crisis in England convinces Adolphe that war will continue, and he stubbornly speculates for a fall. This news he keeps to himself, but his parasites follow his lead in speculation: all but Moïse, who scents an end to the war and speculates against his son. Saldagnac, spying on the situation, follows the older Jew's example. Adolphe, finding himself in a precarious position financially, calls in several powerful Jewish bankers, hoping to persuade them to sell stock and thus keep the market down. They easily divine their comrade's situation and at once take advantage of it, promising him aid only on condition that he will give them the lion's share in a mining proposition which he is trying to arrange with the prince Verhazy. Rumors are afloat on the stock exchange that Silberstein is ruined. The bankers, fearful for themselves, turn traitors and cease to sell. Adolphe sees that his fortune is lost beyond hope of recovery. He takes the disgrace tragically, begging his wife to give him the fortune she has in her own name so that he may retrieve himself; but she rudely refuses. Meanwhile Moïse gloats over his son's misfortune and over the fine sum he himself has made. He refuses to help his son, forcing him into bankruptcy, that being according to Moïse a sure way to get a good start in the financial world. Saldagnac, who had followed Moïse's lead, has also made a fortune.

This play is indeed relentlessly realistic. It is too modern a play for the sixties. Not only is the atmosphere of the bourse given, but the whole interest is in the speculator and his dealings. The play is confused, overburdened with details, it is true; but every line adds to the terrible realism of finance.

As we approach the present day, the money interest in drama becomes keener and grimmer, the sums involved vaster. Not only individuals but nations are concerned, and the stock exchanges of one country affect those of another. Yet we still note in the modern money-play the romantic and realistic currents which ran side by side during the nineteenth century. At times the excitement, the size of the speculation, the desperate courage of the speculator carry us into a land of romance where the bourse is a besieged city of priceless wealth; at others the minute business details, the sober facts, the criminal dishonesty force upon us the realism of the stage. Although the tense excitement of the bourse continues to be present, there are fewer observations on the marvelous or devastating bourse. Much that had excited comment is now taken for granted. In the past of almost every financier of drama is an *histoire de Bourse*, which, as interpreted by a certain character, may be called *une histoire de coupe-bourse*. The dramatist ceases to moralize. He presents coldly an immense fraud of one kind or another: "Au besoin on donnerait un petit coup de pouce, un jour, à la Bourse." Thus a twentieth-century speculator drops a hint to his associates. Here

is the realism of *Un Coup de Bourse,* the realism of the
Third Republic, of *Les Polichinelles, Le Cuivre,* and *Les
Sauterelles.* Although perforce intimately connected with
the bourse, these plays are more interesting because of
their industrial companies and will be handled in a later
chapter. Such companies gradually replace individual financiers in the control of the stock exchange.

Bertrand

CHAPTER VII

THE BUBBLE COMPANY

De la Bourse, théâtre où se joue la grande comédie de l'époque, passons à la commandite, officine où se compose le drame, où se combinent les coups de théâtre.—PROUDHON, *Manuel du Spéculateur à la Bourse.*

FRANCE, having not yet forgotten the Mississippi Bubble and the failure of the Caisse Lafarge, was, at the opening of the nineteenth century, still dubious about credit schemes, taking but cautious interest in the new insurance and industrial companies; but as some of these proved highly successful, bitter memories of past disasters grew dim; and a new era of "paper prosperity" began when every promoter set about applying "his science-illumined genius to the blowing of bubbles, the bursting of which sent many a poor devil to jail, the workhouse, or the bottom of the river" but left the promoter rolling in riches. When once awakened to the alluring dividends offered by companies of various sorts, the public forgot all previous caution and invested with utter recklessness. In 1821 the speculator Brûlot of *Les Joueurs* remarks on the effort made by the newspapers to stir up popular interest by printing every morning the prospectus of a new insurance company. His own suggestion is that an international agency to insure peace be created:

> For the sake of capital
> Companies we plan,
> And insurance can be had
> On the life of beast or man.

What finer enterprise
Than that all wars should cease
And people sign insurance
To live henceforth in peace!

—Scene 10

By the thirties France had become the prey of numerous industrialists who, by a system of shares, extracted money from purses that had never before been tapped. *Actions* were issued for every conceivable and inconceivable thing under heaven. Had Chimborazo been put into shares, says Louis Reybaud, they would have found purchasers. Mercadet refuses to pity this gullible public, holding it as much to blame as the promoter for "tous les deux, ils veulent être riches en un instant." One of the actual schemes proposed by a *tapeur* was the forming of a company for roasting potatoes under the ashes of Napoleon I. Some of the early enterprises in England were equally wild, as, for instance, the exporting of skates and warming-pans to Rio (which reminds one of the snow shovels that later went to Panama) and the subscription of loans to an imaginary South American republic.

Among his *Bubbles of the Day,* played in 1842, Jerrold satirizes such speculation in the schemes of Captain Smoke who is about to lease Mount Vesuvius to make lucifer matches. He is also promoting a company to get the civet out of asafetida and is developing the magnificent project of a trip-around-the-world company. There will be every possible accommodation for everyone, including the luxury of a parson for engaged couples. The children will be put on shore for a week in each country in order to learn the language. The third venture is a cemetery in the Serpentine River: floating tombstones, "water lilies and aquatic plants gemming the translucent crystal, shells of rainbow brightness, a constant supply of gold and silver fish, with right of angling secured to the shareholders." The chairman's bonus is to be a family vault in the river.

The promoter of the thirties and forties is the most impudent, and, at the same time delightful, rogue of drama. He has no sense of honesty, no morality, but he is endowed with a most refreshing imagination and a genius for getting out of scrapes, admiration for which makes the reader forget or despise M. Gogo, the victim. These swindlers are comically earnest in their self-justification. Mercadet, evidently recalling Panurge on debt, cites the perpetual indebtedness of the earth to the sun as a precedent for his own habitual inability to pay his creditors. Mr. Touchandgo of *Crotchet Castle* reasons with perfect logic that, owing half a million, he had better retain the trifle still left in his pocket, for how could this trifle ever find its rightful owner among the creditors? He, therefore, coolly takes it with him to Dotandcarryone Town in Canada where it serves him to set up a bank among the inhabitants of the place, all of whom had, like himself, run away from debt. In the second half of the century, when the novelty of this new character had begun to wear off and the French Touchandgos—Mercadet, Robert Macaire, and many others—were swindling on a larger and larger scale, drama ceases to find them amusing and likens them to animals with enormous throats swallowing up thousands of tiny creatures too small to defend themselves, men who exploit industry, refusing to lend it support unless promised the lion's share of the profits.

Drama pays little attention to the serious importance and true value of the credit system, which should, of course, not be lost sight of. Never without the establishment of a *Banque de France,* a *Crédit foncier,* a *Crédit mobilier,* the work of the Péreire brothers, a *Société générale,* a *Crédit Lyonnais,* and reputable industrial companies, could the great constructive projects of the age have ever been realized. Here again we recognize the foresight of the Saint-Simonians who during the thirties and forties were impressing on the public the need of such institutions of credit, most of which were not established till the time of Louis Napoleon.

Unfortunately the joint-stock company offered almost unlimited opportunity for dishonesty, particularly the *société en commandite* which was not under the supervision of the Code of Commerce. It became legal to make out share certificates to bearer in the companies with share capital. These bearer certificates being easily transferable, swindling was a simple matter. Drama makes little or no attempt to be explicit as to whether a company is a *société anonyme* (a true joint-stock company which might or might not have limited liability according to its constitution) and the sleeping partnership (a *société en commandite* or a *société en commandite par actions*). In either case the directors (*gérants*), either secretly or through proxies, speculate with the money of their stockholders; and when the crash comes, they sell their enterprise and skip out of the country, only to return later for fresh operations. The *société en commandite* was the chief speculative instrument of the forties and fifties, the *crédit mobilier* age. Railroads, mines, canals, newspapers, loans, insurance, and countless inventions were financed in this way.

The first important joint-stock company of drama seems to be that directed by the unscrupulous and resourceful Piffart of *Les Actionnaires,* by Scribe and Bayard (1829). Piffart shows well enough that if you were to ask for money you would get none: but just create a few shares and Paris will fight over them and beg you to take her gold in exchange. Having already gone through a fortune made from *l'argent des autres,* Piffart is on the point of creating an industrial company when his cousin Gustave arrives, a cautious young man as yet untempted by any financial speculation. But Gustave, much in love with the rich Estelle Kernokek, who is in Paris with her aunt, Mme Desperriers, joins his cousin in the new enterprise, hoping thus to make a fortune and win Estelle. The company is duly formed, with Piffart as director at a salary of 30,000 francs and Gustave as cashier drawing 15,000. The ten remaining employes will receive 1,200 each. The capital is to be three million. There will be created one thousand real shares and five hundred remunerative ones to be divided between the director and the cashier. Gustave is amazed at such sums of money and such high-handed distribution of shares, but Piffart assures him that it is the enviable privilege of the stockholders to pay all the bills of the company and that he himself has a right to the five hundred extra shares, for the stockholder can lose only what he puts into the company whereas he, the director, is liable to lose what he does not even possess.

As yet no one, not even Piffart, knows the purpose of the company. He and his partner, Labourdinière, go over a mass of projects which might serve their purpose. Why not buy up all the theaters of Paris and rent or sell them along with their actors? If not that, perhaps a hydraulic enterprise would do, one which should supply all the houses of Paris with water. Another suggestion is the building of an enormous omnibus which should hold five hundred people and be drawn by elephants, a scheme "quite à la mode" says Labourdinière. An even more beneficial project is the reclaiming of the arid plains of Les Sablons by means of

artesian wells. Dikes and canals will transport Holland to
the very gates of Paris. The property owners will have
dairies and a monopoly on beefsteaks and cutlets. Piffart is
much taken with this scheme; but Gustave, after making
investigations and finding that it is wholly impractical,
warns Mme Desperriers, who has thrown herself into the
speculation with great enthusiasm. He also informs Piffart that the artesian wells must be abandoned. Piffart,
however, is not caught without resources. He has bought
from M. Kernokek a château on some wooded property in
Brittany, which, being worthless in its present condition,
Kernokek had sold to Piffart for 600,000 francs. When the
company of stockholders is assembled, Piffart replaces the
former scheme with that of exploiting the forests on this
property. Kernokek, angry at having let the land go so
cheaply, informs the company that there is no shipping
center anywhere near. Piffart meets this attack with the
proposition that the old château be turned into an iron
foundry, which would be inexpensive, as wood could be had
for nothing; and as for the shipping, a railroad could be
cheaply established thanks to the foundry. The shareholders, Crifort, Hardy, and Clairénet, impressed with the lith-
ographed prospectus and finally convinced that there is a
clair et net profit to be made, fight with one another to obtain shares. In a short while Piffart has made a fortune, for
he loses no time in selling his own shares. When asked by
Gustave who among the stockholders really make any
money, he cynically replies: "Ceux qui ne le sont plus."

Close on the heels of Piffart comes the rejuvenated rascal, Robert Macaire, one of the greatest "progressive"
characters of the century, whom we meet here in his famous rôle as director of a joint-stock company against
thieves. He originated as a common thief in the melodrama

L'Auberge des Adrets, by Benjamin Antier, Saint-Amand, and Paulyanthe, played at the Ambigu-Comique, July 2, 1823. The play was reproduced at the Porte Saint-Martin, January 28, 1832. Frédéric Lemaître, who had acted Robert in the *Auberge des Adrets,* noting the trend of public taste, turned the thief into a swindler and revised the play, which was produced under the name of *Robert Macaire* and had a great success in 1834 at the Folies-Dramatiques. The story is told that the actor, Lemaître, found the idea for his new popular hero in a ragged dandy whom he observed on the streets of Paris draw from his pocket an impossible handkerchief and use it with the utmost grace. The actor followed the ragged jaunty figure until the fellow's gestures and costume were impressed on his memory; and he appeared thus on the stage as we still see him in Honoré Daumier's delightful cartoons, which first appeared in *Le Charivari* from 1836 to 1838. Robert Macaire is thus described by Ludovic Cellier: "A high cravat over his chin, a patch on his eye, a heavy chain at his vest, a battered hat, a silk handkerchief dangling from his pocket, proudly planted on his legs, ready to entice trade, in the person of the naïve fool who may fall into his clutches." Macaire is no longer an ordinary thief, but the great incarnation of modern charlatanism: a quack doctor who insults his patients if they die, a dentist who pulls out good teeth to insert false ones, a broker cheating his clients, and finally the director of a fraudulent insurance company against thieves.

The plot of *Robert Macaire* is, in brief, as follows: In the forest of Bondy near a charcoal-burner's cabin, Macaire and his faithful follower, Bertrand, meet after their flight from the inn, the Auberge des Adrets. The wild beat of horses' hoofs is heard. Macaire rushes forth and rescues Baron de Wormspire and his daughter Eloa. The Baron then invites the two scamps to ride in the carriage with himself and his daughter. Bertrand, during the ride, proves himself so skilful with a jimmy when there happens to be occasion to pick the lock of a trunk that he and Macaire feel it advisable to escape from the Baron. The second act shows a public ball at which people are gathered to hear certain political candidates. Disguised in costumes taken from a property trunk they had stolen, Robert and Bertrand address the crowd. Their ruse is discovered and again they are obliged to flee. The third act contains the joint-stock company scene already alluded to. Macaire has, meanwhile, become engaged to Eloa, whom he supposes to be rich. The fourth act gathers our friends at the Neuilly fair. The Baron, who is a brother swindler, appears there as a *coco*-vender. The group of rogues is reunited in a most intimate way, for it is discovered that Eloa is Bertrand's deserted daughter, and Robert Macaire the Baron's son. The happy family reunion is disturbed by the police in search of the convicts, and Macaire and Bertrand escape in a balloon over the heads of the crowd.

But we must return to the meeting of the stockholders which Robert Macaire is haranguing after this fashion:

Gentlemen, at a time when evil passions seem to be sweeping over our social order with the rage of a torrent; in a century when everyone is trying to slip his hand surreptitiously into his neighbor's pocket, the idea of founding an insurance agency against thieves was both tremendous and philanthropic. Mine is the honor of having conceived this idea, but, Gentlemen, yours is the honor of supporting it with your capital and your enthusiasm . . . .

After this cynical exordium, the master thief explains with inimitable candor the ideal management of a company. You buy up some new enterprise, good or bad, paying the minimum for it; you advertise it widely, realize the capital, pocket the money, and leave the country, declaring the company bankrupt. Having thus plenty of funds, the director may repeat the same process. The shareholders are delighted with the prospectus which is presented to them. Macaire then calls for an extra five millions to form a new company to control the police! This is, in reality, a second call for funds; and one of the *actionnaires*, M. Gogo, accuses Robert of this and demands dividends. Macaire faints away with sorrow and indignation that he should be so misunderstood, and Gogo is at once put out of the meeting by the faithful shareholders.

Virmaitre relates similar behavior on the part of an actual financier of the eighties who when asked by a shareholder to show him the forty shares of Lyons railroad stock which he had intrusted to his care, bursts into tears at being so doubted. The shareholder relented and said that he would be satisfied if only the financier's private secretary would say that he had seen the stock. The financier led the secretary and the objector to his safe where the securities were supposed to be. He opened it up, showed a few papers to the secretary, and asked him if he did not see the securities. The secretary refused to lie and the financier fell back in his chair sobbing. His secretary no longer trusted him: he was lost. Virmaitre adds that not the financier but the securities were lost.

The public was delighted with the cynical *blagueur* Robert Macaire, who was only the embodiment of the worst in itself. As Jules Guex observes, the public seemed to have an unhealthy taste for what Heine called "Robert Macairianism," a tendency to find vice amusing and to scoff at decency. Balzac modeled his Vautrin upon Macaire. The type created by Lemaître will live, says Lenient, for Robert Macaire has taken his place beside Mandrin

and Renart, Patelin, Panurge, and Cartouche, legendary
heroes of rascality, "en les égalant ou les surpassant tous,
sinon par le génie, au moins par le cynicisme et l'immoral-
ité."

The popularity of *Robert Macaire* recalls the great interest manifested by the French public of 1721 in *Cartouche, ou les Voleurs,* a three-act prose comedy by M. le
Grand. *Le Mercure* wonders how posterity will judge the
taste of the times when it learns that this play was preferred to *Esope à la Cour.* The harangue of Cartouche,
the robber, to his comrades has much the same spirit as
Macaire's oratory. Cartouche begins by wishing his companions money and a good appetite, but not honor, for they
can easily do without that. After describing the stormy sea
upon which they are embarked, he reminds them that the
whole science of their profession consists in two things:
"taking and not being taken." Moreover, "Everybody's
property is ours," says he, "if we are but clever enough to
get it." The real Cartouche was at this time in prison,
where the author of the play visited and observed him.

The character, Robert Macaire, became so popular
that every theater insisted on having the hero; and many
sequels[1] were written, among which is a one-act *folie, Robert Macaire et Bertrand,* by Jules Vizentini and Auguste
Jouhaud (1849). The celebrated pair is in the French village of Risquons-Tout on the border of Belgium, to which
haven the thieves are repairing for safety. They, however,
spend the night in the French village, disclose their identity by talking in their sleep and are arrested.

[1] Other plays of the cycle are *La Fille de Robert Macaire, Le Fils de
Robert Macaire, Le Cousin de Robert Macaire,* and *Une Emeute au Par-
adis ou le Voyage de Robert Macaire.* Cf. Jules Guex, *Le Théâtre et la
Société française de 1815 à 1848* (Paris, 1900), p. 103.

The activities of a Macaire demand a Gogo who will take enthusiastic interest in all the worthless shares the swindler sees fit to offer. We have already found the hero of Bayard's *Monsieur Gogo à la Bourse* thus occupied. He also becomes involved in a company. Vaudoré, the Macaire who plans this *société en commandite par actions;* a certain Baron ————, the counterpart of Baron Wormspire; and a Bilboquet, the model for whom we shall encounter shortly, meet at Gogo's house to discuss the project. Gogo is nervous, dreading the return of his wife who is opposed to speculation. The purpose of the company is to exploit *toutes les industries.* Vaudoré, the first to arrive, describes to Gogo the other gentlemen who are to be their companions in the enterprise. They are all distinguished persons, well known in Paris, but who, for idle reasons, are not allowed at the bourse. There is the Baron ————, the greatest proprietor of the age; his son-in-law, the greatest industrial of the age; and finally Bilboquet, the wittiest man of the age. All these superlative personages congregate at Gogo's house; and plans for the new company are well under way when Mme Gogo returns and all the speculators are promptly shown the door.

Monsieur Gogo, by Paul de Kock and F. Lemaître, although far removed from *Robert Macaire* in its attitude toward rascality, contains two fraudulent companies. The speculator, Boursicoff, is dreaming of a magnificent affair —platinum mines in the Pyrenees, where millions are to be made. Gogo, who is still a fool, exclaims: "Millions! That's a sure thing. You promised to stick me—no—to put me into your deal." To which Boursicoff kindly replies, "You bet. I'll stick you in it." Gogo eventually becomes astute, tricks the *fripon,* and recovers his money.

In 1831 there swaggered on to the French stage one of

the most impudent scamps of the century, the clown Bilboquet, hero of *Les Saltimbanques* by Dumersan and Varin. Never was anyone more blissfully unaware of the
meaning of "mine" and "thine" than this charlatan who

Charlatan Bilboquet complains that Charlatan Macaire has stolen his
public.

typified the then prevalent spirit of *blague* and trickery in
all phases of life, and whose name signifies a balanced toy
that when upset will always right itself. The landlady demands her pay, and he offers her a worthless check; if another person's truck is within reach, he feels that it "must"
be his and acts accordingly; when furious creditors storm
one door, he takes his departure, bag and baggage, through

the other, seizing his drum with the proverbial phrase of the swindler—*Sauvons la caisse!* He advertises painless dentistry, and at the protests of his suffering victims explains the advertisement as meaning that the operation is painless to the dentist. When accepting a new musician into his troupe, he asks if the youth, Sosthène by name, is the equal of Paganini. To the young man's reply that he does not even know where Paganini lives, Bilboquet joyfully decides to advertise him as a pupil of the great master. Bilboquet speaks no truer word in the whole play than when, pocketing the fifteen francs which Sosthène has lent him, he exclaims touchingly, "C'est quinze francs que je vous dois ... jamais je ne m'acquitterai envers vous." Bilboquet is just the sort of man to have started a joint-stock company, but that is left to his friend Cabochard and is but a slight episode in the play. Cabochard forms a company for the extraction of corns. He secures quite a few shareholders among shoe merchants; but, says Bilboquet, who had lent his friend his signature, "cette entreprise pêchait pas sa base" and poor Cabochard failed; in fact, everything is lost and what remains goes to the creditors.

Two ludicrous companies are mentioned in *La France et l'Industrie:* one, a company insuring against hoarseness in opera singers, the other a company for the extinction of insects. Equally farcical is Lombard's Bankruptcy Company of *L'Assemblée de Créanciers,* which, it will be remembered, furnished decoy creditors for fraudulent bankrupts. The Company will answer for the honesty of these fake creditors, but the said Company will retain one-fourth of the financier's receipts to cover office expenses, one-fourth for the director, one-fourth for interest, one-fourth for registration, and also one-fourth for the poor—one must be philanthropic!

Contemporaneous with Lombard's company is the partnership of Gondolfin and Plumcake described by Scribe and Vander-Burch in *Japhet*. Honesty was the one form of speculation that company had never tried. Since its dissolution Tristam Plumcake has given up swindling as too full of anxieties and dangers, not to mention the tax it puts on one's wit and imagination. Honesty is much less exhausting. It is not only a refuge and rest; it is a *bénéfice clair et net*. Scribe depicts a fraudulent railroad company in *Le Veau d'Or*. Ledoux, promoter and capitalist, has drawn into it his enemy the Duke, with the intention of ruining him. Indeed the enterprise is calculated to ruin all but its directors. Scribe, writing with Duport, again treats a bogus company, this time in *La Tutrice*. Conrad, an industrialist who insists on being called a capitalist, is on a tour among the rich trying to sell stock in the Société Conrad et Cie, investing in the manufacture of woolen and cotton goods. Of course the enterprise is a veritable gold mine which it is a pleasure to share with one's compatriots. Conrad's daughter, Florette, is puzzled that her father should part with shares in so valuable an operation, but he explains to her that shares are rarely profitable if one holds them. That is why Conrad is so eager to associate others in this plan which is national, patriotic, and exceedingly useful to industry. "To yours!" exclaims Florette. "Without doubt," replies her father: "c'est l'industrie de chacun qui fait celle du pays!"

Balzac's notable Mercadet[2] a man after the author's own image, is engaged in a desperate struggle to keep him-

---

[2] Balzac completed *Le Faiseur*, of which Mercadet is the hero, in 1844; but it was not played until 1851. The lengthy original version was reduced to three acts by Adolphe d'Ennery and renamed *Mercadet*. It was published in 1851 at the Librairie Théâtrale. The play as written by Balzac appears in his *Oeuvres Complètes*, Vol. XVIII (Michel Lévy, 1870).

self afloat in the troubled waters of financial difficulties. He is beset by sharklike creditors with hungry teeth, apparently forever deserted by his partner, and much hampered by an honest wife. His assets are a marriageable daughter, wits and enthusiasm. He schemes to marry his homely daughter for money, uses his wit to outwit his creditors, and expends his enthusiasm on stock in numberless enterprises for "les mines d'or ne sont plus au Mexique, mais place de la Bourse."

Mercadet is the true genius of the industrial company: what companies are not in actual existence are well developed in his brain. To reassure his maid Thérèse in regard to her unpaid wages, he promises her as a husband one of the future employees of his insurance company against being recruited for military service. To quiet the troublesome creditor Pierquin, Mercadet blithely offers pink shares in a newspaper which might be successful if it should appear; or blue shares in a mine which has failed; or yellow shares in a paving which cannot be used for barricades. This idea is found in D'Ennery's stage version of 1851, and the reviser probably had in mind the street frays of 1848 when he gave Mercadet the inspiration of the *pavé conservateur*. Mercadet, hunting for a way to appease his creditor Violette, and even to get money out of him, dazzles the old usurer with the classic formula of promoters: "Figurez-vous, mon cher, l'invention la plus brillante, la spéculation la plus magnifique, la découverte la plus sublime ..." But what is this project to be? Groping about in his fertile mind, Mercadet hits upon the conservative paving—a paving which will not admit of barricades. Naturally, all governments anxious to keep order will take shares. Kings, princes, ministers will be charter shareholders and with them all the gods of finance: even socialists, seeing their business ruined, will be obliged to take shares. Violette's eyes are stretching wide to see all the millions as Mercadet concludes: "C'est sublime et philanthropique! ... et dire qu'on m'a refusé quatre mille francs pour répandre les announces et lancer les prospectus." The upshot of this eloquence is that Violette hands over to Mercadet 6,000 francs.

The speculator is promoting Les Asphaltes, La Providence des Familles, and Le Gaz Verdelin. He is heartily in favor of the modern insurance company. Everyone's future, says he, is in the public savings-bank: a girl gets her dowry there, a woman depends on that rather than on her husband; a man pays his debts to his country by means of a company for slave traffic in whites. On the whole we may say that all our duties are taken care of by shares. In spite of all his apparently miraculous sources of wealth, Mercadet is on the verge of bankruptcy and affiances his daughter to the supposedly well-to-do La Brive, who is, however, like most adventurers, in search of a rich wife. While Mercadet is putting off his creditors with the promise of a son-in-law who will satisfy their demands, La Brive is quieting his own creditors with the prospect of his fiancée's fortune. There comes the fatal moment when Mercadet presses La Brive for an exact description of the property which he claims to own in the south of France. Nice sandy land, salt marshes covered with pine, says La Brive. Mercadet beams: "Why not form a company to exploit the salt!" Further questioning brings to light the fact that the salt marshes are only a synonym for "sea" and that La Brive's land is very much under water. Poor Mercadet! Even he hesitates to "mettre la mer en actions!" But there is no reason for being discouraged; they can use the sand to make glass.

With the help of La Brive, Mercadet carries out a coup de bourse in Basse-Indre mining stock. He first spreads the rumor that the stock is dropping, but he secretly hints to his friend Verdelin that the report of the engineers is excellent. No one knows this, so the opportunity offers itself to debase the stock, buy up a quantity, and, when the certain rise comes, make a fortune. Verdelin, in order to force a lowering in the price, sells his stock at a loss of 25 per cent. Mercadet then begins buying in the name of his absent partner Godeau, giving his broker, Berchut, to understand that Godeau has returned wealthy. Mercadet's hope is to scrape together enough money to pay for this stock which is bound to be valuable in time. Very fortunately, indeed, for him, in those desperate minutes which bid fair to be the last of his financial life, Godeau does return from Calcutta with a fortune "incalcuttable." This money to the rescue is the *deus ex machina*, the only true god of Balzac's novels, according to Jules Janin. Money pours in, a veritable Pactolus, "et ça coule, et ça coule avec une rage incroyable."

Lenient calls Mercadet the Turcaret of the nineteenth century, finding him, however, shrewder, keener, less ridiculous than his predecessor. Mercadet belongs to a new period: "Here we have the reflection of a new age, an age of banks and fictitious credit organizations, joint stock companies, imaginary insurance agencies, losing investments, fantastic enterprises sold by shares, and finding purchasers at par or at a premium." Mercadet is more moral than Turcaret, having those bourgeois qualities of respectable family life so popular from 1830 to 1848. He is neither rascal nor honest man, but a typical *faiseur*.

Mercadet had his admirers, among whom is the speculator Coquelet, of *Les Oiseaux de la Rue*, a comedy by

Lambert, Thiboust, and Delacour. Coquelet is in financial straits, but he assures his wife that he can save himself by means of his friends and credit after the fashion of Mercadet of the Gymnase. His wife protests that Mercadet is a rogue. But her husband insists that *Mercadet* is the best play he has seen since *Robert Macaire,* that it is M. de Balzac's masterpiece: "What a great man Mercadet is! What a genius! Always falling on his feet. O Mercadet! You are my master and I am worthy of you!" However, there is no food left in the house, and the grocer has refused further credit. Coquelet bethinks him of his marriageable daughter Anasthasie who is something of an imbecile. He tells her to put paper flowers in her hair and look as intelligent as possible while a wealthy young man comes to call. But Coquelet's endeavors are all failures, and he is obliged to make his escape to Belgium.

Mercadet reappears in the last decade of the nineteenth century under the name of Brignol in the charming comedy by Alfred Capus, *Brignol et sa Fille.* There is the same insouciance with regard to debt, the same innocent criminality, the same certainty of millions tomorrow, but there is by no means the same genius for business. For twenty years Mme Brignol has been condemned to a life of continual expectancy and disillusionment, sure that her husband's creditors will some day march him off to prison. The rent is long overdue, and the proprietor is angry; but Brignol has fifty affairs started, any one of which should make the family rich. He does not care to be a millionaire; he will be content to give Cecile a dowry of 100,000 francs and have an income of 12,000 for himself. The "affairs" remain quite vague. It is Brignol's nature to be vague. His practical and honest brother-in-law laments that Brignol has no vices—vices can be recognized, classified, and combated—but Brignol is neither good nor bad and will commit crimes without the least evil intent. He has already lost the 30,000 francs intrusted to him by his friend the Commander, and is both surprised and hurt to hear himself called a rascal. He has no sense of responsibility and refuses to think of the future. When a good position is offered to him, he declines it as too easy, too simple for a man of genius like himself who needs a vast and complicated sort of work but—nothing regular. "Il ne faut pas que je sache ce que j'ai à faire." It is the obliging suitor of Brignol's delightful daughter who plays the rôle of Godeau and rescues this Mercadet, enabling him to turn to the wearisome preaching sister-in-law with a triumphant "Didn't I tell you so!"

Plays of the forties teem with railroad companies. The droll Quincampoix, whom we have already met shopping in the big stores of Paris, had left Dijon to protest against the violation of his property by a railroad company. Quincampoix is determined that his house shall not be cut in two. He intends to show that trains shall not be run through his dining room, even if he has to stop the locomotives with his own hands! He goes at once to a meeting of shareholders to make his protest. What a mob there was! What excitement! They were actually dealing in millions to hear them talk, and such plans: "We'll cross this river and step over that mountain, a bridge here, a viaduct there! Why, there are fortunes in sight! Get your stock now!" It was enough to make anyone lose his head, and Quincampoix lost his to the extent of a hundred shares. His shame is unbounded: he had entered that assembly as pure as a virgin, with the sole purpose of defending his dining-room, and here he is with all these shares! Two hours later he receives 200,000 francs in dividends. The money weighs horribly upon him and he swears that not for an empire will he keep it.

La grande Bourse et les petites Bourses by Clairville and Faulquemont, mentions a great variety of railroad stock:

A line from Paris to Berlin
And one from Strasburg to Pékin:
From Madeira and Venice there
Run lines to Bordeaux and Nanterre.

Shares make up these many lines
And the public ne'er declines
The alluring bait adroitly flung—
In reach of foolish suckers hung.

—Scene 11

In addition to these are named roads from Astrakhan to Peking and from Kamchatka to Carcassonne. Dutillet, being obliged to invest, chooses the railroad from Pamplona to Toboso, stock in which goes up 100 francs, making the fortunate fellow a millionaire. Other magnificent projects are exposed: a Paris subway through the Catacombs, cutting across Rue Amelot and the boulevards from the Capucines to Bonne-Nouvelle; a Paris elevated from the cupola of the Pantheon to the Observatory with a branch line to the towers of Notre-Dame; and finally a road encircling Paris. A colossal affair, a gigantic project, positively Napoleonic, is hinted at—a road from Cairo to Calcutta, passing via Darfour, with an extension along the Isthmus of Suez.

The rogue Périnet of Doucet's *La Chasse aux Fripons,* keenly alive to the possibilities of speculation in railroad stock baits his victims with all the *grands mots du jour,* such as premiums: Strasburg and Lyons shares!—shares of every sort; and even *promesses d'actions* and *promesses de promesses!!* Another scapegrace of the vaudeville,

Saint-Laurent, a promoter of companies, is cleverly described as a "prince of industry," a "king of finance," and the "immortal inventor of an insurance company against the extinction of poverty." Flammèche of *La Chasse aux Millions* is pestered at the bourse by questions about railroad stock:

> How much is North? What's Pampoux worth?
> Should I, sir, buy up Espelette,
> Or Strasburg, or Bordeaux to Cette?

> Dear sir, I'll take today
> Some Rouen and Calais,
> And Avignon,
> For me, Vierzon
> And me, Lyon
> And me, Dijon
> etc.

—II, 5

Evidently all the stage speculators of the forties agree with Marcel of *L'Argent* (1846), who declares that railroads have restored him to life; that they are an unheard-of phenomenon yielding in one minute more gold than the furnaces of Satan could ever melt. He is winning *à la vapeur* and will stake everything on railways. The excitement cools down eventually, but railroad stocks continue to figure in financial drama.

In a thrilling melodrama of 1847, *Le Fils du Diable,* by Paul Feval and Saint-Yves, there is a certain Reinhold, once the bandit Regnault, whom his wife calls "un speculateur froid, avide, implacable, un tortueux agioteur de honteuses affaires." Reinhold, in order to put money in the strong box of the gang to which he belongs, proposes that they institute a *tontine du travail,* that is, a workingman's

joint-insurance company. Mira, another of the conspira-
tors, calls the plan sheer folly. "Folly!" exclaims Reinhold, "why it will put ten millions in our hands inside of
two months, for I am not going to ask the rich for money
but the poor, the workingmen . . . . these are trustful
because they are honest." Reinhold convinces his hearers,
and the company is formed. The first meeting takes place
in the speculator's *hôtel*. In the foreground is a table
around which the stockholders meet; in the back is a window where money transactions take place. In this setting
Reinhold addresses the assembly: Great capital is suspicious and therefore immobile, but small capital is, more
easily set in motion, and amounts in time to a great sum.
He, Reinhold, is proposing a "magnificent and gigantic operation" which will in a few years decuple the capital of
those who have invested in this enterprise, which is "moral,
gilt-edged, paying, and social." The dramatist says no
more about the *tontine*, and we are left to suppose that a
number of poor men are ruined. Poetic justice finally pun-
ishes the gang. There is something far more sinister in this
glimpse of a company deliberately planning to rob the poor
than in all Mercadet's magnificent, impracticable, rascally
schemes, which, barring the rascality, resemble so closely
Balzac's own schemes for making a fortune.

A fire insurance company with the picturesque name
"La Compagnie de la Lune" plays considerable part in
Les faux Bonshommes. All went well at first; but its
founder, the speculator Lecardonnel, wishing to have more
shares and to get them at a lower rate, complains of the in-
competent director and cashier, says the affair will be a
total loss to stockholders, and sells out. Shares drop from
1,000 to 125 francs. But Lecardonnel is secretly buying up

stock at the reduced rate, planning eventually to become the director. He succeeds in making a goodly sum and then decamps with the money of Péponet and many others, making a hole in the Moon Company.

In *La Question d'Argent* there is perpetually in prospect a company which never materializes owing to Durieu's suddenly awakened scruples about tainted money. Had he not been hampered by a moral wife and an honest nephew, he would certainly have gone into the partnership of the Maison Giraud, Durieu et Cie, although toward the end of the play he weakly protests to his wife that he had never intended to become an associate of Giraud's. In the first act Giraud hands Durieu the draft of the deed of partnership; in the second Jean asks if he has read it, and explains more fully Durieu's position. The company is to be constituted for one year, and Durieu is to have one-fourth of the profits, which should amount to 150,000 or 200,000 francs; and he is to put in only 100,000 francs. Durieu has not that much available, and intrusts 40,000 to Giraud, who promises to net him 20,000 by a coup de bourse at the end of the month. It is this coup which ends the relations between Giraud and Durieu and thus terminates the partnership. Giraud informs Durieu that he is to serve as a prospectus because of his honest name, but this human "prospectus" gives up a profit of 50 per cent a month for the slow and virtuous path to fortune which is lined with 3 per cent bonds.

Jean suggests another joint-stock company, half jestingly, half seriously. Durieu's son has just signed his father's name to a check and been sent to Clichy, and Jean has freed him by paying his debt (not for love, be it understood, but because the son of an associate must not be in prison). A propos of this incident, Jean proposes that all young heirs form a joint-stock company with a capital of two millions or so in *lettres de change* which they would have cashed by usurers at the usual rates of 25 or 30 per cent; then he, Jean, being the banker of the association, would invest the money so as to bring in 60 per cent. It would be a sure speculation; shares could be created—secret ones, of course, "comme toutes les bonnes actions." That is an "idea," Jean concludes proudly.

Back in Jean's past is a company swindle which René airs in the light of day, accusing Jean of having discovered mines, emitted shares, and then of having bought back the shares at 75 per cent below the price of emission. Giraud sees no harm in the three million francs gained thus at the expense of the shareholders.

Mention of this mining company of Jean's brings us to the particular interest about which centered the swindling of the fifties and later years—the exploitation of natural resources, particularly mines. When Silberstein feels the ground slipping from under his feet, he clutches at the prospect of exploiting the Hungarian mines owned by Prince Verhazy. His methods are interesting. He first orders his newspaper reporter to write at great length and glowingly of Hungary, its natural resources, its industries, and so on. He then buttonholes the Prince and explains just how he can make the proposed company succeed:

We will begin by creating a number of shares, of which you as proprietor will have the greatest number. We will declare the very first day that the subscription is closed. The newspapers will boom the affair. The public will get excited; we will part with a few shares at a time until speculation takes hold; then buy back our shares and the premium will rise still higher. We will sell four or five times as many shares as we have issued and shall be able to control the market.

Silberstein is refused the concession.

Régulus Popincourt, of *Les deux Millionnaires,* a rare speculator who, like Augier's Maître Guérin, has a taste for Latin quotations, also forms a company to exploit mines. A meeting of shareholders is held, ostensibly to discuss the further purchase of land. Now Popincourt, who presides, has two hundred shares of stock, and the other stockholders have only two hundred shares among them; hence the meeting is an obvious farce, as the president can always cast the deciding vote. But Popincourt harangues the assembly with the utmost gravity, reminding the members that their company, which is developing the resources of magnificent Auvergne, is contributing to the prosperity of France. Indeed, the conception of this Company of the Mines of Champagnac is not only lucrative but "humanitarian, social, and national." The president then proceeds with the so-called deliberation concerning the acquisition of land. The shareholders, having no voice, obediently sign the document presented to them, and Popincourt carries on the farce to the end by thanking the gentlemen for their intelligent assistance. Unfortunately no more is said of the speculator and his company.

Among the projects of the ill-starred Barreau of *Les Parasites* is a company of submarine boats for the exploitation of naphtha lakes in Asia Minor—capital, 20 million francs; director, Barreau himself. Barreau speculates on his shares and is about to fail when Providence rescues him at the slight cost of a marriage with his mistress.

A formidable company appears in 1868 with Crisafulli's play, *Les Loups et les Agneaux.* The title tells the story.

The principal wolf is the speculator Callot, who, hoping to inveigle the honest banker Tourbonne into a disgraceful speculation, endeavors to get the banker under his control by seducing his wife. In this he fails, but he throws a cloud of suspicion over her character, so that the banker, in despair and disgust, seeing nothing left in life but the excitement of making a fortune, consents to help form the company. Callot is interested in the Grand-Pré mine, a not very successful enterprise. Copper has, however, been discovered there by one of his associates. Callot at once plans to discredit the old company, reduce the shares to nothing, and then secretly buy them up. When he and his companions shall have bought these apparently worthless shares for a song, they will announce the new discovery, form a new company, and become millionaires. Callot counts on Tourbonne's services as banker, but he does not count on his shrewdness. Tourbonne buys up stock till its price rises too high for Callot himself to buy it. The company is duly formed. The Marquis de Rizerolles and Valdepenas Santiago are put on the board of directors because of their sonorous names. The statutes are read, the question of dividends discussed. The Marquis settles that by saying *Nous promettrons*. Tourbonne then explains the ABC's of "promising": "Je promets, je formule des craintes, je ne tiens pas." As nobody is willing to risk funds in the affair, it is decided that shares will have to be issued; the *actionnaires* will be the scapegoats, as usual. The meeting is suddenly interrupted by Georges de Sterny, who had been invited to be a member of the board of directors. He bursts into the room, furious that his name should be connected with a speculation which he knows to be infamous: "Let these gentlemen continue to attack other people's money! They will succeed at it. The sheep of Panurge will always take the road to the wolf's lair." The tone of this last play marks quite clearly the later attitude toward the fraudulent company: it is no longer amusing to watch the wolves devour the sheep and the financial dramas of the Third Republic, most of which are concerned with a colossal company scandal, are extremely impressive in their grim reality.

"Conductor!" cries the unhappy passenger from his lofty perch, "I'm sick! Stop the train!"

CHAPTER VIII

SWINDLES IN DRAMA UNDER THE THIRD REPUBLIC

Ah! les grosses affaires ..., où l'on brasse les hommes à pleines foules ... et les millions à pleines mains ... les millions des autres ... hé? .. les travaux gigantesques ... les ponts ... les ports ... les mines ... les tramways ... j'aime ça. C'est ma vie.—OCTAVE MIRBEAU, *Les Affaires sont les Affaires,* Act I, scene 5.

MANY of the enterprises projected during the reign of Louis Philippe had, by the seventies, been realized. Ferdinand de Lesseps had successfully launched the Compagnie du Canal de Suez, his "fantastically extravagant" enterprise, in spite of the unfavorable reports of English engineers and the petty war of the French *agioteurs,* who, unable to forgive De Lesseps for constituting his company without their assistance, made every effort to discourage the shareholders. But the canal was finished in 1869, to the honor of De Lesseps and the profit of France. This was but the realization of a Saint-Simonian dream of Père Enfantin, who had, in 1846, formed a company to build the canal after the efforts to construct a dam had proved unfruitful. It is typical of the colossal conceptions of the Saint-Simonians that Père Enfantin had advocated the tossing of a pyramid into the Nile to effect the desired dam.

The history of the ill-fated Panama Canal project, undertaken with so much assurance by the courageous De Lessups, is especially valuable to us, as many of the causes of its failure are such as figure in the great swindles of drama which we are approaching. When De Lesseps decided to undertake the project, the enthusiastic French people oversubscribed the first call for funds. It appears that the ultimate catastrophe was due far less to the unfavorable attitude of the United States than to faulty administration of the company's finances. Money was spent lavishly in the erection of buildings in Panama, and enormous salaries were paid. Sanitation was neglected; and though hospitals were erected, the care of the sick was crude. Much useless machinery was bought, including the notorious snow shovels. Panama became a dumping ground for merchandise that could find no market elsewhere. When the crash came in 1888, the work, only two-fifths done, had already cost $400,000,000; whereas the completed canal had been promised for $120,000,000. It is estimated that one-third was spent on the canal; one-third was wasted; and the remaining third stolen, some of the money reaching the hands of senators and representatives bribed to assist the weakening enterprise. De Lesseps, ignorant of much that had been going on in his company, was prostrated and died in 1894.

These canals of Suez and Panama are but two among countless projects, some honest, many more dishonest, which absorbed the savings of the French people under the Republic. Much of the excitement over railroads had given place to the exploitation of mines, particularly in the colonies. During the reign of Napoleon III the mineral wealth of Africa had come to the attention of financiers who were soon bidding for concessions from the colonial governments to work mines and build railroads in that rich land. In these contracts politicians work hand in hand with the financiers "pour la chasse aux écus," aiding them to secure advantageous concessions and making valuable hauls. Big swindles are not infrequently concealed by a political screen. Politicians attack solid enterprises in the Chambre des Députés in order to send the price of stock down so that their financial friends can buy up shares at a low price, or they raise a great disturbance over some minor swindle to conceal from the public a serious financial crime.

France, like her sister countries, has seen numerous *sociétés, banques, crédits,* and *comptoirs* with the most engaging titles and the most brilliant prospectuses sink suddenly out of sight leaving a wreckage of shares behind them and now and then a prison sentence. When reproached with having deceived the public, Baron d'Erlanger, twenty times a millionaire, is said to have retorted: "Il n'avait qu'à faire attention." Perhaps the public is in reality as much to blame as the swindlers, since it refuses to learn wisdom from any of the rigorous lessons so generously given by these crooks. A gullible public provokes dishonesty. It is related that the financier M. de Morny, one day accosted by an engineer who wished his aid in collecting a capital of twenty-five million francs to work a mine situated in the Spanish province of Reinosa and who offered to show him at once all the plans and guarantees, replied, "I care nothing about all that. I wish to know but one thing. Does the province where your mine is really exist?"

Literary men did their share toward protecting the public from these swindlers, but doubtless Louis Reybaud's satire on the Imperial Bitumen Company of Morocco, in his *Jérome Paturot à la Recherche d'une Position sociale,* had as little effect as any of the actual frauds reported in the newspapers. The author, both economist and man of letters, has his hero, Jérome Paturot, persuaded by a luxury-loving and dissatisfied wife, go into business with the promoter Flouchippe. When Jérome penetrated into the office of Flouchippe, he found the room littered with prospectuses of the railroads of Brives-la-Gaillarde, coal of Perlimpinpin, a castle in Spain to be raffled off, paper of flour, iron of straw, rubber paving, and so on. This was evidently the office of an homme d'affaires. On the advice of Flouchippe, Jérome decides to launch the *Bitume impérial de Maroc,* railroads and coal being out of date and this the day of bitumen. Jérome's name is changed to Napoléon Paturot, and he is speedily installed in a handsome office with a cashier and clerks. A magnificent prospectus is published in the newspaper with the fabulous tale of the discovery of certain marvelous lakes of bitumen: how a European ship sprung a leak on the shore of Mogador where these lakes are situated, and was about to sink when an eruption of bitumen (a common occurrence it appears) caulked the ship's leak, so that she was able to sail straight out to sea again and even circumnavigate the globe. There then follows a list of the uses of this product which are indeed universal. Napoléon Paturot is praised for having risked his life to make this great discovery which he is offering to the world. The emperor of Morocco, Muley XXXIV, has granted him the exclusive privilege of exploitation. The *comité de surveillance* for the company has three representatives and ten peers, and among the guarantors are Messrs. Picksous of Berlin, Godichson of London, and Lazarilla of Madrid. The capital is six millions, the shares 1,000 francs each. One day, after the public has had time to sink its money in this brilliant venture, Napoléon discovers, upon going to his office, that M. Flouchippe has decamped with the cash. And so ends the Imperial Bitumen Company of Morocco.

Such are the schemes in this Paris of the Third Republic, which M. Claretie, writing in 1880, describes as a city *qui brasse des millions,* which is filled with the business palaces of financial companies, with stairs of stone and marble colonnades, as if they would prove to the subscriber the solidity of their enterprises. But for all the trustworthy appearance of the façade, the frauds behind it are more frequent and much more stupendous than before. M. Claretie echoes earnestly what so many characters of drama had been saying for years: Money! "Voilà ce qui a pris le pas en ce monde ... C'est la Force succédant à l'Idée."

Henry Becque is among the first playwrights to make a financial swindle the principal subject of a drama. He began working on *Les Polichinelles*, probably about 1884, and set it aside definitely in 1893 still unfinished. Becque gives as his reason for leaving this play incomplete that in it he had proved all too good a prophet; that all of Panama was in his play; and that he did not wish to have the play acted, as he would be accused of depicting the scandals of the day; and, having faith in the Republic, he did not wish to give its enemies so much satisfaction. The play was, nevertheless, completed by Henri de Noussane and published in 1910. The spirit of the continuator is wholly different from that of the author, and the finished play can hardly be at all what the author intended. Becque himself published extracts from his play in 1893 and 1894. The play, as he left it, appears in his *Oeuvres Complètes* (Paris, 1924), Vol. IV, which is the edition here used.

The financial enterprise exposed in *Les Polichinelles* is the founding of the Banque Napolitaine, the concession for which the protagonist Tavernier obtains from the Italian government. We are shown the building up of this swindle the inevitable ruin of which we must imagine for ourselves. Tavernier calls together in the new and luxurious palace of the bank the board of directors for the company now legally constituted. The emission of shares and publicity are to be discussed. A member of the board stipulates at once that the secretary of the meeting is to record as little as possible and to avoid mentioning names. The concession from the Italian government is then rapidly read. Permission is given the banker Tavernier to found the Banque Napolitaine, to establish branches, and to engage in any industrial enterprise except the manufacture of weapons which might be used against the Italian government—an injunction which amuses the board. But less amusing is the final article which stipulates that the Italian government shall in no wise be held responsible for any dishonesty on the part of the bank and that, in case of failure, no shareholders may have recourse to it. This clause the board unanimously votes to suppress in the summary of the concession to be published. Business has progressed thus far when the meeting is interrupted by the arrival of Tavernier's mistress, Marie, and some of her companions, who effectively put an end to that day's affairs.

Tavernier, after dismissing the others, has a consultation with the promoter Legras who has been recommended to him by the disreputable financier Cerfbier. Legras takes himself and his work very seriously. He engages to sell any kind of stock whatsoever, be it Honduras, Mississippi, or the moon. The worse the affair is the more he devotes himself to it. His accounts are impeccable: so many shares sold, so much salary. But he must have good pay; he will not stoop to any bargaining. As a matter of fact, after a demand of 40 francs a share for himself, he agrees to accept 25. When Tavernier begins to tell him about the Banque Napolitaine which he is to promote, Legras with a professional air, questions the banker, commenting on each answer. The title? Yes, it is as good as any other: during the past twenty years every country, city and town has given its name to some enterprise which has disappeared leaving its administrators rich and its shareholders ruined. The first call for funds will be for 10 million francs. Out of this sum Legras will not promise to raise more than 3 million because the big capitalists will sink their money only in projects (whether honest or fraudulent) in which they have some guarantee, and the small investors have been so thoroughly bled that they will not have much money to give. Moreover, objects Legras, Tavernier is making the mistake of having an ordinary board of directors: no senator (to make the affair look important); no representative (the government is devoted to its representatives!); not even a general! (the childish public feels more confidence if there is a soldier on the board). But Legras finally consents to promote the enterprise as the bank claims to have influential support in Italy and as the Comptoir Européen has ordered two thousand shares (thanks to Cerfbier, one of its directors, who receives an excellent commission from Tavernier).

Out of the 700,000 francs' worth of subscriptions secured in Italy, Tavernier gives 10,000 francs to his mistress and intrusts her with 100,000 more to be kept for him in case of disaster. The third act takes place in Marie's new residence, a gift from Tavernier paid for by the Banque Napolitaine. Elise, Marie's mother, remarks that it is a pity that the *gogos* cannot see what is done with their money! Tavernier also publishes an advertising sheet, *Le Tuteur*. What with all these expenses and Dubler who absconds to Belgium with the funds of the Banque Napolitaine, Tavernier thinks it wise to join the Crédit National and launch a fresh operation. Plans are already made for this merger when the police raid the Crédit National. One of its directors, M. Lafosse, also director of the Banque

Napolitaine, packs his trunks and hurries to Spain to await the outcome, "preferring the climate there." It is also hopeless to count on merging with the Comptoir, as it has been taken over by established financiers who will run no unnecessary risks. Tavernier grows nervous and regrets the unimposing board of directors which he had selected in order that it might be subordinate to himself.

The dénouement of the Banque Napolitaine can be only conjectural. It is opined from notes left by the author that the play was to end with a catastrophe in the form of a *faillite* or liquidation, in a scene between the two financiers Tavernier and Cerfbier in which they would expose one another's conduct, or in a *grande scène* at the meeting of the board called by Tavernier. There might even be an invasion of the creditors whom we meet in various scenes apparently leading up to a finale. Incomplete as it is, the play is vastly preferable to Henri de Noussane's version, into which are introduced a complicated plot, a coup de bourse whereby Tavernier makes 3 million francs, and the incredible reformation of the financier who gives up his mistress, takes back his wife, and pays his debts.

The milieu into which Becque leads his audience is as disreputable as any in financial drama. A little argot, a few deft gestures of impudence, a brazen insolence, and the marionettes of this *bas-monde* dance before us worked by the strings of their only desires, money and pleasure. Cheating and deceit are the natural resources of this company. The presence of the sheriff in the first three acts is a constant reminder that these business affairs are of a type to land their directors in the police court. The men themselves—all too often in money-plays mere replicas of each other—these polichinelles of Becque's, have character, from the insolent secretary Dubler, who edits the company paper, criticizes the creditors, patronizes the sheriff, and absconds with the cash, to the president, Tavernier, who has ideas "très avancées en matière de crédit." There is Cerfbier the millionaire, accustomed from birth to being arrested, who always resells for 200 what he has bought for 100 francs, who is involved in every *sale affaire* at the bourse and yet resents Dubler's absconding, for, "What protection will business men have if their subordinates are dishonest?" Mont-les-Aigles is a man of pleasure inextricably bound up with Cerfbier, Tavernier, and the rest, with a history of political jobs won by pull and lost by an inability to respect the government's funds, endless expenditures, costly mistresses, and ultimate dependence on crooks. Lombard, the sheriff, characterizes the group as "decadents of the worst sort."

The *gogos* are little better than the rogues. Lombard's first call at Tavernier's business office is on behalf of Cretet who had borrowed 2,500 francs on securities. When he had paid back the loan and claimed his bonds, Tavernier refused to restore them, alleging, when forced to explain his conduct, that as Cretet had gone into bankruptcy it would be better to keep the bonds. Cretet, who brings suit against Tavernier, says later to the latter's office boy that he would not have objected if Tavernier had said in the beginning that he was hard up and had sold the securities, but he did mind that he should reproach him with his bankruptcy, the finest thing he had ever done, undertaken "pour obliger une pauvre petite malheureuse." Cretet is a socialist with ideas on free love which keep him from marrying his devoted mistress, Virginie Lacerteux (sister of Germinie!). The last scene of the play, as it stands, shows this mistress of Cretet's claiming of Tavernier the securities for which Cretet is suing him and which he had stolen from Virginie.

Becque has done an unusual thing in drawing his *cerf-louviers* not only in their business but in their pleasures. In contrast to the Tavernier who, after intending to cheat the small fry, refunds their money in order to be free to swindle the public on a big scale, is the Tavernier in the arms of his mistress. There is no sentimentality about Marie. Her inclination is always toward the lover with the biggest profits to share. As mistress of Cerfbier she obtained an *hôtel* which she sold, feeling squeamish about inhabiting it with Tavernier. Mont-les-Aigles deserted her because of her business dealings with a lawyer, a broker, and a sheriff, hardly becoming in the mistress of an aristocrat. Marie and her satellites take possession of Tavernier's office at will, while Mme Tavernier is reprimanded by her husband for disturbing the sanctum. Again the worlds of business and pleasure meet at Marie's house-warming in the new residence given her by Tavernier. Into this group of *cocottes* and speculators, which is so admirably painted, glides the ubiquitous Lombard with an order of arrest. Thus the party and the play come to an abrupt end. Incomplete as it is, *Les Polichinelles* has left almost as large a posterity in drama as either *Les Corbeaux* or *La Parisienne;* and practically all the plays which follow bear traces of its influence.

At the time when Becque relinquished work on *Les Polichinelles,* Léon Hennique, a playwright of the Théâtre-Libre and a favorite with the public in the eighties and the nineties, staged his *L'Argent d'autrui,* written much in the manner of Zola's *L'Argent* and having for milieu a financial world like that of Becque's play. The plot turns about a swindle known as the Banque Catholique, launched by the speculator Lafontas, a great admirer of Law. This new bank is to be a business center in opposition to the Jewish financial group. Lafontas has the "superb idea" of confronting a few very rich interests with many smaller ones. There will be risks, of course, but the proverb says: "Semez de la graine de niais, il poussera des actionnaires." And even if the venture fail, it may enrich the directors. This Banque Catholique is to involve not only the Catholic capital of the world but also the funds of the Protestants who will flock to the bank through hatred of the Jews. What tremendous possibilities! This Banque Catholique will become a crusade against the infidel, and in ten months the shares will be sky high. The new young bank will represent David slaying the Goliath of Judaism.

With the 30,000 francs lent him by his mistress, Catherine, Lafontas wins the confidence of the Davannes brothers who, though Protestants, consent to become his associates, as "business is business." The American grisette Kate is employed to decoy the banker Tamisey into the enterprise, which is soon under full sail. An architect draws plans of a magnificent Greek temple to house the bank—"a temple of Fortune with allegorical statues." The third act takes place in this luxurious palace hung with pious pictures. Here Guillaume Davannes figures out the gains made in a rise of 70 francs a share in the Banque Catholique stock, and Lafontas gloats over the slow-moving *bons bourgeois* who would find it difficult to believe that these financiers, the pivots of the Banque Catholique with a capital of 50 million francs, were a twelvemonth before but petty stock brokers. Lafontas draws a salary of 30,000 francs as director; Guillaume, in charge of stock exchange orders, receives 15,000; Edouard, clerk of deposits, 12,-000; and Pierre, postal clerk, 2,400. The rise is soon explained. Lafontas has hired a straw man to buy stock for the company so that the stockholders' own money is paying the company's dividends. Notwithstanding this fact, Lafontas says loudly, as the office boy throws open the door to the customers, "This bank has no secrets." Among the clients who arrive, is an old lady with an offering of holy water from the Jordan for Lafontas and a picture of the Pope. Lafontas thanks her ceremoniously, rejoices that the Pope is encouraging an enterprise, the sole aim of which is the ultimate triumph of religion.

This good fortune alters when a mysterious Catholic, L'Inconnu, representing the Jewish bank, supplied by Kate with the information that Lafontas has sunk the money of one mistress in his enterprise and is passing another off as his wife, uses this scandal and a promise of a large sum and a position in the rival bank to persuade Lafontas to betray the Banque Catholique. The speculator regrets after the departure of the stranger that he had not tried to interest the Jews in his Catholic enterprise, which is not such a bad affair and with which they could accomplish marvels.

The fourth act is staged at the bourse where crowds are buying and selling. Stock in the Banque Catholique has begun to drop. An individual, ruined by the fall, declares that only suicide is left to him. Lafontas, with the customary astuteness of the speculator, has sold his own stock; and when the *krach* comes, he is safe, while the Davannes brothers are ruined. One of them strikes him; a duel ensues, in which Lafontas is wounded. Fearing his wound fatal, the terrified swindler proposes to make restitution. Kate, whom he has promised to marry, is much alarmed at her lover's sudden honesty but is reassured by L'Inconnu. Lafontas will be given the position offered him by the rival bank, and Paris will soon forget his "petite, grande, et comment dirai-je? audacieuse? non, coutumière aventure." And then, addressing the audience, L'Inconnu bids the spectators remember that they have been warned once again.

The authors of *Le Cuivre*, Paul Adam and André Picard, develop their problem play about a question of war and finance. During a conflict between the South American republics, Quesitado and Equatoria, the Banque Cosmopolite of France, represented at Quesitado by the banker Vogt, had bought three monitors, intending to resell them at once to Quesitado whose fleet had been destroyed. European powers intervene before Quesitado has completely crushed her rival, and bring about an armistice. Quesitado no longer needs the monitors but promises to buy them in case hostilities are renewed. In the meantime the stock of the Banque Cosmopolite is falling and the upkeep of the vessels is proving costly. Seven months pass, and the monitors remain unsold. War must be stirred up again in order to insure their purchase and to save the bank.

It is with this purpose in mind that Vogt invites the diplomatic corps of Quesitado just arrived in France on its vacation, to dine with him at Bordeaux. It is here in his handsomely furnished office hung with marine charts, pictures of vessels and such paraphernalia as would be appropriate to an outfitter of ships, that Vogt sets going his plot to reopen the war. The guests include the chargés d'affaires of France and Russia; their families; and the millionnaire speculator and idealist Humphry, an Englishman, director of a copper company commissioned to supply the armies and navies of various countries with copper goods. This company has a contract with Equatoria for copper, and on the sale of this copper Equatoria is depending for the money with which to pay her indemnity to Quesitado. Vogt's plan is to force Humphry to cancel the contract so that Equatoria will be unable to pay and so that war will be renewed.

Vogt has summoned to his assistance the speculator Martin, a man of the same stamp as himself, with whom he, Vogt, is furious because none of the schemes in which Martin has interested him seem to promise any profit. It is true that in launching the Palmyra Railroad Vogt had made the rich haul of five million francs, but the railroad is not yielding dividends at present; the stock of the Banque Cosmopolite has fallen because of the purchase of the three vessels recommended by Martin. This would prove a good investment could the ships be resold, as they had cost but little, having been refused by the French government for their lack of speed, though the official reason given out, thanks to Martin's diplomacy, had been unsanitary ventilation, a minor matter which would not deter the president of Quesitado from making the purchase. Vogt had made sure that Quesitado would need the monitors by selling torpedo boats to the enemy with which to destroy the Quesitado fleet. That country, being poor, would have to buy the ships on credit and would need about twenty years to pay the debt, which, at compound interest, would be quite worth while to the Banque Cosmopolite, especially as that company owned all the telegraph lines and railroads in Quesitado. No one could have foreseen, complained Martin, the untimely end of the war. How could Quesitado have won that land victory, which caused the intervention of foreign powers, when her soldiers, equipped and fed by Vogt, had useless guns, bad shoes, and poisonous food which killed more men than the enemy itself.

The immediate problem is now to force Humphry to cancel his contract with Equatoria. Martin sends a French socialist to stir up trouble among the workmen in Humphry's factories. It would be ruinous to continue to buy copper with the men on a strike and supply orders canceled. In addition to this move Vogt telephones the Banque Cosmopolite at Paris to buy up copper stock in order to control the market and force the price down at the critical moment. The strike is declared, and Humphry faces ruin; but he persists in refusing to cancel the contract with Equatoria, knowing that the result will be war. Humphry is, however, in love with the beautiful and intelligent Anne Vogt, her brother's accomplice, who is using her influence to break down the Englishman's resistance. Humphry becomes engaged in a duel with Daniloff, the Russian chargé d'affaires, a renowned swordsman, because of an insult to a woman. Anne, now interested in Humphry, orders Vogt, who is eager to have Humphry killed, to stop the duel, threatening to disclose to the editor of the *Révélateur*, her brother's arch-enemy, proofs of the scandal regarding the Palmyra Railroad. Vogt laughs at the threat, saying that, as the whole Legion of Honor is involved in the scandal, the matter would be dropped at once. He does, however, promise to save Humphry if Anne can obtain from him the cancellation of the contract. Anne is successful, and the last scene shows Humphry looking out at the bay of Quesitado into which war ships are steaming, watching bitterly the destruction of his ideal of peace. Since the declaration of war, stock in the Banque Cosmopolite has gone up 10 points, to the joy of the victorious Vogt.

Far less important as drama, but valuable as a money-play, is Bernstein's *Samson,* in which a powerful financier carries out a great coup de bourse. The wealthy speculator Brachart discovers the love affair between his wife, who had been forced to marry him for his money, and the rake Le Gouvain, to whom he had been giving lessons in speculating. Brachard refuses the duel offered him as a satisfaction to his honor. Does his rival take him for a fool that he thinks he is going to risk a wound in addition to all that he has already suffered! He secretly plans a far more spectacular revenge—a ruinous fall of Egyptian copper stock in which his wife's lover has invested heavily: "La baisse sera rapide, brutale, foudroyante. Les cuivres égyptiens tomberont aujourd'hui même de deux cent cinquante francs." To carry out the coup without his rival's knowledge, he invites Le Gouvain to a hotel, wines him, and dines him until he is lost to the world. Then Samson, while his enemy sleeps, pulls down the pillars of the bourse in a tremendous crash of stock which ruins himself along with his rival and many other speculators. By this heroic act he wins the esteem of his wife! His broker had begged him to desist, as this speculation falling on the eve of liquidation would render it impossible for speculators to meet their obligations. To this, Brachart scornfully replies that he is not the guardian angel of these gentlemen and that speculating is a risk at best.

In spite of all the insistence on realistic detail, there is much truth in Jean Richepin's observation that this Samson is at heart but a romantic hero of Hugo, or Balzac, or Sue—a superman, a "bloc de boue avec une petite fleur bleue poussée dedans." It is the romanticism of the play which has won the public.

The form of speculation in which Guillaume Bourgade of Bernstein's *Après Moi* becomes desperately involved is the forming of an oil trust to include the producers and refiners of oil in France and Central Europe. In preparation for the realization of his project he begins buying up oil stock with his own money, expecting in a short time to see the trust formed. For five years the project has been under consideration. His own personal fortune exhaused, Bourgade invests the funds of the Aloy-Bourgade Refining Company in oil stock, presenting each year a fictitious balance sheet to the board of directors. This financier, who had always considered his honesty impeccable, finds himself a swindler. But, as he explains to Mme Aloy, the chief loser, when a financier begins cornering stock he must continue to buy until his operation is completed or fail utterly. The crash comes when three vessels bearing 10,000 tons of oil arrive in Marseilles. In order to keep the oil off the market, Bourgade contracts to buy it; but rumors are already circulating against his financial status, and he is unable to raise the necessary money. An investigation follows, and ruin and punishment are ineluctable. Bourgade is told officiously that he will not be prosecuted if the Aloy family makes no complaint and if he will exile himself from France.

It must be confessed that Bourgade is an exceptionally uninteresting financier, for in this play Bernstein has failed to convey the excitement of high finance: the ruses, the resources of the usual speculator.

The most powerful modern writer of financial plays is Emile Fabre, who studies with unflagging interest and depicts with remarkable skill the preponderant rôle of money in the Republic. His *Les Ventres dorés* (the title is a name used to designate the Turcarets and the Laws of business) is one of the few plays which deal with money to the almost entire exclusion of love. The play represents a war between two barons of finance, De Thau and D'Urth, in which is wrecked the Nouvelle Afrique, an enterprise for the development of the African territory Mauritania. In the tragedy of this company, the true protagonist of the play, the audience is made acquainted with a modern industrial undertaking which involves huge sums and which, through the machinations of speculators, is strangled at the bourse.

The implacable enemy of the Nouvelle Afrique is De Thau's former partner, Baron d'Urth, whose wife De Thau had seduced. D'Urth, in his plans for revenge, finds capable and willing assistance in Princess d'Holsbeck, his sister, a widow whose advances Baron de Thau had rejected, unwilling to engage in a love affair and ignorant of the extent of this business woman's power.

Although inaugurated with all the canonading of twentieth-century publicity, the Nouvelle Afrique appeared to be a dignified enterprise; and Vernières, its *administrateur délégué*, a man of spotless character who had proved too honest for politics, praised it in all good faith as an undertaking which would extend French influence and open a great country to civilization. The contract with Mauritania was leak proof: in exchange for the construction of ports and 1,200 kilometers of railroad, the company was to receive from the emperor two-thirds of the profits and permission to exploit any possible mines that might be found along the route. The rumor of gold mines had already increased the value of the stock. Newspapers had been paid extremely well for publicity, and a member of the Institute had been commissioned to produce scientific articles about the riches of the country. To all this advertising, the public had responded with an enthusiasm comparable to that shown for the Panama Canal project. The company's third call, for 80 million francs, had been oversubscribed to the extent of 40 million. Klobb, a German Jew and a director of the Nouvelle Afrique, a man experienced in founding companies and acquainted with the responsiveness of all the European peoples, considers the French the most gen-

erous. After losing more than 2 billion francs in twenty
years they had found 250 million to intrust to the directors
of the Nouvelle Afrique. Most of these investors are shopkeepers, tradesmen, *rentiers*--people from the most prudent class.

The action of the play begins with the break in stock
caused by the bear campaign which the hostile D'Urth
wages in his paper, *La Quotidienne*. Baron de Thau calls
an informal meeting of the board of directors to plan a defense for the stock which is fast becoming speculative. The
meeting takes place in the council room of the expensive
building erected to house the Nouvelle Afrique. The walls
are hung with maps of Mauritania and a picture of the Emperor; the company's safe stands in one corner. The old
clerk, Chavard, before the arrival of the members, begins
croaking about all the companies he has seen go down,
companies whose shares he never bought, thank Heaven!
Of course stock will go up again surely, but so did shares in
the Banque Universelle, just a week before the crash.

The council convenes with De Thau presiding. Present
are the nervous Klobb; the crafty Carrier, who has just
courted public favor by founding a hospital for scrofulous
children; the anxious and foreboding Vernières; and Chauvelot, the speculator par excellence. Chauvelot is described
as seventy years of age, smooth shaven, white-haired, and
with the small head of a bird of prey. He has picked the
bones of many a dead company. He knows the story of the
Culebra Canal whose office building was worth 2 million
francs, and which had expended a fortune before a single
workman had lifted a pick. Call it a national disaster, if
you like, says he, but the directors managed everything so
perfectly that no inquiries were made. Chauvelot once had
to fly from the principality of the Danube, disguised as a

Turkish merchant, because the revolutionists whom he had set against King Kostova and to whom he had sold sand cartridges, wished to impale him. When, in a heated discussion some days later, Carrier reproaches Chauvelot with having an evil eye and bringing bad luck to every company he enters, Chauvelot slings several handfuls of mud at the rest of the group. The Northern Coal Company had failed with Carrier as its president; the boosting of his Banque des Deux Mondes had cost the shareholders 35 million francs; and he had pocketed 6 million in the Harrar loan. Brianne and Klobb had had straw men representing them on the financial syndicates paid to support the Nouvelle Afrique, and they had demanded scandalous advantages. And if he, Chauvelot, a director of the Western Steel Company, had made the Nouvelle Afrique pay high for rails, at least they had the rails, which was better than wasting money on Veurettes for writing scientific lies, or squandering 200,000 francs on advertising in Carrier's paper, *L'Impartial*, which nobody reads.

But to return to our meeting. In spite of continual interruptions Vernières reviews the sins of the Nouvelle Afrique: a building much too expensive (necessary to inspire confidence, objects Klobb); millions paid for the support of newspapers, financiers, and banks (these things must be done, "ce sont les moeurs du temps," answers the Baron); and the expensive trip given Veurettes and other members of the Institute to Mauritania (a scientific mission needed to impress the public, interrupts Klobb). When Vernières would curtail expenses, the objection is general. There must be more, not less, publicity, in spite of the high price newspapers will demand for advertising a now doubtful enterprise. Vernières offers his resignation, which is refused because the people, confident of his rectitude, would be thrown into a panic. In the midst of the discussion a message is received by telephone from the bourse. Stock is crashing down. News has come of a raid by Négou-Abdou on the railroad under construction in Mauritania. The situation is desperate. The fall in stock must be counteracted. To Vernières' horror the consensus of opinion is that the company must speculate with the money of its shareholders and push up the price by "wash sales" to give the impression of heavy buying. Shareholders must be kept from unloading their holdings or by the next day the Nouvelle Afrique will be ruined in a bourse panic.

Chauvelot now comes forward with a plan to save the company. That plan is war. If France can be persuaded to send her soldiers to Mauritania to defend the rights of her citizens there, the success of the company is assured. France must be stirred up by talk of humanity, civilization, progress—the great task that awaits France in Africa. A generous people like the French always fall for this kind of "bunk." The adherence of the government can be assured by the press, which controls the government and lives off of just such enterprises as the Nouvelle Afrique. Besides, elections are near and three hundred thousand Frenchmen own stock in the enterprise.

Vernières is astounded at the idea of creating war to support a financial undertaking. Is it possible that a company could plunge nations into war? Why this is mere fancy, a novel! It is history, replies the Baron, the history of modern expeditions: today we fight over questions of money. And Chauvelot checks an admission that at least ten times he has been employed himself to stir up similar quarrels. The Chambre des Députés convenes in a week. A week! "Time enough," says Chauvelot. "In a week, twenty years ago, I was able to hurl the Balkan Confederation on the principality of the Danube." The forty members of the group of commercial interests in the House must be won over, by bribes if necessary. Vernières continues to protest that the shareholders had not paid in their money to meet such expenditures and that they, the directors, as honest men, must not have recourse to such means. We are financiers, objects Chauvelot, and we are acting as financiers within the limits of financial morality, every other financier would do the same in our position. Just then a telegram is brought, announcing that De Thau's son, who is with the French army in Algeria, has been wounded by the tribesmen of Mauritania under the leadership of Négou-Abdou. Here, at last, is a justifiable pretext for war—Mauritania fighting on French soil. Quick! Telegrams, articles, a visit to the Ministry of War! The Nouvelle Afrique will be saved!

A few days later in the office of the president, members of the council come and go anxiously awaiting the events of that day's bourse. It is clear enough by this time that Baron d'Urth is trying to destroy the Nouvelle Afrique before the imminent meeting of the Chambre, when war might be declared and the company saved. From the windows can be seen the crowds of frightened shareholders watching the building. If the market could be supported on the Brussels Bourse, there would surely be an improvement on the Paris Exchange. Chauvelot again draws from a well-stored past a description of the killing of the Crédit Général when a bear campaign on the exchanges of Lyons and Brussels sent stock hurtling down at Paris. De Thau, in spite of Vernières' scruples, orders the purchase of stock at Brussels.

In this expedient 8 million francs are wasted. There is madness, panic, at the Paris Bourse. The directors of the company try to stem the tide of selling by purchasing stock there, but in vain. False rumors drive the people into greater terror. The engineer and workmen in Mauritania are reported massacred, and an "extra" announces the death of De Thau. The shareholders push from the outer office into that of the president, demanding to see the board members, to know if De Thau is really dead. Chauvelot faces the situation coolly. Had he not held two hundred such persons at bay when the Grand Comptoir failed?

In they crowd with white faces, asking stupid questions, furious, dejected, tragic. The air is filled with bitter recriminations, useless demands, threats of vengeance, pleas for reassurance. A peasant has read in the paper that gold grows in this country of Mauritania as thick as beets in the fields, and whatever the paper says must be true! One shareholder accuses Vernières of ignorance in business because the company had not been speculating on its own shares! A credulous man laments that he had not known a few days earlier what was going to happen so that he could have unloaded on some *gogo*. He is, indeed, himself the M. Gogo of the play, having invested in the fatal Culebra, in the Crédit Général, and even in the galleys of Xerxes—a project to raise those sunken ships reputed to be full of gold and treasure, a project of Baron d'Urth. When, a few moments later, De Thau drives back from the bourse with the good news that stock has gone up (the supporting of the Nouvelle Afrique had proved temporarily successful), our Gogo rushes off to buy more shares, followed by the now rejoicing crowd of men and women.

Again the president's office. A few terrible days have elapsed, in which the Nouvelle Afrique has been forced into bankruptcy; shareholders have committed suicide; the office staff is demoralized. Vernières, determined to force the directors to reimburse the shareholders, refuses, unless they promise a reimbursement, to allow the destruction of the incriminating papers in the safe. He has a stroke, however, and falls dead, leaving the others just time enough to burn the papers before the arrival of the police.

Six months later Baron de Thau, who has been traveling in foreign countries in search of a purchaser for the Nouvelle Afrique, pays a fleeting visit to Paris. Knowing that without the Baron's assistance, nothing could be saved from the wreck, the receiver into whose hands the company had been put made no effort to bring the directors to trial, in order to leave De Thau free to save something if possible for the investors. In the meantime a report has been prepared by an expert, in which the company is accused of having wasted much of its capital, of having intentionally overestimated the possibilities of the project, and of having speculated with its own money. The first two accusations cannot be proved, as the company's books were destroyed and all the blame of the third can be laid on the dead Vernières, whose wife is easily persuaded to give up the only piece of evidence against the company, a letter written by her husband shortly before his death, and to leave his name dishonored. An Anglo-Belgian company has promised to buy the Nouvelle Afrique on condition that the emperor of Mauritania will grant the same excellent terms to them that had been enjoyed by the previous owners. Only the Baron can negotiate this, and the syndic will not bring him to trial until he has had an opportunity to secure the purchase.

While in Paris, De Thau receives a visit from Princess d'Holsbeck, who proposes that he marry her in exchange for a code telegram from Africa which would convict her brother of having instigated the attacks of Négou-Abdou.

Armed with this weapon, De Thau easily defends himself
against a threat of blackmail for three million francs which
D'Urth claims that De Thau owes him. D'Urth had hoped
to drive De Thau quite out of the financial field in order to
reign there himself, but De Thau laughs at him for thinking that a single financier can any longer be master of
Paris. An isolated man is helpless; only trusts are strong.
D'Urth is persuaded to become De Thau's partner again.
Les Ventres dorés ends with the beginning of a new enterprise, concerning the Isthmus of Malacca. "Voici, mon
cher. Il s'agit de trouver cinq cent millions ... ," says Baron
de Thau to Baron d'Urth.

In *Les Vainqueurs*, which came three years later, Fabre
has developed a modern condition already indicated in *Les
Ventres dorés*, the close relation existing between monetary
and political interests. The author has conceived an ingenious financial trap into which falls an ambitious politician.
A speculator, Redan, obtains from the Greek government a
concession to work a copper mine at Corfu. The enterprise
is in fact a good one, but Redan had failed in a previous
speculation on phosphates in Tunis, and a pack of creditors
is after him. He had expected to hold them off for several
years until the copper mine should be a paying proposition,
but they refuse to wait and threaten to seize the mine. He
then brings suit against an imaginary creditor, Count Fir-
miani, in reality a fruit vendor of Sicily, for an equally
imaginary debt of three millions. He intends to amuse his
creditors with this fake lawsuit for several years until he
shall have made his fortune on the mine. But as luck would
have it, when Redan appealed his case, the creditors investi-
gated the identity of the Count and discovered the hoax.
The only possible escape for Redan and for his lawyer, the
would-be minister, M. Daygrand, who is of course drawn

into the scandal, appears to be to raise the three million francs and prove by the payment that the lawsuit has been a bona fide one. The scheme works, the financier pays his creditors, and the lawyer receives his coveted portfolio, but only at the cost of family dishonor and the loss of his son.

Fabre's *Les Sauterelles* portrays the exploitation of an imaginary French protectorate in China, the Nouvelle France. Although not a *pièce à clef*, *Les Sauterelles* indicates a thorough study of colonial press reports of mismanagement and graft by French officials and a determination to arouse in the French mind a realization of the great value to France of these colonies rightly governed. In a speech by Carvin, the admirable governor-general of this Nouvelle France, Fabre reproaches France with her indifference to the great deeds accomplished by her explorers, engineers, soldiers, and colonists, an indifference due to profound ignorance of the gigantic struggle engaged in to redeem these vast territories of swamps and mountains and hostile tribes to productiveness and civilization; due also to the failure of the French people to comprehend the commercial value of these lands upon which France must depend if she is to hold her own with the rest of the world and not sink to a subordinate position. Carvin, the ideal governor, generous toward the natives and honest toward his own country, is sent to another post, through influence in ministerial circles, because he refuses to give his consent to the floating of a loan which would entail the further taxation of the already overburdened Tmère people. Carvin withdrawn, the unscrupulous officials—"grasshoppers," as the natives call them—lose no time in obtaining the loan, the squandering of which is the subject of the play.

It is Souriciau, banker and representative of the Banque des Colonies, founded by a group of financiers and having on its board of directors two representatives, a senator, three ex-ministers and the honorable M. Dupont-Dutertre, who negotiates the loan. The bank promises a loan of 225 million francs provided that peace in the colony can be guaranteed and that the troups of the bandit Moung Bâ are dispersed. The bank wishes also to know how the funds will be expended. Souriciau ventures to recommend to the colonists the building of a railroad which would be undertaken by the Société de Puteaux, at the head of which is the honorable Dupont-Dutertre. The discussion of the spending of the funds before they are obtained seems premature; and Souriciau's suggestion is set aside for a consideration of means to pay back the loan, perhaps through a company to which would be sold a monopoly on the sale of salt and opium. Souriciau sees no objection to reserving a certain number of shares for the colony officials themselves, for doubtless these gentlemen would in no way allow a personal interest in the enterprise to affect their attitude toward it and they should have an opportunity to add to their salaries which, for men thus expatriating themselves, are small indeed.

The scene in which is discussed the spending of the loan lays bare the selfishness and shortsightedness of these officials, one of whom, although wholly unqualified in knowledge or character for such a post, had received, by the "pull" of his wife's protector, M. Dupont-Dutertre, the responsible post of *résident supérieur* of Shong Hoï. Of the 225 million, part must be spent to float the loan, 40 million to meet unpaid debts, and 100 million for the construction of the railroad to be built by the Puteaux Company: so that there remain actually only 65 million for improvements in Nouvelle France. Evidently, essential constructions alone must be undertaken, such as a theater (in which the natives could have the opportunity of hearing French masterpieces), a residence befitting the governor-general (the French representative should be housed more grandly than the native emperor in order to impress the people), suitable houses for the rest of the protectorate officials, roads 16 meters wide, and a cable from Marseilles to Shong Hoï (to be constructed by the Puteaux Company). The question finally arises as to the benefit to be derived by the natives from the loan for which they must pay, and the ready suggestion is a new prison, more comfortable than the old one, and a house of correction for wayward native girls. Obviously, for the present it will be impossible to spend anything on the irrigation ditches, the hospitals, and schools so much needed.

The money to meet the payments on the loan is to be raised by renting a monopoly on opium and alcohol to a company at 10 million francs a year. But considerable expense is involved in preparing for this company, which must be protected against smugglers. For this purpose boats must be purchased and quais built. Soon fifteen more million have melted away.

Among the French officials is one skeptic who takes no interest in the loan, Laforêt, once a lieutenant-governor in Africa. At that time he too had negotiated a loan for which he had estimated his expenses with economy. But, when, for the construction of his railroad, he had tried to purchase materials from small industrial companies content with reasonable profits, he had been obliged to buy of the big ones at a ruinous cost as they had crowded the small companies out of business. Every attempt he had made to develop native industries was fought by French manufacturers, and Laforêt was eventually exiled to his present obscure post where, he thanks God, there is neither commerce nor industry.

The final steps in the plot develop out of the loan to the protectorate. It will be remembered that the Banque des Colonies had demanded assurances of peace as a condition of the loan. During the administration of Carvin, the bandit Moung Bâ had become a peaceful farmer settled on the estate given him by the government. Carvin's successor, in order to make the loan doubly sure, sent troops to kill or expel Moung Bâ and his followers, and, as a proof of tranquillity, ordered the return to France of half the garrison of the colony. Moung Bâ is neither killed nor captured but some six months later stirs up a rebellion which bodes no good for the poorly protected colonists. The Tmère officials are incensed at the wasting of the loan for which the money had been collected with cruelty: the projected railroad had had to be abandoned because the route had been badly planned, the quais which were to cost 5 million francs have cost 9 million and are already sunk in the mud; the governor-general's palace, the only building completed, has cost double the sum it should have cost. What good have the French done in the country? True, they have quieted neighboring pirates but where is the gain, since taxes are as high as the former tributes?

Feeling uncertain of the loyalty of the old emperor, the acting governor-general deposes him and puts in his place the ten-year-old prince who has been educated by the French. This is the last straw; and the native officials and common people revolt, killing the young emperor set up by the French, besieging the troops in the fortress, and nearly exterminating the French colonists. Thanks to the efforts of M. and Mme Bérigny, the only members of this group who know the language of the natives with whom they are

living, the Tmère troops are kept under command and the
revolt quelled. The telegram which forms the final curtain
of the play is a marvel of diplomacy. The revolt is stated
to have been directed against the emperor and mandarins
by the people who are asking for greater liberty. It is proposed to the minister that the protectorate of Nouvelle
France be annexed to France as a colony.

In *Un Grand Bourgeois* Fabre devotes his attention
less to the big business deal concerned than to the study of
the powerful bourgeois, Maxime Matignon, whose father,
by exploitation of Algerian mines, had laid the foundations
of the fortune which Maxime's son Xavier will one day
squander. Old Matignon, Maxime's father, originally a
workman himself, and imbued with the socialistic ideas of
Saint-Simon and Fourier, had promised his workmen a
profit in the mine and had engaged to pay just taxes to Algeria for the concession. Maxime, having discovered an ad-
jacent mine, takes advantage of an illness of his father's to
have him declared unfit to manage his own business. He
then secures a concession for this new mine at very slight
cost. The shipping of the ore entails also a concession for a
railroad. The socialists of France object to such a concession unless Matignon will model his contract on that which
his father had made with the Algerian government.

Richebais, editor of *L'Egalité*, is also opposed to this
grant on the general principle that the colonial governments give too many advantageous concessions to industrial companies. In spite of Maxime's eloquent account of the
noble work of exploitation, of the industrial poetry in the
development of the great mines hidden away in Algeria,
Richebais remains cold. He can see poetry in the great
projects but not in the enormous profits they yield to their
directors. The speculation on mines is as great, he objects,

as was speculation on railroads under Louis Philippe. Individuals are confiscating national resources. Grouped in companies and banks, the *grands bourgeois* are now all powerful; and everything, including parliament and the press, is under their control. They call themselves "pillars of France," but are not these mere words?

Richebais is a dangerous enemy, and Maxime tries to buy up his shares in the newspaper and persuade him to accept an appointment in Asia Minor. Richebais refuses; and Matignon shifts his attack to the other shareholders of *L'Egalité*, threatening to suppress the publicity of all companies and banks in which he is interested unless Richebais be removed.

In the meantime old Matignon has sufficiently recovered from his illness to consult his lawyer and discover the action taken by his son against him. In addition to this he finds out that the railroad proposed by Maxime as an excellent enterprise for Algeria is to be laid along the route that would coincide with that of future Moroccan lines. Matignon, as proprietor of this road, could set the rates for Moroccan merchandise using the road. Maxime is guilty of a still greater crime which his father uncovers. Unable to handle in his factory at Saint-Denis all the iron from the new mine, and unwilling for any other French company to share it with him, Maxime has sold the ore to a German company at a moderate profit. This is a traitorous act, as Germany would have paid Algeria any price for the much-needed iron. All the papers relating to these facts old Matignon threatens to give to Richebais to publish in *L'Egalité* unless Maxime will consent to the marriage of his daughter Frédérique (who is in reality Richebais' child) with the young mining engineer whom she loves. Maxime yields, but only on condition that Richebais leave the country, which the journalist does so as not to interfere with his daughter's happiness. And Algeria continues to be exploited by the *grands bourgeois*.

All the plays dealt with in this chapter are serious dramatic productions. The vaudeville is too frail a mold to contain the molten metal of modern finance, and it has been poured into the sturdy vessel of the *drame*. Every form of business intrigue that an audience could comprehend is resolutely depicted in as straightforward a manner as possible and with the unflinching purpose of representing reality. Under the Third Republic the barons of finance wage a much more deadly war against one another and against the public than they did in the days of Mercadet and Jean Giraud. Enterprises have become world-wide affairs, even involving nations in war. Press, politics, and finance unite in all important undertakings. But the chief underlying principle of every swindle is that simple one, long ago recognized by Dancourt's Trapolin—deception, the throwing of dust in the eyes of the world, "puff" whose proteiform nature is set forth in the succeeding chapter.

CHAPTER IX

PUFF

C'est le mensonge passé à l'état de spéculation, mis à la portée de tout le monde, et circulant librement pour les besoins de la société et de l'industrie.—SCRIBE, *Le Puff*, Act I, scene 2.

PUFF is one of the most characteristic figures of the modern world. He has his finger in every speculative pie. So many and varied are his disguises that it would be an endless task to count them up. Puff expresses himself sometimes in the façade or the luxurious interior of a place of business, or in an ill-afforded carriage and an opera loge. He is fond of splendid balls; he calls his friends "baron," and attaches with a wink some decoration to an eager buttonhole. Nor does he hesitate to use philanthropy when it best suits him. He gets himself and his doings into print and lies so successfully that his veracity is suspected by few indeed.

Jules Janin, after defining "puff" as the inordinate praising of anything and everything which meets one's eyes on walls, on billboards, in trains and newspapers; the modern substitute for fame; the power that governs finance, politics, and literature; the Prime Minister of speculation, recounts the following allegory:

"Go my son," said a great advertiser to a bastard son of his. "Take this little écu and these 10,000 francs. With the little écu you will hire a cab and go to Lombard Street where you will buy a drug: with these 10,000 francs you will advertise your drug, and your fortune will be made!"

And the son did as his wise father bade him and had no cause for regret.

Drama gives Puff the important place he deserves, and puts him on the stage in human form, whether under the name of Robert Macaire, Piffart, Coquelet, and scores of others, or under his own name of M. Puff. No one knows better than the speculator the value of bluffing. If he can appear wealthy, or take refuge under an honest name, or hide his rascality behind the glowing little button of the Legion of Honor, his fortune is made, for he can draw other people's money with magnetic force. And what would life be without other people's money!! The speculator, therefore, spends most of his energy in "jetant la poudre aux yeux"; thus forming a foundation of lies on which to build his enterprises, which burst upon the world as "brilliant opportunities," "sublime discoveries," and "superb undertakings."

The appearance of success is a phase of progress. Delbar of Picard's *L'Enfant trouvé*, aware of the strides his century is already making in the art of pretence, says that he cannot remain stationary while the age is advancing. People want an eloquent prospectus, and a financier's office must be either a museum or a ballroom. Delbar admits that his clients' affairs gain nothing by all this luxury of his, but the clients themselves are flattered at being so richly received. Goberville advises a carriage, a big diamond, and a loge at the opera—in fact, all things that give people confidence. If you are taken for a man engaged in big deals, capital pours in to you, and by means of display you find yourself rich. Goberville also sets a good table, for business is always more profitable if concluded over good wine. A broker must keep up with racing news, so Didier subscribes to the *Journal des Haras*. He goes to a riding-school because, having clients who are *à cheval*, he feels it necessary to flatter them by riding also in the Bois de Boulogne.

We have Piffart's word for it that no corporation can succeed without a fine building: "Il n'y a pas d'autre moyen d'attirer la confiance." This fact is even truer in the sixties than it was in the twenties. Silberstein hides the precarious financial condition of his bank behind a rich façade. When the secretary, Henri, insists that the bank is a swindle, his credulous uncle raises the natural objection that a house employing twenty-three clerks and having a window for deposits, one for withdrawals, another for bonds, could not possibly be a fraud. The financier Montjoye insists that his protégé, Georges, take better lodgings when he plans to enter business, for concessions must be made to the human weakness for appearances. Roseraye the ruined speculator of Becque's *Michel Pauper,* on the verge of committing suicide, regrets that he will no longer be in the world of finance, with his head held high, his heart full of courage, depending on a "semblance of wealth."

A conspicuous form of display is the financier's ball, which becomes a veritable motif in the money-play. It is, as we have seen, the regular prelude to a fraudulent bankruptcy, under cover of which the speculator retires to Belgium with his creditors' funds in his wallet. Allusion is made in *Le Voyage à Dieppe* to a brilliant fête given by a financier, whereupon a character remarks, "Oui; tout ce qui reluit n'est pas or." These balls are criticized in a vaudeville air of *Les Adieux au Comptoir:* although there is great luxury and opulence, the business men themselves are bores:

> Terpsichore dreads to see
> A Croesus on the floor
> And says of him reprovingly:
> "His purse is really much too fat—
> No one could dance with a load like that!"
>
> —Scene 10

Martigny, one of Picard's bankers, has heard nothing all winter but the balls given by German and Dutch bankers. In order to show national spirit, he too will give a ball —it will cost little and will be money well spent. The very villainous speculator of *Le Facteur* gives a gorgeous party while the man he has ruined is dragged off as a criminal. The bright lights of the house and the merry chatter of guests form the background for the tragic disgrace of the victim. The agreeable swindler Escroc Duplumet is famous for his entertainments, which are the finest in Paris, excellently planned, always adorned by some new lion, such as the Ojibwa Indians. Duplumet, after picking the pockets of his creditors, tries to make the classic escape to Belgium, but is caught and plucked in his turn. The American financiers in Paris are not behind the times, and we find the millionaire Foster of Mme Ancelot's *Marguerite* entertaining his French friends magnificently. Shrewd Thomassin of *Le Gendre d'un millionnaire* depends on his balls for election to a political office. The furnisher Gaudriot, a rank swindler, has a reputation for his excellent parties. Bourtibourg, being heavily in debt, feels the necessity of bedazzling his creditors: "Coolness, nerve, and the usual trick. We'll bluff them with a few fireworks tonight." Thus with fireworks, a banquet, the purchase of a carriage or later a touring car, the raising of servants' wages, the speculator succeeds in blinding the public until Augier has one of his characters say when inviting another to a party: "Un bal d'amis, simplement, et non pas une spéculation d'homme d'affaires."

Though born without titles, the feudality of money soon strives to attain them, partly in imitation of an envied aristocracy, partly for the prestige a title gives to business. A speculator wisely rechristens himself with an aristocratic

name, such as Saint-Gilles, Saint-Laurent, Saint-Joseph, or
Saint-Remy. He may also add to his own name that of his
town or village with the particle between which makes a
"proud name of a ridiculous one." The title "baron" is acquired either by purchase or as a reward from the government. The Vicomte Delbois of *Les trois Quartiers* would
put a stop to the custom of decorating bankers for their
loans, as it instills in them vanity and creates a new feudality. The majority of industrialists, however, feel that their
millions entitle them to enter the aristocracy, for an industrialist of today is as a marquis of yesterday, says Dubourg: he can attain anything. And Dubourg claims the
peerage as a lawful benefit of *égalité*. Durandard of *Un
mauvais Riche* pompously announces his new rank: a
friend addresses him by his simple name, and he explains
that, though he considers the matter of small moment, yet
he must tell his friend that he has bought the fief of Oléron,
as his name seemed to him a trifle vulgar. He begs his
friend to kindly address him in the future as *mon cher
baron,* or simply *baron.* The servants of Jean Giraud use
his new title of baron so excessively that even the crass
Jean realizes what a fool they are making of him and orders them to use the title only in private.

As a financial asset the title is extremely valuable, for
shares emitted by a baron seem much more trustworthy
than those issued by a simple citizen. A board of directors
should be adorned with titles. As Emma remarks in *Le
Duc Job,* she has heard her father, David the banker, say
that in big companies "on est très-friand de grands noms
... honorables." Silberstein says to Prince Verhazy that he
must be a director for the new mining company: "Illustrious names such as yours are rare," says he, "I need yours."
Fallen members of the old aristocracy are not infrequently

hired as directors that their names may attract the public, as, for instance, the Marquis de Rizerolles and Valdepenas Santiago in *Les Loups et les Agneaux*. A financier in an-

The Butler announces the Baron de Bois-flotté

other play rages because so many members of the nobility display their names in business enterprises. He says there is not a single exploitation in which they do not appear; if a railroad company is formed, the director is a duke or a marquis; if a canal is to be built, the treasurer is a baron.

A speculator is sometimes as much interested in the shelter
of an honest name as in an aristocratic one. Jean Giraud
tries to go into partnership with Durieu, under cover of
whose respected name he, Jean, could act safely; and Brassac of *La Bourse ou la Vie* seeks an honest man for a partner, for, "Un nom honorable dans les affaires, c'est le rêve."

The speculator pulls all possible wires for a decoration
of the Legion of Honor. The rosette or the cross announce
to the world that he is a man to whom capital may safely
be trusted. One of Picard's adventurers is hung with medals—two Russian crosses and the order of the *Eperon
d'Or;* he is seeking in addition the *croix d'honneur*. The
cross serves a very definite financial purpose in *Les deux
Raymond*. The evil-hearted Marcel Raymond receives by
mistake a letter from the government awarding the cross to
his brother. Marcel, being in financial straits, claims the
award as his and parades the honor before the financiers on
whom he is relying for assistance, hoping to impress them
and secure their support. Another speculator grows irate
over the way in which the government has neglected him:
"I have an independent fortune, I am a useful citizen, having enriched the state by enriching myself; but what good
has it done me? If I am a baron, it is because I paid for the
title. I have not even the cross, and I have asked for it
twenty times." Similarly, Scribe's Dulistel insists that after his fifteen years of labor to enrich himself, his country
should reward him. Mme Ancelot's Danvilliers boastfully
wears the red ribbon: he is at last officer of the national
guard. Once upon a time a person's activities were limited:
the soldier fought; the judge sat on the bench; the financier counted his money. Now soldiers make laws; a marquis goes into business; and financiers—do everything!
Likewise M. Benoîton of "les sommiers à ressorts compen-

sateurs" feels that after having come to Paris with only
forty sous in his pocket he should be recompensed for having made a fortune.

An homme d'affaires à la mode is cleverly caricatured
in *La Dot de Cécile*. We meet this financial dandy in a barber shop, where he is being perfumed and curled. It is there
that he discusses his title "chevalier," a title of which he is
proud and which he finds very convenient. "In a century
like ours, when the essential thing is to dazzle, I simply felt
obliged to add a title to my handsome face and my good
figure. Who in the world would dispute my right to it at a
time when there are so many chevaliers?" Thereupon
Floridor the barber replies with a song:

> A title goes with every trade
> And carries science onward:
> In art and in the army
> It is a sure reward.
> Knights always are and e'er will be
> The noble pride of their country.

Here Raymond, a count in disguise, takes up the song with
a glance at Beaumont.

> But in their ranks you'll often see
> A thieving Knight of Industry.

—I, 7

Beaumont, this dandy of the bourse, considers himself
"adorable," orders the barber to give him an extra fine curl,
sends his valet to the bourse with his tilbury: "ça vous
classe." Of course he owes the barber and refuses to pay, is
planning to marry for money, and finally proves himself a
coward by backing out of a duel when he hears that his opponent is a good swordsman.

Besides luxurious display and the glitter of aristocratic

titles or the decoration of the Legion of Honor, the speculator often hides himself and his nefarious practices behind
the spreading skirts of Philanthropy. This is truly a very
effective form of puff. Scribe's Desgaudets classifies *bienséance* and *désintéressement* as methods of fooling the public. The speculator subscribes to many charitable organizations (frequently he never pays the subscription); and
when he organizes a company, it is always for the benefit of
mankind.

Etienne introduces us to this hypocrisy in his *Les deux
Gendres,* a modern recurrence of the Lear theme. Dervière,
the capitalist son-in-law, is rich, miserly, and philanthropic.
He is connected with many charities, in whose interest he
expends ink rather than money, thus advertising himself
as a philanthropist while his purse strings remain tied. A
raisonneur of the play asserts that Dervière is not the only
such speculator for whom Paris has cause to blush:

> Once charity was simply done
> But now by it are fortunes won.
> This generous ardor serves for gain—
> A mask for avarice, 'tis plain.

—I, 7

Etienne's shafts are apparently directed at the ambitious
and philanthropic charlatans of the day. The author made
himself quite popular with *Les deux Gendres,* the original-
ity of which, as M. Allard points out, is its use of public
opinion as a driving-force, impelling the movements of the
chief characters, Dervière the capitalist and Dalainville
the politician.

Philanthropy as a means of speculation occurs again in
L'Argent of 1826. The banker Dalincourt and the speculator Chalet are engaged in financial enterprises. Chalet,
of whose acts few will bear scrutiny, hoodwinks the public

by having subscriptions for victims of a fire collected in his name. Chalet, however, does not intend to restrict his profits to a reputation for goodness: he knows that money is like calumny—a little of it always remains. So Chalet will shine before the public as a philanthropist while he coolly does a little grafting on his own account. The same author, Casimir Bonjour, in a political drama, *Naissance, Fortune et Mérite, ou l'Epreuve électorale,* has the financier, Lisieux, run for office against a marquis and an honest man. Lisieux's campaign manager advertises him by having him join the Société d'Encouragement pour l'Industrie and the Société d'Enseignement élémentaire, and also subscribe heavily to the *incendiés du Calvados.*

A banker with the reassuring name of Bonnefonds, in a one-act comedy, *Le Comité de Bienfaisance,* actually parades his speculations in philanthropy before the public. He puts in a breezy appearance before a certain committee with apologies for his tardiness: he has so many affairs, so many matters to see to; a visit to our little orphans; and so on. But what can you expect of a philanthropists' banker and the president of innumerable organizations who must prove to his century that a man can make money and yet be a benefactor? (Incidentally, being a benefactor is a very lucrative profession.)

I am always telling my banker friends to think less of money-making and more of their neighbors. Why, I make more than they do! By being philanthropic I make my name popular, and that brings me credit. While they have sought for wealth in railroads and canals, I have found it in the human heart. Noble passions and generous ideas are a lever in my skilful hands which can pry up gold from the whole world. I do endless good and at the same time have a profitable business, which fact attaches me all the more to the principles of justice and humanity!

Could any rogue prey more openly upon the sentiments of mankind! And yet Charity spreads so thick a robe that no one sees beneath it.

I'm sorry, my good woman, but I can do nothing for you. I belong to the Northern Philanthropists and give only to the poor of Kamchatka.

Such speculation is the theme of a play by Coucy, called *Les Philanthropes*. The protagonist, Daubray, is a contemptible character, hateful and hypocritical. He speculates in philanthropic schemes and takes pains to let his left hand know what his right has done. He scolds his wife for doing her charity in secret. What profit does she get from that, pray tell? Besides, she really spends money on the poor, and he gets credit for it without ever spending a cent. Daubray is characterized by his nephew as a modern Tartufe. Nothing is to be gained today by devoutness as in the time of Molière, so men become philanthropists. Daubray is an assiduous member of charitable committees, and his deeds are cited in at least twenty papers. He is forever talking of the people's comfort, of prison reforms, of humanitarian projects, and advising economy for those who have no bread. Among Daubray's schemes is a workingman's bank, a brilliant project which will yield a dividend of 20 francs on a capital of 20 sous.

Of the four philanthropists engaged in promoting this noble scheme, not one will accept any office except that of cashier. Moreover, a quarrel arises as to who should be rewarded for the original conception. Daubray demands 30,000 francs for the idea; and the doctor, Morinville, at once claims the money as rightfully his. Daubray becomes unpopular, and the others determine to unmask him before the public. His prestige is almost lost when he hears of the noble deeds performed by a hero at a fire in a neighboring town. He brazenly announces himself as the hero, the true hero being as a matter of fact his own nephew. A peculiar form of puff is indulged in by the above-mentioned Doctor Morinville. He is in the habit of always being present at accidents in the street, lending his aid, refusing to give his name that his generosity may remain unrewarded. He will, however (accidentally of course), leave a bill book containing his name and address on the site of the accident.

A financier's philanthropy may take the form of pretended generosity toward people to whom in reality (but the world does not know this) great sums are due. So the miserly Dubuisson of Scribe's *O Amitié* with ostentatious charity shelters a woman and her daughter while to the woman's husband he owes a fortune made at the bourse. Again the disagreeable M. Pinchard in Dugué's play by that name makes great show of protecting his wife's young protégée, though as a matter of fact he is trying to hinder her marriage in order that he need not pay her the dowry willed her by his wife.

No company prospectus is complete without the dubious statement that the enterprise is to be undertaken for the good of humanity. Ledoux's railroad swindle is a "noble enterprise founded in the interest of the country and of national glory." Mercadet considers his protective paving "sublime and philanthropic." Daubray's workingman's bank, a rank exploitation of the poor, is advertised as a blessing to the laboring class. The suave banker Aveïro, a member of the coalition of bankers in *Un Coup de Bourse,* carries his hypocrisy into the very center of this pack of cheats who are trying to trouble the waters of the bourse the better to fish therein.

Let us not enrich ourselves too publicly. If we trouble the waters of the bourse, we do so for the good of our country! It is we who have made possible railroads and canals; we who have rebuilt towns. And yet people object to our just compensation, and because we make money they say that we are depreciating the value of stock and that our enterprises are not on a solid foundation! Our devotion, prudence, and morality deserve a better reward. But we shall find this reward in the peace of our consciences. Our consciences are untroubled, gentlemen, because we are less interested in our personal fortunes than in the good of others. Let us be as devoted as missionaries and as disinterested as soldiers!

Silberstein storms in an aside: *"Farceur!* Fifteen years ago he was hard up; and now, thanks to his 'philanthropy,' he's worth fifty million and more."

Balzac ironically excuses this philanthropic thieving in a scene between Quinola and his partner Monipodio. The former, scheming to profit by the invention of Fontanarès, secretly procures duplicates of the parts of the steam engine, with the excuse that, if the inventor should perish, he would have saved his invention for the good of humanity. Monipodio interprets Quinola's philanthropy justly by saying, "The more so, as, according to an old author, *we* are humanity."

The greatest and most characteristic form of puff which the nineteenth century stage derides is printed publicity. Not that self-advertising in the newspapers appeared then for the first time in drama. M. Lanson calls attention to Boursault as the first dramatist to bring journalistic publicity before a theater audience. Boursault represents the public of 1683 passing through the office of the *Mercure Galant* and besieging the editor for notice in the journal's pages. The plebeian Michaut demands an aristocratic ancestry; Mme Guillemot wants her good qualities praised (she will write the article herself); the fraudulent Longuemain, whom the reader will remember as a seventeenth century tax-collector, needs a character for honesty; Boniface requires advertising for his artistically printed funeral notices, hoping by this means to make a fortune if the year is "rich in deaths"; Du Mesnil asks the editor to condemn the French nobility for learning foreign languages when they do not know the tongue of Normandy which he is prepared to teach them; and Du Pont has an infallible cure for gout which he wishes to have advertised, a cure which drives away the gout but sends the patient to another world.

Printed publicity, a novelty under Louis XIV, becomes a rage two centuries later. Sainte-Beuve describes the expansion of newspapers and the birth of advertising: the infancy of the *annonce* was like that of Gargantua, he observes, "elle passa vite aux prodiges." It soon found its way into all newspapers, reviews, annuals, guides, almanacs, not to mention innumerable posters of every sort. Posters had been greatly improved through the invention of the chromolithograthic machine, thanks to which the Chéret brothers were able to dress Paris walls out in gaily colored sheets. Improved methods of paper manufacture were in part responsible for the rapid multiplication of newspapers. Banks, stores, companies, began to issue their own papers, which bore such enticing names as *La Bonne Foi, La Confiance,* and *La Justice.* Toussenel, in 1847, writes bitterly of the *annonce,* saying that it has become indissolubly entangled with stock-jobbing and bourse orgies. He blames it for disastrous speculations, for having created the *faiseur,* for having put political influence into the hands of *agioteurs de bas étage,* for having increased tenfold the power of the financial aristocracy, and for having placed the directing of the intellectual movement in the hands of speculators.

About the time of this assault on advertising the first advertising agency was formed, and some two decades later there existed the Société Générale des Annonces, a powerful publicity trust. French newspapers depend much more on financiers and the publicity they purchase for their enterprises than on straight advertising, so that they are less independent than American and English papers. The financial columns are frequently sold outright to a financier or a company, and used not so much to convey reliable information to the public as to push the sale of certain stock or blackmail other financiers.

Drama alludes frequently to the private newspapers of

business men. It is suggested to the millionaire Pierre that, since he is ambitious to become powerful, he establish a newspaper, a literary review, or a theater, by means of which to direct letters, art, and politics. The people will then receive from him, not only *panem et circenses* but opinions and *tissus imperméables* at a reasonable price. "Dites-moi," says his interlocutor, "si ce n'est pas là une royauté réelle." The newspaper is treated in *Un Parvenu* of 1860 as the speculator's latest luxury. Bidart, who has risen from poverty to wealth, boasts of his residence and his carriage, and then exclaims:

> And men own papers as they do a coach!
> They once kept works of art upon display;
> But founding papers is the thing today!

Bidart is going to run a complete newspaper—literature, art, bourse, railroads, commerce, and *feuilletons*. His assistants are a couple of adventurers who try their hands at anything and everything, but the editor-in-chief is too ignorant to realize their incompetence.

The newspaper becomes less of a luxury and more of a necessity as the century advances, and it plays a leading rôle in company enterprises of the Third Republic as we saw in the last chapter.

The vaudeville eagerly seizes on the puffist types. There is M. Gobetout of *Les Actualités,* who, among other novelties, gulps down the *annonce.* In order to advertise one of his schemes he sends his servant out on the street dressed "entre le lancier rouge et le chinois de paravent" to distribute prospectuses. This, explains Gobetout, is a form of *actualité.* Gobetout is bent on speculating with his daughter's dowry, and his wife threatens to take the matter to court. So much the better, cries Gobetout, rubbing his hands to-

gether—that means a little scandal which is only another
phase of *actualité*. Thus it is that Gobetout keeps pace
with his century.

In 1838 appeared a vaudeville called *Le Puff*, printed
with the parody *Ruy-Blag*. The characters are M. Puff
himself and his two charming daughters, La Réclame and
La Blague, whom he is offering well-dowered as the prizes
for some contest or other. M. Puff proudly traces his ancestry back to Baron Wormspire, father of Robert Macaire. He boosts himself enthusiastically as the king of
charlatans, the great contractor of Macairisms, of suc-
cesses and trickery, always well received by good Parisians
and welcomed at the bourse. Miss Blague is his eldest
born; Miss Réclame is the loveliest thing in creation, his
finest offspring:

> The first Puff
>   Came quietly enuf:
> A little breeze
>   Followed the second Wheeze.
> Since then the race has grown so
> That on the Judgment Day there'll blow
>   A final Puff.
>
> —Scene 3

Miss Réclame chirps her little song too:

> I'm just a little ad—
> But pillar of the paper;
> And over every new success
> I cut a little caper.
>
> —Scene 2

The scant plot of the vaudeville turns on Puff's treatment of Dame Truth: he has driven her quite out of the
country, but she returns in beggar's rags. Miss Blague offers her some Provençal bread at which Dame Truth turns
up a scornful nose: Provençal bread, indeed! It was baked

right in the Rue Feydeau! M. Puff and his daughters will
not stand for that, so they throw poor Truth into the well
of Saint-Pétrin; and M. Puff, slightly upset by the occurrence, strolls off to the bourse to regain his composure.
And so ends this nineteenth-century allegory.

A similar skit, *La France et l'Industrie,* has among its
characters Enterprise, a Confidence Man, and Advertising.
The last named sings:

> First a handfull of dust in their eyes
> (That is the needful thing today)
> And if the ad's of sufficient size
> The speculator will have his way—
> But remember! Throw dust in their eyes!
>
> —Scene 4

The Confidence Man explains how he helps business: he
talks loudly about advertisements, stands before billboards
and gets very much excited. When a crowd of gulls has
gathered, he persuades them all to invest their money.

Every tangle of the plot of Scribe's *Le Puff,* which is as
complicated as most in La Scribie, is twisted about some
form of bluff. The honest and ingenious Albert d'Angre-
mont, an officer in the African army, returns to Paris to so-
licit funds for the widow and orphans of his general. His
success is meager, for a simple tale of suffering brings no
response from his auditors. Fortunately, an homme d'affaires, versed in the ways of the nineteenth century, drums
up a little scandal about Count de Marignan and the general's wife. Public interest is roused and money begins
to pour in, when Albert spoils everything by indignantly
denying the lie. Shortly after, the above-named count gives
a reading from his new book, the *Mémoires* of the dead
general. Albert, who had followed the general throughout

his campaigns, is present at the reading; and his indignation knows no bounds, for he recognizes the wild adven-
tures related as those which he himself had once invented
for a novel, the sheets of which had evidently fallen into
the hands of the count. Albert is about to uncover the deceit but is persuaded to keep silent for the sake of the general's family in which so much interest has been aroused
that its future is assured. Thus lying Puff triumphs over
Honesty.

There is also a poor man called Desgaudets who has by
some chance acquired the reputation of being a miser and
is believed to have much gold hidden away. He is very
much sought after, and indeed has as much power as if he
were in reality wealthy. When the young speculator Max-
ence secures Desgaudets as a member of the board of directors for his railroad company, the success of the company is assured. Puff is resorted to in order to boost this
company, not only by means of Desgaudet's name, but by
means of a lie regarding the shares. It is advertised that
they are all gone in the very beginning, and this so whets
people's desire that the shares go with great celerity. Puff
is indeed proteiform: Desgaudet's blue-stocking daughter,
Corinne, adopts it for her schemes; the editor Bouvard explains to Albert the use he makes of it. An author, for instance, wishes to print a book and he pays both for the
printing, which is a slight matter, and for the advertising,
which is more costly. Bouvard writes to all the newspapers
that the Bouvard printing house has just bought for, say,
50 or 100 thousand francs the exquisite collection of poems
by Mr. So and So, which have been impatiently expected.
Thus the book is well advertised, and no one knows that
the author printed it at his own expense.

Before quitting Scribe's *Le Puff*, it would be well to quote Des Granges, who shows how very applicable the play was to the conditions existing in all walks of life before the Revolution of 1848:

> It was, I believe, even more timely and more true, in its satire of boosters of every sort, at the approach of that Revolution of 1848, which was at first an indignant protest against the Tartufes of liberalism, the Robert Macaires of law, the Bertrands of finance, the Bilboquets of politics . . . . only to be immediately confiscated by the same band which had gone to change costumes in the dressing-room.

Mr. Arvin ranks this play of Scribe's very high, for it marks a transformation in the writer's manner: he at last pays "more attention to the painting of manners and to the portrayal of character than to the development of the plot."

The light, sparkling comedy by Edmond Gondinet, *Les Tapageurs* of 1879, overflows with the puff or *tapage* of a number of society people grouped about the swindler Cardonat who is launching the Danube Company. The chief asset of this company is the name of the honest financier Jordane who is lured into the enterprise by Olga, the speculator's mistress. When it became known that Cardonat had dined at Jordane's and that Jordane had consented to become a director for the company, shares went sky-rocketing up. Cardonat proclaims that he will promote his company with a great deal of noise: for advertising is now ennobled and replaces Fame. Even Jordane admits that an affair is no longer judged by its true value but by the disturbance it makes at birth. There is no time to let an enterprise grow up and develop. This is the fault of the newspapers which for twenty years have been creating *petits grands hommes* of all dimensions. Fire a gun! That is sufficient; "C'est le règne du tapage."

Cardonat advertises himself with equal fervor by talking of buying the Trocadero or the Bois de Boulogne and by boasting that within twenty-four hours he will be not only the best-known man in Paris but in the whole universe. The Danube Company is already engaged in a law suit, and Cardonat seeks the reputable Bridier to defend it, because, even if the suit were lost, the weight of his name would be a great protection. After examining the telltale papers of the company, Bridier refuses to take the case; but Cardonat has already bruited the honest lawyer's name about as the "Company's lawyer." Bridier accuses Cardonat of trying to attain fame and fortune through *tapage;* "You are perhaps treating your contemporaries as they deserve," he adds, thinking of the loss which the shareholders in this enterprise must sustain when Cardonat shall have sold his own shares, as he obviously intends to do. Fortunately for the investors, the honest Jordane reimburses them for the two million francs which Cardonat carries off with him when he leaves suddenly to study at Brussels the navigation of the Danube.

Among the friends and acquaintances of Jordane are amusing fourflushers. Valentine, the young widow of M. de Folny, whose husband loved quiet as much as she herself loved excitement, intends to remain a widow but is frustrated by her dead husband who has willed his property to her only on condition that she remarry, as he does not wish her to use his name as an asset. She has founded a charitable institution for wayward girls which must have M. de Jordane as president, the celebrated Dr. Bajol as its physician, and the big booster Cardonat as treasurer. Dr. Bajol consents on condition that two other doctors be appointed so that no one would suppose he were doing any of the actual work. The doctor, who keeps himself before the public by dinners, receptions, horses, pictures, and eccentric friends, is not averse to attending Cardonat, who is certain to get himself talked about; and it matters nothing whether the gossip be good or ill.

Mme Descourtois, in order to push her stupid husband, turns him into an *homme profond*. She makes him shave to appear bald and teaches him to look wise and say nothing, so that the papers are forever repeating the magic phrase "M. Descourtois made no reply." Having been taught by his wife to keep himself in the public eye, he invests heavily in the popular Danube Company, without, however, first consulting Mme Descourtois. As she had married him only for his money, she sees to it that he sells these dubious shares at once.

Balistrac has fairly lost his mind over *tapage*. He runs about, seeking in every possible way to draw attention to himself; but most of his efforts are futile. When he engages in a duel for the sake of notoriety, the combat is called off; when he acts the clown at a society ball, someone else is given credit for the rôle by the newspapers; he subscribes for a box at the opera, and his wife rejoices with her friends that as he detests music she will have the box all to herself, but Balistrac announces that he will attend in person for fear the public may otherwise forget him.

Thus in *Les Tapageurs* as in *Le Puff*, everyone is making a big stir about himself, hoping thereby to obtain social recognition, a better clientèle, or a fortune. In Gondinet, pre-eminently a writer of farces, there is, as Léopold Lacour puts it, a *gaulois* sense of *blague* mingled with a Parisian sense of actuality, so that, though poorly constructed, *Les Tapageurs* offers an excellent and diverting view of life leading the audience to agree that "M. Gondinet, avec sa pénétration et sa verve caricaturale, est un des maîtres rieurs d'aujourd'hui."

We must take leave of M. Puff and his twin, Tapage, to examine more minutely than we have yet done the characteristics of the financiers who depend so successfully on bluff and trickery.

CHAPTER X

THE SONS OF TURCARET

C'est encore comme du temps de la Bruyère: nos moeurs ne sont vraiment que les habits de nos passions. La mode change, l'homme reste le même.—PICARD, *Riche et Pauvre*, Act I, scene 1.

STAGE financiers of any period, whether petty swindlers or captains of industry, bear a strong family resemblance to their father Turcaret. The apparent differences between Turcaret and his sons are usually but superficial, depending on the habits and customs of their respective epochs. The style in money-making changes as it does in speech and dress, but the fundamental nature of the man alters little with the centuries. It seems more difficult to give individual characteristics to an homme d'affaires than to men of other professions. There is, perhaps, a leveling power about preoccupation with money which wears away personal peculiarities and graces. At all events, most stage financiers are as little differentiated in their personal qualities as Dante's usurers, recognizable only by the coats of arms on the money bags they carry. Looking over the array of financiers who during the past centuries have walked the boards of French theaters, it would be difficult to distinguish with certainty a Piffart from a Mercadet, a Lecardonnel from a Chicanenville, were it not for the incidents and speculative scheme connected with each.

The progeny of Turcaret have in their names also held strictly to family tradition. Some connection with money is almost always indicated (as usury in the name of Turcaret), either a typical characteristic of the homme d'affaires or some phase of business. Basset, like many a financier, was born in a hovel; and Poirier, Durosay, Verdier, and Péponet are wearisome or ludicrous bourgeois parvenus. Plebeian adventurers in finance wear such names as Saint-Joseph or Du Tillet, or the title of baron. The conventional usurer peers through the mask of Araby, Lombard, Rapinier, Rapinard, Raffle, Matthieu, Gripparville, Salomon, Cogne, and Chavassus. Money has set its defacing stamp on Moses Geld and Vaudoré, Dorvilé, Dulingot, Dargentac, and Silberstein. One is instinctively suspicious of Escroc Duplumet, Chicanenville, Fillerin, Truchelu, Trapolin, and Fich'ton-kan, obviously light-fingered folk. Boursicoff, Duhautcours, and Carottin; Brassier, Brassac, and Lebrasseux, hint strongly at bourse speculation. Brûlot, Accéléré, Faitout, and Tout-Affaire are ever busy promoters. M. Lebègue will stammer his victim into confusion, as Regnard's Bredouille does. Clairénet and Crifort, Gogo, Gobetout, Gobergeot, and Goulard will eagerly gobble shares and cry for dividends. Thus comedy gaily bestows conventional names upon the business man, constructing his individuality in the same set fashion.

The millionaire of drama is habitually the self-made man who entered Paris for the first time in wooden shoes and a peasant's blouse. So they confess one after another. The goad that drove Chalet to success was fear of starvation, as he explains to Mme Dalincourt. Balzac's César Birotteau tells of arriving in the capital wearing a Touraine blouse, carrying an iron-tipped stick, and blessed with a single gold louis; and after forty years, behold he is one of the leading perfumers of Paris. César's brother Tourangeau, of *Un Parvenu,* brags so eternally of his wooden-shoe origin that he is advised to found the Order of the Sabot and attach a golden sabot to his buttonhole as the decoration of the new order. Roussel, too, of *La Ceinture dorée* proudly contrasts his wooden shoes with his acquired millions, and M. Benoîton throws out his chest and boasts of having come to Paris with forty sous in his pocket. Sardou is fond of the type and has given us not only Benoîton but Jonathan of *Les Femmes fortes*. These and others—Delpierre, Riquebourg, Didier, Péponet, and Jean Giraud—begin in wooden shoes to tread the romantic road to millions.

For they all handle millions in reality or in imagination. Limeray of *L'Adversaire* by Capus claims to have been for fifteen years the greatest financier of Paris, the man to whom everyone brings money: "J'ai une situation unique." But this "unique position" is claimed by each one. Lebourg, who has 50 or 60 million francs, is called an arch-millionaire. Vérugna is the "most powerful man in Paris": he has saved a ministry, which is much more difficult than overthrowing one. Isidore Lechat has also the reputation of being "un homme d'affaires remarquable ... le premier de Paris." Nathan Strohmann, of whom we shall hear more later, proclaims himself "le plus gros financier de Paris," declaring that he can rig the market to suit himself. Brachart, a combination of child and brute, who detests nothing so much as useless words, a galley slave of success with the motto "Win or croak," is worth 30 million francs and is hailed by his wife as "un des maîtres du monde." Cerfbier is "et failli et condamné"; but, thanks to the countless gulls on the face of the earth, he is an arch-millionaire. These men who have become *condottieri* of business can all look back from a pinnacle of millions to a wretched beginning in hunger and poverty.

The years of accumulation of wealth are years of adventure in all manner of occupations. Thomassin, who came penniless to Paris, was a sheriff's officer, a store clerk, an unlicensed broker, and finally a business man piling up in his strong box the "penny of the poor and the gold piece of the rich" and marching straight to Fortune. Abraham Strohmann, father of Nathan, has had a still more varied life: son of an Austrian or Polish shoemaker, he became a pedlar in the Balkans; a slave merchant in Egypt, Salonika, and Constantinople; a furnisher of supplies for the Turkish army in 1877; a banker in Paris; and a promoter of Persian mines. Jacques Brachart, better known as Samson, started out as a porter. Fifteen years later he was in Egypt calling himself "Brachart pacha," directing a newspaper and two big companies. He is speculating in oil and then all of a sudden appears in Paris to launch the famous Egyptian Copper Company, which he himself later wrecks. There are conflicting reports with regard to the past history of Baron d'Urth of *Les Ventres dorés*. He is alleged to be a German Jew, naturalized in France and having made his fortune in America. According to another story he is a Catholic, who went to America when only fifteen. There he was groom, grocer, cowboy, and showman. He attracted the attention of Fair Whitelaw, who took him into his bank and at his death willed him his fortune. D'Urth lost his fortune at speculation on the Paris bourse and dropped out of sight until rescued by Baron de Thau, who associated him in his enterprises. He then devoted himself to speculation in real estate, banking, and railroads. During this brilliant period of his life he was given the title of baron by the king of Carinthia, decorated, and promoted finally to commander of the Legion of Honor. A third rumor makes of D'Urth a Genovese Protestant.

It is by no means poverty alone which assured these financiers success. Each possesses an indomitable will and an inordinate amount of self-assurance which carry him lightly over mountainous difficulties. He merits as his device the words of Lechat "Tout ce que j'ai voulu ... je l'ai réalisé." The unusual strength of will found in the business man of the stage is due partly to the fact that his life has but one purpose, *faire fortune,* toward which he directs every atom of energy he has. No other ambitions enter in—at least not until he has made his million—nor is he troubled by any doubts, either as to the ultimate worth of his goal or as to the means by which it should be attained. Each speculator dreams of being a *Napoléon des affaires* and of rivaling Rothschild and Aguado. The financier is immune to discouragement and is imbued with a faith in his own ability which is denied to most men. Montjoye expresses thus the creed of the will: "There can be no great destiny for the weak. That is why, though respecting true social principles, I trampled underfoot from the very beginning that which has always constituted the weakness of the vulgar, all convention, all the parasitic and literary elements with which this poor humanity is pleased to weaken its natural debility, to torment its conscience, and to increase its burden." Chalet declares that were he left penniless he could reconstruct his fortune. How? By following up the method of Newton, that is *en y songeant toujours.* Mercadet fairly radiates self-confidence. In the face of ruin he honestly believes himself capable of becoming a millionaire in twenty-four hours. Bourtibourg, in a like predicament, depends entirely on his own power of scheming to save himself; and he says, tapping his forehead: "Voici la caisse, et celle-là est inépuisable ... ce n'est pas comme l'autre." At the beginning of the play Bourtibourg is on the brink of ruin, but he appears in the last act with his hands full of shares in new and superb projects. Did people think him drowned? Not he! One takes the plunge, but one always comes up again. Praised be Heaven, Bourtibourg is as rich as ever he was; and the hand he extends to his ward's surprised fiancé, will, he declares, one day handle millions.

When the enterprise of the Nouvelle Afrique is facing destruction, the Baron de Thau, whose brain is "like a watch that never stops," refuses to have his career ruined when his mind is teeming with great schemes which will change the face of the world. Never will he let those projects perish, never! Brassac confidently declares that *he* cannot be mistaken, that he is incapable of making unfortunate speculations. Brachart boasts to his wife that people may deceive him but they cannot control him, "c'est moi qui ai les autres." Cardonat, who has returned after a forced exile in the Near East full of *projets gigantesques,* speaks of the absolute assurance which fills him to overflowing.

With the last-mentioned quality, confidence, goes the love of speculation, the *grande passion,* so great often that no lesson of failure, no reasoning of friends, can deliver a speculator from it. The will and daring of the financier plunge him into countless activities which his vivid financial imagination suggest to him as likely means of duping the public and doubling his capital. Speculation is splendidly eulogized by Isidore Lechat as business in which you handle crowds of men and millions of francs, other people's millions, of course. It is the "need to be always creating something new," the "intoxicating joy of overcoming obstacles," described by Lechat, that makes the thread of speculation run like a thread of romance through the most ordinary money-plays.

This passion sweeps before it every consideration of

right. As long as the business man can keep a corner of the mantle of the law over him, he blandly violates all ethical standards. Roussel, when accused by Trélan of having ruined his stockholders, replies arrogantly, "Je ne connais que la loi, moi"; and with the law he has taken care to be *en règle*. The Marquis d'Auberive in *Les Effrontés* says cynically to Charrier of Vernouillet's bankruptcy, "When a man is within the law, what can you say?" Pyat's brigand of the bourse, Oscar, explains the same principle: the wrong is not in stealing but in stealing without the code in one's hand.

Mercadet makes an amusing attempt to trace the hazy line between honesty and dishonesty. In business one has the right to be shrewd. Excessive shrewdness is not indelicacy, indelicacy is not dishonesty; but all these qualities fit into one another like the tubes of an opera glass. In short, safety lies in sticking to the code.

Occasionally the only thing wrong with an enterprise is that it is a little contrary to the laws of the land, as Maurice observes of Limeray's crooked scheme; but more often the laws are such as to leave the financier free to rob his neighbor as much as ever bandit did (or so, at least, Cherance feels about Abraham Strohmann's deceits). More often still, as Richebais says to Matignon, the business man is depicted as so powerful that there is no danger of his honesty being questioned, for whatever he does will perforce be right. The financier, in short, seems to have, as Vernières says, "une mentalité spéciale, et même une moralité spéciale. Ce sont ... ce sont," and the word he cannot find is supplied by his companion, "Ce sont des financiers."

The business man who makes his first million dishonestly has still at heart the desire of the rogue Touchandgo, which is to become a "respectable" man. The locksmith

Burl of Pyat's *Les deux Serruriers,* hired by a banker to commit murder, consents to it for the reward promised: once the murder committed, he will go into honest business; and, says the cynic, "I shall become a banker." Vernouillet justifies himself for the shady operations of his bank by the admission that he merely wanted to get a start and that he intended thereafter to be an honest man. Roussel, taken to task for the tainted source of his fortune, feels that his subsequent honesty is sufficient justification. It is indeed rare for a financier to have a wholly clean financial past. Henri thanks his father, Charrier, for having kept his name unsullied to hand on to his son, but even the banker Charrier's first step had been a dishonest one. When two of Vogt's acquaintances discuss him, the one says that the question of his early honesty is but a relative one, the essential thing being to get a start; and the other adds, "Depuis, il a eu le temps de laver ses langes."

The ethic of the financier is often crystallized by him into terse sayings like the much quoted "Les affaires sont les affaires," used by Mirbeau as a title and found earlier in *Les faux Bonshommes* and *La Famille Benoîton.* Piffart reduces all financial operations to two words, "buying" and "selling": "Vous achetez bon marché; vous vendez très cher; voilà le secret du commerce." These maxims express the all importance of business and the exploitation of the weak: "L'argent est l'argent," "Les affaires avant tout," and "On n'y fait rien pour rien." At the bourse "la fin justifie les moyens." The American motto, as given by Jonathon, is "Chacun pour soi et en avant." Success is obtained according to one of Scribe's characters "en n'ayant jamais de passions et en exploitant celles des autres." Exploitation is naturally the theme of many such sayings: "La victoire appartient à l'adresse"; "Pour que l'argent

entre dans une poche, il faut qu'il sorte d'une autre";
"L'argent roule toujours vers les moins maladroits"; "Les
affaires, c'est bien simple, c'est l'argent des autres"; "L'ar-

M. Gogo's mother reproves him for his rash investments

gent est l'argent, quelles que soient les mains où il se
trouve"; "En affaires il faut plus de malice qu'autre chose";
"Le génie des affaires fait le malheur des autres; tant pis
pour les autres"; "Si l'on n'exploitait pas un peu les imbé-
ciles, il y en aurait trop"; and "Il vaut mieux voler tout le
monde que de ne voler que quelques personnes." It is said

of the swindler Badoulard, who has an agency, that "en faisant les affaires des autres, on fait les siennes." Such are the business maxims which one finds on almost every financier's tongue, and they illustrate admirably his slight preoccupation with an ethic which transcends personal profit and the accumulation of wealth.

The politics of the business man is wholly selfish: he is loyal to no party, and rather prides himself on his ability to change readily with the political winds which blew fitfully enough in the last century. There is D'Ircey, who tried every party in the effort to enrich himself: he was in turn true to the *bonnet rouge*, to the Bee, the Lily, and even to the Barricades! Raymond regulated his political ideas according to the popular mind: in the time of anarchy, a socialist; but since *dévot et royaliste*, undertaking even to establish the inquisition. Abraham Strohmann is *plutôt royaliste*, and Lechat does not attend mass "puisqu'il est anticlérical, cette année." The banker uses his funds wherever they will bring him the most profit, regardless of the merit of any cause. If he is rich enough he can take an active and powerful part in overthrowing or establishing ministries. Dalincourt finds himself taken to task for offering a loan to the principality whose enemies he had once supplied with funds. His answer is, "Mon argent, voyez-vous, n'a pas d'opinion."

Although the financier attemps to acquire the titles of an old aristocracy, he rarely has any idea of abstract honor. If a debt can be evaded, it need not be paid. For instance, Charrier informs Marquis d'Auberive that the debts contracted by a wife in speculation do not have to be met, according to the law, by her husband. But the Marquis makes the noble gesture of paying his wife's debts. M. Poirier refuses to reimburse fully the Jewish creditors of his son-in-

law; he will repay only what was actually loaned; as for
the signature of Marquis de Presles, that means nothing to
him. Duelling is replaced by a lawsuit or financial revenge.
Gaudriot threatens a lawsuit against De Pyange, who has
seduced his wife and has offered reparation in a duel. And
Ledoux and Brachart wreck their rivals at the bourse.
Jean Giraud flatly refuses a duel with René, alleging that
it is beneath the dignity of his millions to condescend to
fight with the impecunious René; but the real reason is re-
vealed in the question: "Est-ce que vous croyez que je suis
assez bête pour me faire tuer par vous?" René recounts
the tale of Jean's having been slapped at the bourse, on
which occasion, instead of avenging himself with a duel,
he had the settlement of the insult carried over as one carries over a deal. When Lechat's son tells his father of a
debt of honor, the latter storms: "Honor!!? The devil
take honor! Where money is concerned there is no honor.
There is only business; and that can be arranged." This is
to be expected from a man who had ruined a friend dishon-
orably at the bourse and who refuses to consider himself
bound by anything he says: "Il n'y a de bon que ce que
j'écris." The speculator has no scruples about taking advantage of women in a financial way. Jean Giraud speculates with the funds of a woman placed in such a position
that a public scandal would have ruined her. D'Estrigaud
also uses a woman's money to pay his debts at the bourse,
and Lafontas accepts his mistress' for a speculation.

The money-play concerns itself very little with the
question of sex, as the mind of the speculator is too completely engrossed in business to consider woman anything
but secondary. Love is a pastime and very incidental: "Ça
repose des affaires," says Lechat. In respect to moral questions the modern speculator has no more scruples than had

Turcaret who, keeping his wife in the country, passed himself off as a widower and enjoyed his amours unhampered.
César Birotteau is much shocked that the financier Raguin
should countenance the fact that Du Tillet is his wife's
lover, and he remarks that a man who allows dishonor in
his household is not to be trusted in business. But César is
an exceptional homme d'affaires, being honest in all points.
The banker Verdier wishes to have his fling and courts an
opera singer.

> Seem I a creature of so little wit
> That you should think me but for figures fit?
> A dull man whose austere and arid thought
> Makes much of business and of loving naught?
>
> —*Les Aristocraties*, IV, 7

The evil brother in *Les deux Raymond* is guilty of seducing and deserting a girl of good family. Philippe de
Noras, speculator in *Le Duc Job*, consents, for a sum of
money, to save the reputation of another man's mistress by
marrying her. Montjoye refuses to marry the woman he
had betrayed, and who is to all appearances his wife, that
he may remain unhampered in his *affaires d'amour* as well
as in business. Barreau does not see fit to marry the mother of his son until he realizes that it would help his new
speculation to do so. Becque's financier Roseraye deceives
his wife. Jean Giraud brags loudly about his mistress,
thinking to raise his standing in high circles. Baron de
Thau seduced Mme d'Urth, his partner's wife, merely to
prove that there is no *honneste dame*.

In none of these cases have we a serious *grande passion*. The love affair is apart from the financier's true interests. One cannot call him moral or immoral. As for marriage, it is invariably a speculation. A dowry is the prime

object of matrimony, and no speculator remains faithful to a girl whose father has lost his money.

Viewed in relation to his family, the financier of drama is not prepossessing. He is sure to be wholly engrossed in business and usually of uncertain temper, "gloomy when he makes money, cross when he loses, and melancholy when he is doing neither," as Scribe's Coelie says of her broker brother-in-law. Or he is depicted as so obsessed with affairs and so indulgent with money that his wife and children are morally wrecked. So, in the notorious Benoîton family: father and son-in-law always at the bourse, mother and older daughter at card parties and races, Théodule a fop at school, and little six-year-old Fanfan a leader of gambling among his playmates. At a certain moment in this play Marthe is compromised, her younger sister Camille has eloped, Théodule is in prison, and Fanfan intoxicated. Equally terrible is the home circle imagined by Fabre in *L'Argent:* Reynard, a manufacturer of adulterated chocolate goods, drives his wife to a liaison with a rich banker for the sake of his support; his extravagant daughter has become involved with a lover at the instigation of her husband; his son is a ne'er-do-well; and his son-in-law a swindler. Reynard has a stroke, and his children try to secure his fortune, leaving their mother penniless. When reproached with her early liaison, she replies by threatening a suit against Reynard for adulteration of foods. A compromise is reached, and Mme Reynard is given 150,000 francs; but it is the intention of her children to cause this donation to be ultimately revoked.

The wives are either spendthrifts and flirts, pawning their jewels for their lovers, like Mme Ardan, or timid browbeaten creatures like Mme Mercadet, Mme Guérin, Mme Lebourg, and Mme Lechat, weak women in the hands of overbearing men. Henriette, the mother of Montjoye's children, states the truth baldly when she flings at the financier the accusation that she and her children and the entire world are but the instruments of his fortune or pleasure which, when weary of, he will cast aside. A daughter is a chattel to be sold to the highest bidder or exchanged for a title to satisfy a father's social ambition. Verdier tries to disguise this fact by putting his daugher on a par with princesses who must sacrifice themselves for the good of the state, the "state" being in this case Verdier's fortune. Lebourg who has made 50 million francs in copper, and blushes at his origin of tradesman, eager to shine in high society, is very exacting about his wife's etiquette and forces his daughter to marry a count whom she does not love. When Lebourg discovers that his daughter has taken a lover, he is pitiless to wife and daughter, but covers up the scandal for his own sake. Isidore Lechat is exceptionally cruel: he tortures animals, is harsh to all who come near him except his overindulged son; and his daughter says bitterly that she is merely "fluctuating stock."

A financier's son is apt to be ruined by indulgence and encouraged to make a display of wealth as an advertisement for his father. Ardan's sons enjoy themselves in the coarsest fashion without any refinement in their pleasures, and young Lechat is a rake.

The financier of drama hopes by inordinate display to make his entry, though a disputed one, into the ranks of the aristocracy. The parvenu is inextricably blended with the speculator, but in most of the plays of finance the interest in the man as a parvenu is incidental. Many of the crass traits of the modern *nouveau riche* closely resemble those of Turcaret. Scribe's Dorbeval praises the magnificence of his salon, which is gilded from top to bottom, and his own taste in arranging it, and names the cost: "C'est d'un goût exquis: de la dorure du haut en bas." These lines read like a quotation from the lips of Turcaret, who, telling his mistress the price of his gifts to her, adds, "Ils sont d'un goût exquis; je les ai choisis moi-même." Bourville in *La Manie de briller* gives as a birthday present to his wife his own bust done in biscuit. He surrounds himself with books, though everyone knows that his library is but a *meuble de parade* like that of Saurin's parvenu Géronte. Verdier of *Les Aristocraties* is so jubilant over his wealth and acquired nobility that he decorates with his new escutcheon the carriage that bears him to the bourse. Poirier is probably the most familiar parvenu of the modern stage, with his big *hôtel*, his aristocratic and expensive son-in-law, his hankering for the peerage, and his execrable taste. His idea of a good picture, as everyone will remember, is a dog barking over a sailor's hat which has been washed ashore—"C'est simple et touchant"; and his notion of furthering the arts is to let all artists starve, the lazy dissolute fellows! It is delightful to hear Poirier roll upon his tongue the delicious title "baron." Baron Peartree! Isidore Lechat pushes his love of the aristocracy to the point of naming each room of his château for a French king.

Society resists the financial intruder less as money becomes more powerful. Ardan, the parvenu of Donnay's *La Douloureuse*, has made a dishonest fortune and yet is received everywhere. Is he happy? queries one of the characters, noting Ardan's manner of walking with his hands in his pockets, his thick neck sunk between his shoulders, and his shifty eyes. Though he may not have conscience enough to feel the scorn with which he is regarded, he at least shows embarrassment. Vogt, one of the blackest scoundrels of drama, whom we met playing fast and loose with the republics of Quesitado and Equatoria, the beginnings of whose fortune lie in a dark *histoire de bourse,* who does not hesitate at bribery, theft, murder, and war to gain his ends, is everywhere received with his sister in society, because they are rich, or seem to be, because they entertain well, and because for some years doubtful persons have been in style.

An important parvenu problem of the Third Republic is the influx of the Jewish financiers. They were powerful in French finance by the forties, as Toussenel points out, showing them already in control of railroads and canals, regulating the money market, and directing the press, for many of the Saint-Simonians were Jews. But the great Israelite speculator is not introduced into drama until Feydeau brings on his Silberstein in 1861. In recounting the lives of the Péreire brothers, Hippolyte Castille explains the success of the Jews in finance as due to their superior daring. The Christian must see and touch before he can believe, while the Israelite is capable of both prudence and audacity at the same time.

The banker, Baron de Horn, of Lavedan's *Le Prince d'Aurec,* represents the old-fashioned Jewish usurer who has "put on gloves" and entered the drawing-room of a prince, to whose wife he lends money with the *arrière pensée* of seducing her. Horn is a suave gentleman in perfect control of his temper, swallowing insults for the sake of ultimately satisfying his desires and ambition. He is thoroughly conscious of the contempt and fear in which he is held by reason of his millions, which have unlocked private doors to him though the social club to which he aspires remains closed.

The problem of a marriage between an Israelite financier and a daughter of ruined nobility is treated in Guinon's

Décadence. The modern parvenu, says Marquis de Cherance, is the *juif-gentilhomme;* and Abraham Strohmann, to
whom he refers in particular, is straightway given the sou-
briquet of Jourdain-Strohmann. Jeannine, daughter of the
decadent Duc de Barfleur, says of the Strohmanns, to
whom scant courtesy has been shown, that they may as
well wait awhile as they are used to it, having been waiting
since the time of Moses; but Cherance replies that since
1870 they have been "catching up" very fast. And he
grumbles at the Jews for having no other country than
their counters and no countrymen but their shareholders.
Both Abraham and his son Nathan have a bad repute in
business and are known to make use of a strawman, Nie-
derclauss, for their anomalous business deals. They are
both immensely wealthy, and both wear the rosette. Jeannine laughs at their sumptuous residence in which the furniture and hangings are in deplorable taste, "Ce n'est pas
un salon, c'est un mémoire de tapissier." To this Mme de
Luçon agrees, admitting that there is perhaps too much
gold displayed even for a financier. Poor Abraham feels
the vulgarity of his unhappy name of Strohmann, but Nathan has determined to make the haughty and extravagant
Jeannine wear the name, and he succeeds by buying up her
father's debts and offering her either marriage or disgrace.
When, after the marriage, she tries to elope with Duc de
Cherance, Nathan draws her back with the glitter of his
wealth.

Bernstein in *Israël*, recalling the Dreyfus affair, sets a
pack of young society men barking at the heels of the inof-
fensive but, unfortunately anti-clerical, Gutlieb whom the
young men, under the leadership of Thibault de Croucy,
Prince de Clar, determine to hound out of the club as part
of their crusade against the moneyed aristocracy. Thi-

bault's uncle defends the persecuted race, declaring that the old aristocracy long ago died out of public life, that there exist now but the bourgeois and the proletariat, and that, against the latter, Jewish finance is an important defense. No, says the hot-headed Thibault, France must sacrifice the wealth of these Israelites if she is ever to establish a harmonious society, which can never be done while they are present. Here the dramatist drops the social question to develop the personal tragedy of Thibault, who discovers himself to be the illegitimate son of the man he is persecuting.

To deal further with the parvenu would lead us too far afield, as the interest in the accumulation of wealth is here superseded by the ever recurrent social problem of adjustment between wealth of long standing and newly acquired millions.

Among the sons of Turcaret are a few who, though unmistakably of the same family, have been endowed by master dramatists with more than the usual share of personality. No financier of the stage is more skilfully depicted than Teissier, the blackest raven of *Les Corbeaux*. Teissier's very name is surrounded by the atmosphere of loathing and fear that attends his repulsive person when he slinks into Mme Vigneron's drawing-room, shifty-eyed and watchful, afraid to trust his hat out of his sight, ill at ease in the presence of confidence and affection. In the corner he seems to crouch, waiting for his prey. He forces the nefarious lawyer Bourdon to be his accomplice in the swindling of the Vigneron family; buys up the silence of the dead Vigneron's contractor, who could have given information as to property values; forces the only son, Gaston Vigneron, to enlist in the army by threatening him with prosecution for a forged check; and reduces the widow and her three girls to absolute dependence on himself. The business trickery is clear enough to all but the untrained eyes of the women who, though semiconscious of his perfidy, are unable to escape from the net of intrigue he so swiftly spreads over them and their inheritance. This is in the form of shares in a factory which, as partner of the deceased, according to the Code (which Teissier carries about with him), Teissier had a right to sell and in real estate on which M. Vigneron was having buildings put up, paying for them by mortgages. It takes no great effort to harass the widow into a sale greatly to the profit of Teissier who pays but half the real value of the land. With the help of the lawyer, Teissier sees to it that Mme Vigneron has not even ready money enough to pay her inheritance tax, so that she, who should have had a small fortune, is reduced to penury.

Teissier, too stingy to pay a servant, and too old to live much longer alone, finds the practical and charming twenty-year-old Marie Vigneron very attractive. In spite of his sixty-odd years, he is still able to distinguish "la brune d'avec la blonde." He invites Marie and her family to visit him, stipulating that they have lunch before leaving home and return home in time for dinner. He assures Marie that he is not afraid to entertain her and her sisters, as they are no longer children and will, he feels sure, spoil nothing in his house. Too vulgar to realize the possible effect of his proposal, he hints that Marie come and live with him, half promising to marry her some day. When Marie is driven by the abject poverty of her family to accept the offer of marriage which Teissier finally makes to her, she inquires of Bourdon if Teissier is *un honnête homme*. Bourdon, mistaking her meaning, hastens to warn her not to trust her fiancé's word but to make sure of his money in the marriage contract. As to his money being tainted, it is no more so

than most people's money. By marrying him, Marie will
but make a bargain, or, to be more polite, a "speculation,"
for marriage is nothing but a business matter anyway.
Teissier is so genuinely a rogue that he is unconscious of
the hypocrisy of his protection when he says to his betrothed, after she has been presented with a false bill by
one of her dead father's creditors, "Vous êtes entourées de
fripons, mon enfant, depuis la mort de votre père."

Teissier is very like Augier's Maître Guérin, who,
though educated and physically less repulsive, attempts to
rob a childish old inventor and his daughter of their château by an underhand trick which would have put him in
possession of the property at two-thirds of its real value.
But Guérin works more slowly than Teissier, and his son
has time to rescue the victims. Alfred Capus describes
Guérin as a bird of prey which watches its victim, trying
to tame it, and lets it escape; whereas Becque's business
man belongs to another epoch, having the coldness and cal-
culation of the twentieth-century swindlers. He is swift,
and his prey never escapes. Canny Maître Guérin, who
knows the difference between a *billet fictif* and a *contre-
lettre,* is one of Augier's finest creations. He is a tyrant
over his wife and son, crafty and yet fairly good-natured,
mingling Latin quotations with his hard bargains. Lemaître finds him admirably conceived: "Maître Guérin is indeed a living character; he lives fully, frankly, richly, brilliantly. He is good to behold. He is so lifelike that one
cannot call him hateful, for no matter what he does we get
the impression that he is doing it because of his physical
and moral makeup and that he could not help doing it."

Although Capus has not the fondness for big speculations and dramatic financial catastrophes such as Paul
Adam and Emile Fabre delight in, he has drawn an amus-

ing gallery of swindlers as individual as Teissier and Guérin though less complete, who fill his plays with the jargon
of the bourse and the excitement of mushroom fortunes.
The crook Limeray does not like the noisy sport of hunting, preferring to wait silently for his victim and land him
with a sure jerk of the line. Perhaps he likes fishing so
much because it reminds him of his business methods. Fat
Brassac, nicknamed Bébé, is full of *bonhomie*. He introduces himself as "le financier sympathique, bon enfant et
très parisien." He uses the familiar *tu* with three thousand
persons—friends and enemies alike. In fact, his acquaintance is so numerous that he has to go along the street with
his hand outstretched to receive the friendly hand shakes.
He even invents special sandwiches for his clientèle. Poor
five years ago, he is now driving a car, directing a bank,
manipulating irons in a dozen affairs, charming his clients
who are the choicest cocottes in Paris, trying to get into a
fashionable club, using dishonest means in his enterprises,
but sure that he not only has but merits the confidence of
everyone. M. Piégois, though an adventurer and a homme
d'affaires, is at heart unspoiled. After studying medicine,
he drifted for ten years, founded several sport papers, and
finally made his fortune by directing a casino. He is kind,
honorable, shrewd, proud, and generous, risking ten times
his fortune to save the financier into whose traps he had
been too keen to fall. Piégois does not wish a limitless fortune: "Tout homme est capable d'absorber une quantité
d'argent déterminée; s'il la dépasse, il est étouffé infailli-
blement." Luck, says he also, is but unconscious theft, and
the man who is too lucky is sure to be pinched some day.
M. Doumic considers Piégois, *chevalier d'industrie* and
hero at the same time, "the most inconsistent puppet created by the caprice of M. Capus." But, if M. Bordeaux

has rightly interpreted Capus, he is a pessimist considering all things a matter of chance in this unstable modern society of ours, which is like a gambling house; and there, where chance rules, it is not disconcerting to find a confidence man heroic.

All fundamental characteristics considered—will power, bouyant courage, unscrupulousness, unity of purpose—there is little difference in the financiers of late drama and the hated tax-collector of Louis XIV's reign. Turcaret's sons have had, thanks to great economic developments, a much wider scope for their activities and have in consequence become shrewder men less likely to be duped themselves. Confronted by an audience better versed in business, they are more at liberty, become expansive, and talk shop freely. They seem in a sense bigger than Turcaret, because their swindles are on a so much larger scale. What with newspaper advertising and the improved means of communication afforded by the railroad, steamboat, telegraph, and telephone, they reach thousands of clients, where Turcaret reached a handful. Turcaret, working in the limited field of the French tax-farming system, is a national character; whereas the modern speculator, engaged in the same pursuits as other speculators in England, Germany, Italy, and America, with whom he is in contact, has become an international figure.

CHAPTER XI

MONEY-PLAYS OLD AND NEW

L'argent craint moins de se dissimuler, puissance formidable qui se fardait jadis de quelque apprêt, se masquait de grands mots, et se découvre aujourd'hui, impitoyable et vengeresse.—LÉON SÉCHÉ, *L'Evolution du Théâtre contemporain* (1908), p. 239.

THE audience which attended *Turcaret* in 1709 was delighted to see its enemy the financier worsted, delighted to see ridiculed the ignorance, the immorality, and the unjust fortune of this oppressor of the people. A century and a half later a French audience watches with eager sympathy and intelligent understanding the desperate financial struggles of Mercadet. The audience has learned much since the days of the tax-collectors. Modern enterprise has put wealth within the reach of all; and everyone present is engaged in making a fortune, each with problems like Mercadet's to meet, needing to gain time, to deceive creditors, to persuade the public to take stock in his undertakings. Each auditor understands this imagination which conceives millions and this jaunty insolence which comes of close contact with the general stupidity of mankind. This audience has had a taste of wealth and is insatiable for more. It is like the negro of the Soudan. He needs nothing; give him a shirt, and he will be happy. By no means, objects the psychologist, give him a shirt and he will want to have his picture taken. A competence begins to look like poverty; and countless sacrifices of honor, honesty, and happiness are laid on the altar of the god Million.

An audience personally interested in money-making demands financial realism on the stage. It must be told in just what sort of an enterprise a speculator is engaged, why he fails, and how he succeeds. We find the stage representing scenes that would have been hissed or but coldly tolerated a century earlier: the interior of a shop with clerks selling goods; a factory cluttered up with the models of an inventor; a mine where workmen pass to and fro about their business to the sound of steam-driven machinery; the luxurious office of a fraudulent promoter where the audience may hear the details of a swindle only too like some in which it has made or lost money; and the magic bourse where fortunes are won and lost in a single day. As the making of money has passed out of the hands of a comparatively few into the grasp of the masses, so crowds invade the stage of the money-play: shoppers, factory hands, miners, and the more interesting groups of stockholders and speculators at the bourse. Pierrot and Scaramouche, in their long black cloaks and crêpe-banded hats, mourning for their money, give place to the anxious creditors who fill the fourth act of *Duhautcours*. Out of this modest creditor group develops one hundred years or so later the great scene of the irate stockholders who besiege and enter the private offices of the Nouvelle Afrique.

There is now heard on the stage much more frequently than in the past the clink of coins and the crackle of banknotes; interest and stock exchange profits are calculated before the spectators; stockbrokers run about scribbling in their little notebooks, hurling forth the latest market quotations and prophesying the probable rise and fall of stock. Robert Macaire passes an *acte de société* around for his stockholders to sign, and the account books of a bankrupt are studied on the stage. Vernières faces his angry partners with his back to the safe which contains the papers testifying to their culpability, and old Matignon keeps under his hand the incriminating contract with which he can force his son to do his bidding.

Drama has materially increased its business jargon also. To the few terms dealing with bankruptcy and the discounting of paper money passed down from the early farces have been added the vocabulary of the bourse, the names applied to brokers and stock-jobbers, the precise terms describing their activities, and the names of stocks on the market. The very names of the characters, are, often, as we have seen, drawn from the terminology of finance; and the plays in which they figure bear in their titles some indication of the world of money. And not infrequently these speculators express their wit in puns on *actions* and *fin courant*.

It is true that all the essential elements of these modern and highly developed money-plays are present in Dancourt's *Les Agioteurs:* the theme of speculation, the milieu, the infamous swindlers, and their activities. But the milieu has widened from a Paris bucket-shop to the markets of the world; the rogue is now a banker or a promoter who victimizes hundreds of people by a glowing advertisement or a false prospectus: and speculation has come to include the exploitation of manufactured and natural products the world over. The unassuming financial vaudeville seems to be caught up in the tremendous industrial growth of France and increases proportionately to accommodate the swiftly growing importance of money.

The attitude of the dramatist toward the homme d'affaires fluctuates with public opinion. Under Louis XIV, when everyone expected the financier to be a scamp, he was so depicted by the authors of farces and light comedies.

A century later, the business man having acquired education and having become more gentlemanly, public opinion softened somewhat toward him; and Sedaine and Beaumarchais in their bourgeois dramas represent these men in a very kindly light. During the storm of 1789 the stage financier was almost lost sight of, but he reappeared most actively when the New Régime had settled down into commercial life. Then Picard and Scribe in their comedies and vaudevilles gave him most flattering attention, for he bid fair to become an important figure financially, politically, and socially. When the great excitement over speculation grew feverish under Louis Philippe, the interests of the speculator were echoed by the popular vaudevillists of the day. These do not moralize; they are content to represent the cheerful roguery of a Piffart or the cynical *blague* of a Robert Macaire. Although these character sketches are not profound, they are *pris sur le vif;* and the author does not make the mistake of reforming a born rogue. He makes a Brûlot, for instance, pat his pocket-book when his dishonesty has been discovered, and say: "Well, well! I have lost my partner and my fiancée; but as long as *this* is intact a speculator is easily consoled!"

With the *coup d'état* of February the favor of the public veered away from the shameless representation of rascality which it had so applauded in *Les Saltimbanques.* The stage began to moralize again, and the Ecole du Bon Sens, arose. Public opinion approved of the sermonizing of Ponsard's *La Bourse* and the niceties of Feuillet's *Montjoye* and the condemnation pronounced by Augier against the homme d'affaires. The changed attitude is strikingly evident in *Monsieur Gogo à la Bourse,* of 1838, and *Monsieur Gogo,* of 1859. By the time the second of these plays was written, the craze over new inventions and the progress

of industry had lessened, France had begun to frown upon
Robert Macaire and his ilk, and was weary of seeing honest, trusting souls cheated. Monsieur Gogo is no more the
beaming, gullible, amusing, likable fool of the thirties, but
has changed into a venerable *terre à terre* bourgeois who
suddenly develops the astuteness of a rogue and outwits the
villains who endeavor to filch his money. Gogo then reads
the swindler Boursicoff a little lecture incorporating the
sentiments of France of the fifties: "Don't be forever making fun of these good Parisian bourgeois who haven't your
air and your ways! The worm turns occasionally. It is all
right to laugh, but never at the expense of honor and honesty." It is patent enough from Gogo's sermon that morality now has, temporarily, at least, the center of the stage. It
is, in a way, a protest against ever increasing materialism
which men of letters hoped to stem by praising virtue. Their
financiers, therefore, converted by their children, develop
consciences after years of dishonesty, and reform and make
restitution. It must be admitted, however, that fortunes
continue to drop from heaven and a marriage is always
blessed by a rich dowry. Augier fills his whole theater with
a protest against money: "There where he would paint virtue he is perfect only in painting vice." It becomes a fad to
harp on the money question, and every author wished to
have a voice in condemning speculation.

Society changes much with the Third Republic. Finance and politics have united, and money is more truly
than ever the ruling power in France. The financier fuses
with the politician into a social being, breaking down a caste
distinction just as by his cosmopolitanism "he is preparing
the way from nationalism to humanitarian international-
ism." Money walks boldly forward, and millionaires establish themselves socially. The ambitious parvenus of the

Second Empire become ministers. With the aid of politics, of constantly developing industry and ever more astounding inventions, the amassing of tremendous fortunes becomes one of the chief interests of the present day. Drama no longer moralizes, but represents with documentary exactness the vast swindles of her financiers. The time has passed in which a financier of the stage reforms. Neither need he escape to Belgium. By political pull he shifts responsibility for his disastrous failures and, with the unabated confidence of a Mercadet and with better chance of success, undertakes a new enterprise.

My dear sir, since the public is so stupid,
let's fleece it

BIBLIOGRAPHY

PART I. PLAYS

This list is chronologically arranged according to the date of production. Information concerning each play is given as follows: year of first performance (or of publication when play was not produced); title; description; author(s); theater and date of *la première* where possible; publisher. Roman numeral following name of author indicates volume of collected works (see "Oeuvres") in which the play occurs. Collections of plays are added in parentheses. Paris is the place of publication, and the date of production and publication coincide, unless otherwise indicated.

ABBREVIATIONS

THEATERS

Amb.-Com.:	Ambigu-Comique	Pte. St.-A.:	Porte Saint-Antoine
Dél.-Com.:	Délassements-	Pte. St.-M.:	Porte Saint-Martin
	Comiques	Renais.:	Renaissance
Fol.-Dram.:	Folies-Dramatiques	Th.-Fr.:	Théâtre-Français
Gymn.:	Gymnase	Th. du Vaud.:	Théâtre du Vaude-
Imp.:	Impératrice		ville
Pal.-Royal:	Palais-Royal	Var.:	Variétés
Pan.:	Panorama	Var.-Pan.:	Variétés-Panorama

TYPES OF PLAYS, ETC.

a.:	*acte*	Livr.Th.:	Librairie Théâtrale
com.:	*comédie*	livr.:	*livraison*
dr.:	*drame*	mélo.:	*mélodrame*
fol.:	*folie*	p.:	*pièce*
Ill.:	*Illustration*	tab.:	*tableau*
impr.:	*imprimerie*	v.:	*vers*
libr.:	*librairie*	vaud.:	*vaudeville*

COLLECTIONS OF PLAYS

Chefs-d'oeuvre du théâtre moderne
La France dramatique au XIXe siècle (Fr. dram.)
Magasin théâtral (Mag. th.)

239

Magasin théâtral illustré (Mag. th. illus.)
Musée dramatique (Mus. dram.)
Pièces de Théâtre
Répertoire général du Théâtre-Français (R.G.)
Théâtre contemporain illustré (Th. cont. illus.)
Théâtre moderne

LIST OF PLAYS

1661 *Les Fâcheux.* Com. 1 a., v. Molière. Vaux, Aug. Pal.-Royal, Nov. 4. (R.G., XIX.)

1662 *Le Riche mécontent ou le Noble imaginaire.* Com. 5 a., v. Chappuzeau. Hôtel de Bourgogne. (Cf. Frères Parfaict, *Histoire du Théâtre-François,* IX, 91 ff.)

1668 *L'Avare.* Com. 5 a. Molière. Pal.-Royal, Sept. 9. (R.G., XXI.)

1671 *La Comtesse d'Escarbagnas.* Com. 1 a. Molière. St. Germain, Dec. (R.G., XXIII.)

1682 *La Rapinière ou l'Intéressé.* Com. 5 a., v. Jacques Robbe. Th.-Fr., Dec. 4. (Cf. Frères Parfaict, *op. cit.,* XII, 338 ff.)

1683 *Le Mercure Galant ou la Comédie sans titre.* Com. 5 a., v. Boursault. Th.-Fr., Mar. 5. (R.G., XXXVII.)

1685 *L'Usurier.* Com. 5 a. De Visé. Th.-Fr., Feb. 13. (Cf. Frères Parfaict, *op. cit.,* XII, 457 ff.)

Les Façons du Temps. Com. 5 a. M. de Saintyon. Th.-Fr., Dec. 3. (Published in Holland, 1696, as *Les Moeurs du Temps,* by M. de Palprat. Cf. Frères Parfaict, *op. cit.,* XII, 491.)

1686 *La Coquette et la fausse Prude.* Com. 5 a., v. Baron Th.-Fr., Dec. 18. (R.G., LVI.)

1687 *Le Banqueroutier.* Com. 3 a. Noland de Fatouville. Th.-Italien, Apr. 19. (Ghérardi, *Le Théâtre-Italien* [Amsterdam, Michel Charles le Cene, 1721], Vol. I.)

La Désolation des Joueuses. Com. 1 a. Dancourt (IX). Th.-Fr., Aug. 23.

Le Chevalier à la mode. Com. 5 a. Dancourt (I). Th.-Fr., Oct. 24.

1690 *L'Eté des Coquettes.* Com. 1 a. Dancourt (I). Th.-Fr., July 12.

1695 *Le Tuteur.* Com. 1 a. Dancourt (III). Th.-Fr., July 13.

1696 *Le Joueur.* Com. 5 a., v. Regnard. Th.-Fr., Dec. 19. (R.G., XXIV.)

1697 *La Loterie*. Com. 1 a. Dancourt (IV). Th.-Fr., July 10.
Le Retour de Officiers. Com. 1 a. Dancourt (IV). Th.-Fr.,
Oct. 19.

1699 *Le vert Galant*. Com. 1 a. Dancourt (IX). Th.-Fr., Dec. 18.

1701 *Esope à la Cour*. Com-héroique. 5 a., v. Boursault. Th.-Fr.,
Dec. 16. (R.G., XXXVII.)

1706 *La Joueuse*. Com. 5 a. Dufresny (II). Th.-Fr., Oct. 22.

1707 *Le second Chapitre du Diable Boiteux*. Com. 2 a., prologue.
Dancourt (VI). Th.-Fr., Oct. 20.

1708 *La Critique du Légataire universel*. Com. 1 a. Regnard. Th.-
Fr., Feb. 19. (R.G., XXVI.)

1709 *Turcaret*. Com. 5 a. Lesage. Th.-Fr., Feb. 14. (R.G., LVIII.)

1710 *Les Agioteurs*. Com. 3 a. Dancourt (VII). Th.-Fr., Sept. 26.

1728 *Le Triomphe de Plutus*. Com. 1 a. Marivaux (I). Th.-Italien,
Apr. 22.

1760 *Les Moeurs du Temps*. Com. 1 a. Saurin. Th.-Fr., Dec. 22.
(R.G., LXIII.)

1764 *La jeune Indienne*. Com. 1 a., v. Chamfort. Th.-Fr., Apr. 30.
(R.G., XII.)

1765 *Le Philosophe sans le savoir*. Com. 5 a. Sedaine. Th.-Fr.,
Dec. 2.

1770 *Les deux Amis, ou le Négociant de Lyon*. Dr. 5 a. Beaumarchais (I). Th.-Fr., Jan. 13.

1771 *Le Fabricant de Londres*. Dr. 5 a. Falbaire de Quingey (II).
Th.-Fr., Jan. 12.

1773 *L'Indigent*. Dr. 4 a. Mercier (III). Dijon, 1773. Th.-Italien,
Nov. 22, 1782.

1776 *La Brouette du Vinaigrier*. Dr. 3 a. Mercier (III). Th. des
Associés. Th.-Italien, Oct. 13, 1784.

1789 *Les Modernes enrichis*. Com. 3 a., v. Pujoulx. Th. de la République, Dec. 16.

1795 *L'Agioteur*. Com. 1 a., v. Charlemagne. Th. de la République,
Oct. 30.

1800 *Les Moeurs du Jour, ou le bon Frère*. Com. 5 a., v. Collin
d'Harleville (III). Th. de la République, July 27.

1801 *Duchautcours, ou le Contrat d'union*. Com. 5 a. Picard (III)
and Chéron. Th.-Louvois, Aug. 6.

1803 *Le pauvre Riche, ou la Séparation de biens.* Com. 3 a. Ch. G.
Etienne. (Not played.)

1806 *La Manie de briller.* Com. 3 a. Picard (V). Th. de l'Imp.,
Sept. 23.

1810 *Les deux Gendres.* Com. 5 a., v. Ch. G. Etienne. Th.-Fr., Aug.
11. Le Normant, 1811.

1816 *Le Bateau à vapeur.* Vaud. 1 a. Henri Simon, Carmouche, Cot-
tenet, and Rozet. Pte. St.-M., May 8. Huet.
Les Montagnes russes, ou le Temple à la mode. Vaud. 1 a.
Scribe (V*a*). Poirson and Dupin. Th. du Vaud., Oct. 31.

1817 *Le Combat des Montagnes, ou la Folie-Beaujon.* Folie-vaud.
1 a. Scribe (III*a*) and Dupin. Var., July 12.
Le Café des Variétés. Epilogue en vaud. Scribe (III*a*) and
Dupin. Var., Aug. 5.

1819 *Le Fou de Péronne.* Com.-vaud. 1 a. Scribe (IV*a*) and Dupin.
Th. du Vaud., Jan. 18.

1820 *L'Ennui, ou le Comte Derfort.* Com.-vaud. 2 a. Scribe (VI*a*),
Dupin, and Mélesville. Var., Feb. 2.

1821 *Le Voyage à Dieppe.* Com. 3 a. Wafflard and Fulgence. Odéon., Mar. 1. Barba.
Les Joueurs, ou la Hausse et la Baisse. Com.-vaud. 1 a. Moreau, Lafortelle, and Francis. Var., Aug. 18. Barba.
Un Jeu de Bourse, ou la Bascule. Com. 1 a. Picard, Wafflard,
and Fulgence. Gymn. Barba.

1823 *Le Plan de Campagne.* Com.-vaud. 1 a. Scribe (X*a*), Dupin,
and Mélesville. Gymn., Apr. 14.
L'Avare en goguettes. Com.-vaud. 1 a. Scribe (XII*a*) and Delavigne. Gymn., July 12.
Le Fabricant, ou la Filature. Com.-vaud. 1 a. Francis and Brazier. Var., Oct. 29. Bezon.

1824 *Les Adieux au Comptoir.* Com.-vaud. 1 a. Scribe (XIII*a*) and
Mélesville. Gymn., Aug. 9.
L'Enfant trouvé. Com. 3 a. Picard and Mazères. Odéon. Bar-
ba, 1825.

1825 *Le Roman.* Com. 5 a., v. M. de la Ville de Mirmont. Th.-Fr.,
June 22. Barba.
Les Entrepreneurs. Com.-vaud. 1 a. Brazier, Dumersan (XI),
and Gabriel. Var., Aug. 16.

1826 *Le Capitaliste malgré lui.* Com.-vaud. 1 a. D'Artois and Saintine. Var., Mar. 10. Barba.

Le Banqueroutier. Mélo. 3 a. Nezel, Overnay, Berrier, and Brahain-Ducange. Gaîté, Apr. 29. Pollet.

L'Anonyme. Com.-vaud. 2 a. Dupeuty, de Villeneuve, and Joslin de la Salle. Th. du Vaud., May 29. Bezou. (Pièces de Théâtre.)

Le Spéculateur. Com. 5 a., v. F. L. Riboutté. Th.-Fr., June 24. Vente.

L'Agiotage, ou le Métier à la mode. Com. 5 a. Picard and Empis. Th.-Fr., July 25. Béchet aîné et Cie.

La Fin du Mois. Com.-vaud. 1 a. Mazères. Madame, Aug. 26. Quoy.

L'Argent. Com. 5 a., v. Casimir Bonjour (I). Th.-Fr., Oct. 12.

Paris et Bruxelles, ou le Chemin à la mode. Com.-vaud., 2 a. Théaulon, Etienne, and Gondelier. Var., Dec. 4. Barba.

1827 *Les Passages et les Rues.* Vaud. 1 a. Brazier, Gabriel, and Dumersan (XI). Var., Mar. 7.

Les trois Quartiers. Com. 3 a. Picard and Mazères. Odéon, May 31. Barba.

Riche et Pauvre. Com. 1 a. Picard. Madame, Sept. 7. Barba.

Le Mariage d'Argent. Com. 5 a. Scribe (I*b*). Th.-Fr., Dec. 3.

1829 *Les Rouliers, ou la Route de Bruxelles.* Vaud. 1 a. Dumersan (XIII) and Gabriel. Th. du Vaud., May 21.

Les deux Raymond, ou les nouveaux Ménechmes. Mélo. 5 a. Ducange, Brisset, and Ruben. Pte. St.-M., Aug. 27. Quoy.

Les Actionnaires. Com.-vaud. 1 a. Scribe (XIX*a*) and Bayard. Madame, Oct. 22.

1831 *Les Saltimbanques.* Com.-parade. 3 a., with verses. Dumersan and Varin. Var., Jan. 25. Stock, 1859.

Naissance, Fortune et Mérite. Com. 3 a. Bonjour (I). Th.-Fr., May 13.

Encore un Préjugé, ou les deux Eligibles. Com.-vaud. 1 a. Saint-Hilaire, Brunswick, and Thérie. Pte. St.-M., July 2. Riga.

1832 *Louis-Bronze et le Saint-Simonien.* Com.-vaud. 3 a. Vander-Burch and Langlé. Pal.-Royal, Feb. 27. Barba.

Les Chemins en fer. Vaud. 1 a. Arago and Alhoy. Th. du Vaud., Dec. 31. Barba, 1833.

1833 *Le Voyage dans l'Appartement, ou l'Influence des Localités.*
Com.-vaud. 5 tab. Scribe (XXV*a*) and Duport. Var., Jan. 18.
L'Escroc du grand monde. Com. 3 a., with songs. J. Ancelot
(I). Th. du Vaud., Apr. 10.
Les Actualités. Vaud. 1 a. Dumersan (XII) and Brazier. Var.,
Sept. 5.

1834 *Le Brigand et le Philosophe.* Mélo. 5 a. Pyat and Luchet. Pte.
St.-M., Feb. 22. Duvernois.
La Passion secrète. Com. 3 a. Scribe (III*a*). Th.-Fr., Mar. 13.
Le Facteur, ou la Justice des hommes. Mélo. 5 a. Desnoyers,
Boulé, and Pothier. Amb.-Com., Dec. 9. Barba, 1838. (Fr.
dram.)
Robert Macaire. Vaud. 4 a., 6 tab. Saint-Amand, Antier, Paulyanthe, and Frédérick Lemaître. Fol.-Dram., June 14. Barba,
1835. (*Robert Macaire,* précédé de l'*Auberge des Adrets,* re-
manié par MM. P. Gille et W. Busnach. Pte. St.-M., Mar. 1,
1889. Stock, 1910.)

1836 *Le Diable à Paris.* Fol.-fantastique 1 a. Brazier and Gabriel.
Gaîté, Dec. 29. Nobis. (Mus. dram., I, No. 1–20.)

1837 *La Dot de Cécile.* Com.-vaud. 2 a. Gabriel and Angel. Pal.-
Royal, Oct. 30. Impr. Mervel. (Mus. dram., IV.)

1838 *César Birotteau.* Dram.-vaud. 3 a. Cormon. Pan., Apr. 4.
Impr. Mervel. (Mus. dram., IV.) (Balzac's novel was also
dramatized by Fabre in 1910.)
Monsieur Gogo à la Bourse. Vaud. 1 a., 1 tab. Bayard. Var.,
May 16. Marchant. (Mag. th., XXV.)
Le Puff, orné de Ruy-Blag. Revue 3 tab. Carmouche, Varin,
and Huart. Var., Dec. 31. Marchant. (Mag. th., XXIII–
XXIV.)

1839 *Le Comité de Bienfaisance.* Com. 1 a. Ch. Duveyrier and Jules
de Wailly. Th.-Fr., Jan. 30. Impr. Dupont. (Fr. dram.)
Industriels et Industrieux. Revue 3 tab. Desvergers, Dubourg,
and Laurencin. Gymn., June 1. Duverger. (Fr. dram.)
La France et l'Industrie. Vaud. 1 a. Tournemine and Guénée.
Pte. St.-A., June 3. Gallet.
Le Ver rongeur. Com. 3 journées, 5 a., v. M. G. Malvoisine.
Delloye. (Apparently not played.)

1840 *La Grand'mère.* Com. 3 a. Scribe (IV*b*). Gymn., March 11.
Une Assemblée de Créanciers. Vaud. 1 a. Théaulon and Lubize.
Gymn., June 2. Tresse. (Fr. dram.)
Japhet, ou la Recherche d'un Père. Com. 2 a. Scribe (IV*b*)
and Vander-Burch. Th.-Fr., July 20.
Marguerite. Com. 3 a., with verses. Mme Ancelot (II). Th.
du Vaud., Oct. 3.
1841 *Le Veau d'Or.* Com. 1 a., with verses. Scribe (XXIX*a*) and
Dupin. Gymn., Feb. 26.
Les deux Serruriers. Dr. 5 a. Pyat. Pte. St.-M., Mar. 25.
Tresse.
1842 *Les Philanthropes.* Com. 3 a., v. F. de Coucy and Th. Muret.
Odéon, Jan. 29. Tresse.
Les Ressources de Quinola. Com. 5 a., with prologue. Balzac
(XVIII). Odéon, Mar. 19.
1843 *La Tutrice, ou l'Emploi des Richesses.* Com. 3 a. Scribe (V*b*)
and Duport. Th.-Fr., Nov. 29.
1844 *Pierre le Millionnaire.* Com. 3 a., with songs. Mme Ancelot
(III). Th. du Vaud., Mar. 2.
Tout pour de l'Or. Dr. 5 a., with prologue. Dinaux (Prosper-
Parfait Goubaux) and Lesguillon. Gaîté, June 17. Tresse.
Satan, ou le Diable à Paris. Com.-vaud. 4 a., prologue, and epi-
logue. Clairville and Damarin. Th. du Vaud., July 23. Brus-
sels, J. A. Lelong.
1845 *Le Gendre d'un Millionnaire.* Com. 5 a. Léonce and Moléri.
Th.-Fr., Feb. 25. Tresse.
Le Lansquenet et les Chemins de fer. Com.-vaud. 1 a. Bayard
and Dumanoir. Gymn., May 18. Beck.
La grande Bourse et les petites Bourses. A propos vaud. 1 a.
Clairville and Faulquemont. Th. du Vaud., Oct. 31. Beck.
1846 *La Chasse aux Fripons.* Com. 3 a., v. C. Doucet. Th.-Fr., Feb.
27. Furne et Cie.
La Chasse aux Millions. Vaud. 3 a. Laurencin, M. Michel, and
L. Couailhac. Gaîté, Dec. 25. Maistrasse et Wiart, 1847.
L'Argent, ou l'Ecole des Rentiers. Com. 3 a., v. Julien Coeur.
(Not played.) Dondey-Dupré.
1847 *Une Femme qui se jette par la Fenêtre.* Com.-vaud. 1 a. Scribe
(XXXII*a*) and Lemoine. Gymn., Apr. 19.
Le Fils du Diable. Dr. 5 a. Féval and Saint-Yves. Amb.-Com.,

Aug. 24. Lévy. (Th. cont. illus., livr. 1.)

Les Aristocraties. Com. 5 a., v. E. Arago. Th.-Fr., Oct. 29.
Tresse, 1848.

1848 *Le Puff, ou Mensonge et Vérité.* Com. 5 a. Scribe (VI*b*). Th.-
Fr., Jan. 22.

O Amitié! ou les Trois Epoques. Com.-vaud. 3 a. Scribe
(XXXIII*a*) and Varner. Gymn., Nov. 14.

La Propriété c'est le Vol. Fol.-Socialiste. 3 a., 7 tab. Clairville
and Cordier. Th. du Vaud., Nov. 28. Beck, 1849.

Les Convenances d'Argent. Com. 3 a., v. D'Epagny. Odéon,
Dec. 18. Boulé.

1849 *La Sonnette du Diable.* Vaud. 5 a., 12 tab., prologue, and epi-
logue. Bourgeois and P. de Guerville. Gaîté, Sept. 18. Michel
Lévy frères. (Th. cont. illus., livr. 695.) (From *Mémoires du
Diable,* novel, by F. Soulié.)

Robert Macaire et Bertrand, ou les Suites d'un Cauchemar
Folie 1 a. J. Vizentini and A. Jouhaud. Dél.-Com., Sept. 29.
Dechaume.

1850 *Les Chercheurs d'Or du Sacramento.* Mélo. 5 a., 6 tab. M.
Fournier and P. Duplessis. Pte. St.-M., Jan. 23. Marchant.
(Mag. th., 2ᵉ série.)

Le Courrier de Lyon ou l'Attaque de la Malle-poste. Dr. 5 a.,
8 tab. Moreau, Siraudin, and Delacour. Gaîté, Mar. 16. Lévy
frères.

1851 *Monsieur Pinchard.* Com. 5 a. F. Dugué (III). Galeries St.-
Hubert Brussels, Mar. 11. Lévy frères.

Le Faiseur. Com. 5 a. Balzac (XVIII). (Written 1844. Stage
version, *Mercadet,* by D'Ennery, Libr. Th., 1851, produced at
Gymn., Aug. 24, 1851.)

1852 *Les Coulisses de la Vie.* Com.-vaud. 5 a. Dumanoir and Clairville. Pal.-Royal, May 24. Michel Lévy, 1858. (Th. cont.
illus., livr. 81.)

1853 *L'Honneur et l'Argent.* Com. 5 a., v. F. Ponsard (II). Odéon,
Mar. 11.

Les Enfers de Paris. Com. 5 a., with songs. Roger de Beauvoir
and L. Thiboust. Var., Sept. 16. Michel Lévy frères. (Th.
cont. illus., livr. 98.)

1854 *Les Oiseaux de la Rue.* Com. 3 a., 4 tab. L. Thiboust and Dela-
cour. Var., Jan. 6. Lévy frères. (Th. cont. illus., livr. 150.)
Le Gendre de Monsieur Poirier. Com. 4 a. Augier (III) and
Sandeau. Gymn., Apr. 8.

1855 *La Ceinture dorée.* Com. 3 a. Augier (III). Gymn., Feb. 3.
Un mauvais Riche, ou Bonheur passe Richesse. Dr. 5 a. E.
Serret. Th.-Fr., Apr. 27. Lévy frères. (Th. cont. illus., livr.
183.)
Par Droit de Conquête. Com. 3 a. Legouvé. Th.-Fr., June 7.
Lévy frères.

1856 *La Bourse.* Com. 5 a., v. Ponsard (II). Odéon, May 6.
La Bourse au Village. Vaud. 1 a. Clairville, Lubize, and Siraudin. Var., July 2. Libr. Nouvelle.
Les faux Bonshommes. Com. 4 a. Th. Barrière and E. Capendu. Th. du Vaud., Nov. 11. Calmann Lévy, 1893.

1857 *La Question d'Argent.* Com. 5 a. Dumas *fils* (II). Gymn.,
Jan. 31.
Le Diable d'Argent. Com. 4 a., 3 tab. Bourgeois, Brisebarre,
and Laurent. Th. Impérial du Cirque, Feb. 19. Libr. Centrale.
Avez-vous besoin d'Argent? (Parody of *La Question d'argent*).
Siraudin and Bourdois. Pal.-Royal, Mar. 21. Michel Lévy.
(Th. cont. illus., livr. 314.)

1858 *Les Lionnes pauvres.* Com. 5 a. Augier (IV). Th. du Vaud.,
May 22.
La Balançoire. Com. 1 a., with verses. Dumanoir and La-
fargue. Gymn., Aug. 2. Lévy frères. (Th. cont. illus., livr.
557.)

1859 *Le droit Chemin.* Com. 5 a., v. Latour Saint-Ybars. Odéon,
Mar. 28. Michel Lévy.
Le Testament de César Girodot. Com. 3 a. A. Belot and M.
Villetard. Odéon, Sept. 30. Barbré.
Monsieur Gogo. Com.-vaud. 5 a. Paul de Kock and F. Lemaî-
tre, *fils.* Luxembourg, Oct. 8. Barbré. (Mag. th. illus.)
Le Duc Job. Com. 4 a. Léon Laya. Th.-Fr., Nov. 4. Michel
Levy. (Chefs-d'oeuvre du théâtre moderne, I, 1873.)

1860 *Un Parvenu.* Com. 5 a., v. A. Rolland. Odéon, Mar. 1. Michel Lévy frères.

1860 *Les Femmes Fortes.* Com. 3 a. Sardou. Th. du Vaud., Dec. 31. Nouvelle éd., Michel Lévy, 1869.

1861 *Les Effrontés.* Com. 5 a. Augier (IV). Th.-Fr., Jan. 10.
Un Coup de Bourse. Com. 5 a. E. Feydeau. (Written 1861. Not played.) Michel Lévy, 1868.

1862 *Les deux Millionnaires.* Com. 4 a. F. Deschamps. Th.-Fr., Apr. 12. Rouen, Libr. Nouvelle.
Les Fous, ou la Vie à outrance. Com. 5 a. E. Plouvier. Gymn., Sept. 11. Michel Lévy. (Th. cont. illus., livr. 628.)

1863 *Montjoye.* Com. 5 a., 6 tab. Feuillet (II). Gymn., Oct. 24.

1864 *Maître Guérin.* Com. 5 a. Augier (VI). Th.-Fr., Oct. 29.

1865 *Les Parasites.* Dr. 5 a. E. Rasetti. Odéon, Oct. 2. Michel Lévy, 1866. (Théâtre moderne, II.)
La Famille Benoîton. Com. 5 a. Sardou. Th. du Vaud., Nov. 4. 25ᵉ éd. Michel Lévy, 1867.

1866 *La Maison neuve.* Com. 5 a. Sardou. Th. du Vaud., Dec. 4. Michel Lévy frères, 1873.

1867 *La Banqueroute.* Com. 2 a., v. J. Bornet. (Apparently not played.) Libr. Centrale, 1868.

1868 *Les Loups et les Agneaux, ou les Actionnaires grugés par les Hommes d'affaires.* Com. 5 a. H. Crisafulli and L. Stapleaux. Th. du Vaud., Apr. 20. Libr. Internationale.
La Parvenue. Com. 4 a. H. Rivière. Th.-Fr., Aug. 30. Michel Lévy frères.

1870 *Michel Pauper.* Com. 5 a., 7 tab. H. Becque (I). Pte. St.-M., June 17.

1873 *L'Oncle Sam.* Com. 4 a. Sardou. Th. du Vaud., Nov. 6. Calmann Lévy, 1883.

1879 *Les Tapageurs.* Com. 3 a. Gondinet (V). Th. du Vaud., Apr. 19.

1882 *Les Corbeaux.* P. 4 a. Becque (II). Th.-Fr., Sept. 14.
Le Roman parisien. P. 5 a. Feuillet (IV). Gymn.-Dram. Oct. 28.

1892 *Le Prince d'Aurec.* Com. 3 a. Lavedan. Th. du Vaud. June 1, Calmann Lévy, 1894.

1893 *L'Argent d'Autrui.* P. 5 a. Léon Hennique. Odéon, Feb. 9. Tresse and Stock, 1894.
Le Cuivre. P. 3 a. Paul Adam and André Picard. Com.-Parisienne, Dec. 16. Ollendorf, 1896.

1893 *Les Polichinelles.* P. 4 a. (Unfinished.) Becque (IV). (MS published by Henri de Noussanne, Imprimerie de l'Illustration, 1910 as well as a four-act play drawn from the MS.)

1894 *Brignol et sa Fille.* Com. 3 a. Capus (I). Th. du Vaud., Nov. 23.

1895 *L'Argent.* Com. 4 a. Fabre (I). Th.-Libre, May 6. Stock.

1897 *La Douloureuse.* Com. 4 a. Donnay (II). Th. du Vaud., Feb. 12.

1900 *La Bourse ou la Vie.* Com. 4 a. Capus (II). Gymn., Dec. 4.

1903 *L'Adversaire.* Com. 3 a. Capus (IV). Renais., Oct. 23.
Les Affaires sont les Affaires. P. 3 a. Octave Mirbeau (I). Th.-Fr., Apr. 20.

1904 *Décadence.* Com. 4 a. Albert Guinon. Th. du Vaud., Feb. 18. Libr. Th., 1901.

1905 *Les Ventres dorés.* P. 5 a. Fabre (II). Odéon, Mar. 4.
Monsieur Piégois. Com. 3 a. Capus (IV). Renais., Apr. 5.
La Rafale. P. 3 a. Bernstein. Gymn., Oct. 20, Fasquelle, 1906.

1907 *Samson.* P. 4 a. Bernstein. Renais., Nov. 6. Libr. Th., 1908.

1908 *Qui Perd Gagne.* P. 4 a. Capus (VI). Réjane, Mar. 14.
Israël. P. 3 a. Bernstein. Réjane, Oct. 3. Fasquelle, 1909.
Les Vainqueurs. P. 4 a. Fabre. Antoine, Nov. 25. Calmann Lévy, 1909.

1911 *Après moi.* P. 3 a. Bernstein. Th.-Fr., Feb. 20. Fayard.
Les Sauterelles. P. 5 a. Fabre. Th. du Vaud., Dec. 13. Stock.

1914 *Un Grand Bourgeois.* P. 3 a. Fabre. Antoine, Jan. 25. Illustration.

PART II. OEUVRES

Ancelot, Jacques. *Oeuvres complètes.* H. Delloye, 1838. 1 vol.

Ancelot, Virginie. *Théâtre complet.* Nouvelle éd., Beck, 1848. 4 vols.

Augier, Emile. *Théâtre complet.* Calmann Lévy, 1890–92. 7 vols.

Balzac, Honoré de. *Oeuvres complètes.* Éd. définitive, Michel Lévy frères, 1869–76. 24 vols.

Beaumarchais. *Oeuvres complètes.* Firman-Didot et Cie., 1878. 1 vol.

Becque, Henry. *Oeuvres complètes: Théâtre.* G. Crès et Cie., 1924. 4 vols.

Bonjour, Casimir. *Théâtre.* A. Lemerre, 1902. 3 vols.

Capus, Alfred. *Théâtre complet.* Fayard, 1910–13. 8 vols.

Dancourt, Florent. *Oeuvres*. Veuve de Pierre Ribou, 3ᵉ éd., 1729. 9 vols.

Donnay, Maurice. *Théâtre* (en cours). Fasquelle, 1908.

Dufresny, Charles Rivière. *Oeuvres*. Nouvelle éd., Briasson, 1747. 4 vols.

Dugué, Ferdinand. *Théâtre complet*. Calmann Lévy, 1891–94. 10 vols.

Dumas, Alexandre, *fils*. *Théâtre complet*. Calmann Lévy, 1898–99. 7 vols.

Dumersan, Marion. *Théâtre*. Collection accompagnée de notes autographes pour la Bibliothèque royale, 1837. 16 vols.

Fabre, Emile. *Théâtre complet* (en cours). Flammarion, 1920.

Falbaire de Quingey, Fenouillet de. *Oeuvres*. Veuve Duchesne, 1787. 2 vols.

Feuillet, Octave. *Théâtre complet*. Calmann Lévy, 1892. 5 vols.

Gondinet, Edmond. *Théâtre complet*. Calmann Lévy,

D'Harleville, Collin. *Oeuvres choisies*. Ménard et Desenne, *fils*, 1820. 4 vols.

Marivaux, Pierre de. *Oeuvres: Théâtre complet*. Nouvelle éd., E Fournier. Laplace, Sanchez et Cie., 1878. 1 vol.

Mercier, Louis Sébastien. *Théâtre complet*. Nouvelle éd. Amsterdam: B. Ulam, 1778–84. 4 vols.

Mirbeau, Octave. *Théâtre*. Flammarion, 1922. 3 vols.

Picard, L. B. *Oeuvres*. Barba, 1821. 10 vols.

Ponsard, François. *Oeuvres complètes*. Michel Lévy, 1865–76. 3 vols.

Scribe, Eugène. *Oeuvres complètes: (a) Comédies-Vaudevilles; (b) Comédies-Drames; (c) Opéras et Ballets; (d) Opéras-Comiques; (e) Romans, Nouvelles, Proverbes*. Dentu, 1874–85. 76 vols.

PART III. WORKS ON FRENCH DRAMA

Allard, Louis. *La Comédie de Moeurs en France au XIXᵉ Siècle*, Vol. I, *De Picard à Scribe (1795–1815)*. Cambridge: Harvard University Press, 1923.

Arvin, Niel Cole. *Eugène Scribe and the French Theater (1815–60)*. Cambridge: Harvard University Press, 1924.

Celler, Ludovic. *Les Types populaires au Théâtre*. Liep Mannsshon et Dufour, 1870–75. 3 vols.

Chandler, F. W. *The Contemporary Drama of France*. Boston, Little, Brown and Co., 1920.

Delaforest, A. *Théâtre moderne. Cours de Littérature dramatique (1822–28)*. Allardin, 1836. 2 vols.

Des Granges, Charles-Marc. *La Comédie et les Moeurs sous la Restauration et la Monarchie de Juillet (1815–48)*. A. Fontemoing, 1904.

Doumic, René. *De Scribe à Ibsen*. Perrin, 1896.

————. "La Comédie de moeurs contemporaines," *Revue d'histoire littéraire*, I (1894), 1–7.

Dreyfus, A. *Le Juif au Théâtre*. Maison Quantin, 1886.

Etienne, Louis. "La Comédie contemporaine," *Revue des deux Mondes*, LXXVII, 712–45.

————. "Les Hommes d'Argent dans la Comédie française," *Revue des deux Mondes*, LXXXIX, 513–24, 698–718.

Faguet, Emile. *Notes sur le Théâtre contemporain*. Lecène, Oudin et Cie., 1891. 3 vols.

————. *Propos de Théâtre, 2ᵉ série*. Société française d'imprimerie et de librairie, 1905.

Gaiffe, F. *Le Drame en France au XVIIIᵉ Siècle*, A. Colin, 1910.

Guex, Jules. *Le Théâtre et la Société française de 1815 à 1848*. Eischbacher, 1900.

Hastings, W. S. *The Drama of Honoré de Balzac*. Baltimore: George Banta, 1917.

Janin, Jules. *Critique dramatique*. Michel Lévy frères, 1877. 4 vols.

Lanson, Gustave. *Histoire de la Littérature française*. 15ᵉ éd. Hachette, 1921.

Latreille, C. *La Fin du Théâtre romantique et François Ponsard*. Hachette, 1899.

Leblond, Marius-Ary. "Le Financier de la Troisième République (D'après le roman contemporain)," *La Revue*, XXXVIII, 362–77.

Lemaître, Jules. *Impressions de Théâtre*. Société française d'imprimerie et de librairie, 1888–98. 10 vols.

————. *La Comédie après Molière et le Théâtre de Dancourt*. 2ᵉ éd. H. Welter, 1903.

Lenient, Ch. *La Comédie en France au XVIIIᵉ Siècle*. Hachette, 1888.

Lenient, Ch. *La Comédie en France au XIXe Siècle*. Hachette, 1898. 2 vols.

Lintilhac, E. *Histoire générale du Théâtre en France*, Vol. IV. Flammarion, 1909.

———. "Turcaret et l'Opinion publique," *Revue des deux Mondes*, CXV, 131 ff.

Loliée, Frédéric. "Le Financier sous la Troisième République," *La Revue*, XXXIX (1901), 37–55.

Molènes, G. de. "Les Ressources de Quinola," *Revue des deux Mondes*, II, 136–50.

Muret, Th. *L'Histoire par le Théâtre*. Amyot, 1865. 3 vols.

Nitze, W. A., and Dargan, E. P. *A History of French Literature*. New York: Holt, 1927.

Parfaict, Frères. *Histoire du Théâtre-François*. Amsterdam, 1735–49. 15 vols.

Parigot, H. *Le Théâtre d'hier*. Lecène, Oudin et Cie., 1893.

Petit de Julleville. *Le Théâtre en France*. Collin, 1889.

Poitou, E. *Du Roman et du Théâtre contemporains et de leur Influence sur les moeurs*. A. Durand, 1859.

Sarcey, F. *Quarante ans de Théâtre*. Bibliothèque des annales, 1900–1902. 8 vols.

Séché, A., et Bertaut, J. *L'Evolution du Théâtre contemporain*. Mercure de France, 1908.

Second, A. *La Comédie parisienne*. Havard, 1856–57. 26 livrs.

Soubies, A. *La Comédie française depuis l'Epoque romantique (1825–94)*. Fischbacher, 1895–96. 3 vols.

Waxman, S. M. *Antoine et le Théâtre-Libre*. Cambridge: Harvard University Press, 1926.

Weiss, K. J. *Trois Années de Théâtre (1883–85)*. 2e éd. Calmann Lévy, 1892.

———. *Le Théâtre et les Moeurs*. Calmann Lévy, 1889.

PART IV. SELECTED SOCIAL AND ECONOMIC WORKS

Avenel, Georges d'. *Le Méchanisme de la Vie moderne*. Colin, 1900–1905. 5 vols.

Bled, Victor du. *La Société française du XVIe Siècle au XXe Siècle*, Vol. VII. Perrin et Cie, 1909.

Castille, H. *Les Frères Péreire*. Dentu, 1861.

Chaptal, M. le Comte. *De l'Industrie française.* Renouard, 1819. 2 vols.

Clapham, J. H. *The Economic Development of France and Germany (1815-1914).* Cambridge: Harvard University Press, 1921.

Delord, Taxile. *Les Troisièmes Pages du Journal le Siècle.* Poulet-Malassis et de Broise, 1861.

Duval, Georges. *Frédérick Lemaître et son Temps.* Tresse, 1876.

Febvre, Lucien. "Les Nouveaux Riches et l'Histoire," *Revue des Cours et Conférences,* No. 13 (June 15, 1922).

Guéroult, Ad. *La Liberté des Affaires.* Dentu, 1861.

Lange, Maurice. *La Bruyère, Critique des Conditions et des Institutions sociales.* Hachette, 1909.

Lanzac de Laborie, Léon de. *Paris sous Napoléon,* Vol. VII. Plon-Nourrit et Cie, 1911.

Lavisse, Ernest. *Histoire de France contemporaine,* Vols. IV and V. Hachette, 1921.

Martin, Alfred. *Les Moyens de Transport dans Paris.* Imprimerie nationale, 1894.

Martin, Germain. *L'Histoire du Crédit en France sous le Règne de Louis XIV.* Librairie de la Société du Recueil. Paris, 1913.

Proudhon, P. J. *Manuel du Spéculateur à la Bourse.* Nouvelle éd. Lacroix et Cie, 1876.

Rambaud, A. *Histoire de la Civilisation contemporaine en France,* 6e éd. Collin, 1897-98.

Renard, Georges. *Les Étapes de la Société française au XIXe Siècle.* Marcel Rivière et Cie, 1913.

Toussenel, Alphonse. *Les Juifs, Rois de l'Époque,* Vol. I. Ecole sociétaire, 1847.

Vallée, Oscar de. *Les Manieurs d'argent, 1720-1857.* Michel Lévy frères, 1858.

Vallès, Jules Louis Joseph. *L'Argent, par un Homme de lettres devenu Homme de Bourse.* Ledoyen, 1857.

Virmaitre, Charles. *Paris-Boursicotier.* A. Savine, 1888.

Weill, Georges. *L'Ecole Saint-Simonienne. Son Influence jusqu'à nos Jours.* Alcan, 1896.

INDEX